A RUSSIAN ON COMMANDO

A RUSSIAN ON
COMMANDO

The Boer War Experiences of
YEVGENY AVGUSTUS

Edited by
BORIS GORELIK

Translated by
LUCAS VENTER

JONATHAN BALL PUBLISHERS

JOHANNESBURG · CAPE TOWN · LONDON

The publication was effected under the auspices of the
Mikhail Prokhorov Foundation TRANSCRIPT Programme
to Support Translations of Russian Literature.

Mikhail
Prokhorov
Fund | Supporting the translation of Russian literature   transcript

Published in South Africa in 2022 by
JONATHAN BALL PUBLISHERS
A division of Media24 (Pty) Ltd
PO Box 33977
Jeppestown
2043

ISBN 978-1-7761-9136-9
ebook ISBN 978-1-7761-9137-6

www.jonathanball.co.za
www.twitter.com/JonathanBallPub
www.facebook.com/JonathanBallPublishers

Cover by Johan Koortzen
© Cover images: Photo of Yevgeny Avgustus: *Razvedchik* (1908: 947);
photo of the German corps: National Archives of South Africa.
Other photos courtesy of: Davidson, A & Filatova, I: *The Russians and
the Anglo-Boer War* (Human & Rousseau, 1998), the Ditsong National
Museum of Cultural History, Boris Gorelik, Tinus le Roux, Museum Africa,
the National Archives of South Africa, *Razvedchik* (a Saint Petersburg
military journal), the Russian State Library, *The Sphere* (a British illustrated
newspaper) and the War Museum of the Boer Republics.

Design and typesetting by Martine Barker
Set in Adobe Garamond Pro

Contents

Foreword

When I was approached by Boris Gorelik to write the fore-word to this book I thought: great, I shall place Russia's involvement in the Anglo-Boer War in perspective and explain why Russian volunteers participated in the war (and in such numbers). However, I was pleasantly surprised to find that Boris had written an exceptionally good introduction. Seldom have I come across an introduction that gives the context so well.

Furthermore, Boris's explanatory footnotes are a wonderful contribution, enhancing the quality of the publication. Boris might be correct that Yevgeny Avgustus was the best stylist among the Russian volunteers who wrote their experiences of the war, but he has added some flavour that makes this a magnificent read.

We learn that Russians, unlike the Dutch or the Germans, had no links of kinship with the Boers, so the foundation of Boer-mania in Russia was mostly political and ideological. To them the Boers embodied nationalism and anti-imperialism. The Russian public admired the two small nations in a little-known part of the world who stood up against 'perfidious Albion' as Russians 'might also do some day'.

Boris points out that Avgustus saw the Anglo-Boer War as his chance to escape the routine of garrison life and 'face the formidable, still unfamiliar phenomenon of war'. On 26 January 1900, Avgustus arrived in Pretoria with a number of Russian companions. From there he departed for the Natal front. Like other Russian volunteers who recorded their reminiscences, he recognised the flaws of the Boer military organisation, despite his admiration for the defenders of the republics' independence. And like the others, he tended to criticise the foreign volunteers, even his own compatriots.

Boris remarks that the reminiscences of Avgustus are 'particularly lucid, engaging and evocative'. He quotes the historian RW Johnson, who calls Avgustus 'a gifted writer'. Indeed, Boris decides, none of the other Russian witnesses of that war produced an account of such literary merit.

The reminiscences of Avgustus have been touched upon in English by earlier writers on the Russian volunteers, particularly by Elisaveta Kandyba-Foxcroft in her book *Russia and the Anglo-Boer War* (1981), and by Apollon Davidson and Irina Filatova, who quote long excerpts from his account in their *The Russians and the Anglo-Boer War* (1998).

However, the text presented in this book is a reconstruction of accounts of the war from Avgustus's book in 1902, as well as his articles in Russian newspapers and magazines between 1899 and 1902. Because Avgustus did not complete his war memoirs, Boris skilfully uses six of his texts, partly or in full, to reconstruct what can be considered his war memoirs.

Perhaps Avgustus gives us his experience best in the words: 'For six solid months I fought side by side with the Boers, lay with them in the trenches. Their blood and brains clotted my eyes when deadly shrapnel struck comrades close by. Together we endured all the deprivations and adversities of commando life; they shared their last rusks, their last sips of water with me, and I learnt to love and respect these stern and unfriendly looking, childishly good-natured, wholeheartedly courageous and profoundly religious men.'

Avgustus's first experience of battle in the war was at Vaalkrans between 5 and 7 February 1900 on the Tugela front. Of particular interest are the problems in forming a Russian corps. We take note of the leadership struggle between Alexey Ganetsky and Yevgeny Maximov, which in reality decided the fate of the Russian corps-to-be. The outcome is unfortunately not discussed by Avgustus, but in a very revealing piece Boris eloquently and dispassionately discusses the reasons why the Russian volunteers did not want to serve under Maximov.

Avgustus served in the Johannesburg Police Commando from

early May 1900 until the British occupation of Pretoria. He was wounded during the battle for the capital on 4–5 June and taken prisoner. Thanks to the intervention of the Russian attaché with the British troops, Colonel Pavel Stakhovich, Avgustus was released and allowed to return to his homeland in July 1900.

Although parts of his memoirs appeared in Russian news-papers and even as a book, the longest version was published in the *Varshavsky Voyenny Zhurnal* (Warsaw Military Journal). The last instalment that came out in the *Varshavsky Voyenny Zhurnal*, in June 1902, ended with the phrase, 'To be continued'. But there was no sequel.

Boris then proceeds to give a vivid account of the rest of Avgustus's life until his death in October 1914 in a battle against the Germans in the Great War.

I have had much pleasure in reading this text. There is no doubt in my mind that it adds a great deal to our understanding of this enigmatic war from a very unusual angle.

Fransjohan Pretorius
Professor Emeritus
Department of Historical and Heritage Studies
University of Pretoria

Introduction
by Boris Gorelik

The war between the British Empire and the two Boer republics (the Transvaal, or South African Republic, and the Orange Free State) is possibly the best-researched armed conflict in sub-Saharan Africa. Long seen as a 'white man's war', the conflict is now understood as a battle between the British Empire and a South African community that comprised Afrikaner men and women, their black and coloured scouts, servants, labourers and tenants, and their families.[1]

Apart from the combatants, civilians of various nationalities were involved in the hostilities and suffered from the scorched-earth and mass-internment policies of the British forces. While the South African War, also known as the Anglo-Boer War, has been ideologically important for Afrikaner nationalism and for the development of Afrikaner identity, modern historians have shown that this destructive conflict affected other South African peoples, the majority of the population.[2]

But it would be wrong to assert that most inhabitants of South Africa were actively involved in that war or allied with either of the adversaries. Black people usually preferred to shun the confrontation and observe neutrality, though they could use the situation to their political or economic advantage. Editors of a book on social aspects of that conflict admit that, although they did their best to explore and emphasise the multiracial character of the war, 'it nevertheless remains a pre-eminently Afrikaner struggle against British imperialism'.[3]

The military historian Ian van der Waag suggests that future generations may regard this conflict as a war of South African unification.[4] There is no sign of this yet. As Bill Nasson remarks, 'the legacy of the war remains a sectional business' in South Africa.[5] For example, African nationalist historians tend to see it primarily as a colonial war waged by Europeans on appropriated African land over matters that had no relevance to Africans but led to their further dispossession and disenfranchisement. From this point of view, it was just 'a domestic quarrel between the Boers and the British government and its two southern colonies of Natal and the Cape'.[6] Moreover, the war is nearly absent in the collective memory of black South Africans.[7]

Now that the political and ideological significance of the war in the deeply divided South African society has declined, its historical importance is no longer evident. That conflict is too often seen in South Africa as an internal matter, something that concerns only South Africans and possibly the British. But the South African War matters in global history. It was one of the few times when the world was closely watching developments in South Africa, and when its local events could have lasting consequences overseas. 'From the American Civil War to the First World War, no conflict achieved greater attention in international opinion than the South African War,' states Donal Lowry.[8]

The United States and continental Europe rooted for the two small nations in Africa that challenged the largest empire in the world and defied it for three years. To overpower the burghers, the British carried out their biggest military mobilisation since the Napoleonic Wars both at home and in the colonies.[9]

For the outside world, 'the South African War was much more than a colonial war writ large'.[10] It was the beginning of the end of British imperialism, and the first modern war. It demonstrated the emerging power of international mass media. It excited the imagination of millions of people in Europe and North America, kindled their Anglophobia and inspired mass pro-Boer movements and war volunteering.[11] Imperialists projected onto the Boers their own desire to confront their British rivals. Nationalists and anti-imperialists saw in the Boer republics an example of valiant resistance to foreign domination. Anti-capitalists praised the Boers' 'indifference to gold'.

The conflict captured the attention of people on several continents,

Fraternity Cup, encrusted with precious stones,
a Russian gift to the Boers.

not least in countries with no colonial interests in Africa. The burgher resistance impressed Jawaharlal Nehru, the future first prime minister of independent India, and Sun Yat-sen, the future leader of the anti-monarchist revolution in China.[12] Military agents from abroad hurried to South Africa to learn about new methods of warfare. Young foreign officers volunteered for the burgher armies to see action for the first time in their lives. Men and women of letters discussed the South African War in the context of the situation in their home countries.

Fraternity Cup (detail).

People outside South Africa followed the war for reasons that often had no direct relation to the future of the Boer republics or British colonialism.

Boers become Russian heroes

Before the outbreak of the South African War, the Russian public had shown no particular interest in South Africa. Russian trade with the Cape, Natal and the Boer republics was negligible; Russian goods usually reached South Africa through European intermediaries. Most immigrants from the Russian Empire were Jewish, not ethnic Russian, and the government in Saint Petersburg had little time for them. Besides, Russia had no plans to acquire colonial possessions in southern Africa.

Russian people's ideas of the Cape Colony and the Boer republics had been formed mostly by tales of discovery and derring-do, such as in novels by Henry Rider Haggard or Thomas Mayne Reid, or Jules Verne's *The Adventures of Three Englishmen and Three Russians in South Africa*. As a visitor from Russia had noted half a century earlier, South Africa was 'an entirely different world'.[13]

However, the South African War agitated the public in Russia, as it did people across Europe. As Donal Lowry notes, there had not been 'such international interest in the "moral" issues of a distant war since Garibaldi's South American campaigns and the American Civil War'.[14]

Most European countries had their pro-Boer movements, and Russia was no exception.[15] At the turn of the 20th century, European perceptions of the Boers were romanticised and deeply emotional.[16] Even monarchists and Pan-Slavists found much to love about the two republics: they admired Boer conservatism and religiosity, and also liked the burghers' tendency towards collective decision-making, which reminded them of the similar tradition in Russian villages. Russian journalists closely observed the events of the war and portrayed the Boers as modest, devout and patriotic peasants confronting a greedy, cynical and aggressive capitalist power.

Valentin Katayev, a prominent Russian novelist who was a boy during the war, recounted that the affection of his compatriots for the burghers was irrational. As a child, he hated the British and loved the residents of the Transvaal and the Orange Free State 'because the Boers were simple hardworking people of modest means who loved their African country, the Transvaal. And the rich and cruel English wanted to capture their country and to turn it into their colony and the Boers into their slaves, or something like that.'[17]

Russians, unlike the Dutch, the French or the Germans, had no links of kinship with the Boers, so the foundation of Boer-mania in Russia was mostly political and ideological. To international audiences, the burghers embodied nationalism and anti-imperialism.[18] In the expansionist Russian Empire, which was vying with the British Empire for domination in Central Asia, the anti-British kind

A Russian poster containing the lyrics of the song 'Transvaal, Transvaal' (1900s).

of anti-imperialism was welcomed. The Russian public believed that Britain was their country's most insidious rival. They admired the two small nations in a little-known (to Russians) part of the world who stood up against 'perfidious Albion' as Russians might also do some day.

In Russia, streets were renamed after Boer generals. Services in honour of President Kruger were held in Russian churches. Orchestras played the national anthem of the Transvaal. In pubs and restaurants, patrons had heated arguments about the war. Circuses capitalised on the popularity of the Boers by launching special revues. Writings by burgher leaders were published in Russian, and dozens of pro-Boer pamphlets, articles, essays and brochures came out in various cities. A pro-Boer folk song, 'Transvaal, Transvaal, my country', emerged in those years. Russian churches raised funds for burgher civilians. Expensive presents, such as an enormous porphyry vase dedicated to General Piet Cronjé, subscribed to by

70 000 donors, were sent to Pretoria. Some of the foremost Russian writers, philosophers and public figures, such as Leo Tolstoy, Alexander Kuprin and Vasily Rozanov, spoke out in support of the Boer resistance.

Russian volunteers on the republican side

When covering the conflict, none of the major Russian newspapers, representing a wide spectrum of political opinion – from socialists to ultra-nationalists – supported Britain's goals and actions in South Africa.[19] But the Russian government, like governments of the other Great Powers, were guided by realpolitik, not by the popular sympathy with the Boer republics.[20] Although Tsar Nicholas II toyed with the idea of moving his troops towards the Afghan border and threatening the British Raj in India to force Britain to send reinforcements to Central Asia instead of to South Africa, he never did so. When British Intelligence learnt about the rumours that Russian troops were being mobilised in Turkestan in early 1900, the Russian War Minister promptly allowed a British military attaché to inspect the area and satisfy himself that Russia was not preparing an invasion.[21]

After preliminary negotiations with Germany and France in October and November 1899 on joint representations to Britain, the Tsar, the initiator of the Hague Peace Conference, did almost nothing to bring peace to South Africa.[22] Public opinion favoured intervention, but the Russian government consistently avoided both antagonising Britain and rendering material aid to the Boer republics.

Assistance was provided only by Russian individuals and non-governmental organisations. Two Russian ambulances operated in the republics in 1900. The Russian Red Cross sent over 30 doctors, nurses and other medical personnel to the Boers. During their half a year in Africa, the Red Cross ambulance attended to more than 7 000 patients.[23] The staff of the Russo-Dutch Ambulance, including eight Russian doctors and nurses, was financed by the donations that were sent in from across the country after an appeal by the Dutch congregation in Saint Petersburg.

The only military men that the Russian government sent to South Africa were military attachés and unofficial observers. Meanwhile, from the outset of the war, hundreds, if not thousands, of Russians of various ages and social groups, with or without military experience, wanted to fight for the Boers.

Throughout the 19th century, individual Russian volunteers fought in military conflicts outside their homeland, for example during the Greek War of Independence (1821), Franco-Prussian War (1870–1871), American Civil War (1861–1865), Italo-Ethiopian War (1887–1889), Cuban War of Independence (1895–1898) and War of the Pacific (1879–1884). Russian voluntarism in external conflicts became a mass movement only in the mid-1870s, during the series of rebellions of Slavic peoples in the Balkans against Ottoman rule.

The popular ideology of Pan-Slavism called on Russia to help secure the liberation of Slavic peoples in Bulgaria, Bosnia, Herzegovina, Montenegro and Serbia from the domination of an Islamic power. It inspired more than 4 000 Russian soldiers and medical personnel to take part in that struggle as volunteers.[24] Russian officers and other ranks joined rebel units and teams in the Herzegovina uprising (1875–1877) and Serbian army units during the Serbian Wars for Independence (1876–1878).

In the South African War, the involvement of Russian volunteers was about 20 times smaller than it was during the Balkan Wars of the 1870s, and much shorter. The Transvaal was much further from Russia than Bosnia or Serbia, which is why fewer volunteers could afford to travel there. Besides, the Russian government had adopted an ambiguous attitude towards the Boer republics. While it tolerated pro-Boer public sentiments, it did not expressly endorse military involvement in defence of the republics, including allowing retired soldiers of various ranks to travel to South Africa as volunteers. In the 1870s, Russian Pan-Slavic organisations recruited hundreds of military volunteers and dispatched them to the Balkans. The Tsar declared that Russian officers who retired so that they could fight against the Turks would be, on their return from Serbia, readmitted by their regiments, with the time of their absence regarded as active service.[25] But during the South African War, Russian military volunteers were given no such guarantees.

One or two small groups of Russian volunteers came to the Transvaal with funding from their wealthy compatriots. Other Russian men arranged their journey to South Africa at their own expense. Young officers from the Russian Empire, which had not waged a full-scale war for almost two decades, resigned or took a long leave to be able to escape from the routine and gain practical experience of modern warfare. The British Empire, it was thought, could soon start a war against Russia, and they wanted to be prepared for it.

Their contribution

'Of all the foreign contingents in the Transvaal the Russian was the most serious, the most scientific, the best equipped', remarked the *Daily Mail* correspondent with the burgher forces. 'It cared little for the justification of the Boer, but it cared much for the experience to be gained of actual warfare, and that in battle against the British.'[26]

Still, their air of pragmatism was misleading. Russian officers were also encouraged by the romanticism of pro-Boer propaganda, which presented the South African War as a conflict in which the weaker side required international assistance, similar to the Balkan uprisings and the Serbo-Turkish War of the 1870s.[27] The highest-ranking Russian volunteer on the republican side, Lieutenant Colonel Yevgeny Maximov, had participated in those conflicts and applied that experience in South Africa.

According to Lieutenant Colonel Vasily Gurko, the Russian attaché with the burgher armies, the Russian volunteers who came especially to fight on the Boer side were inspired by the 'freedom struggle of the unjustly oppressed people'. At the same, he continued, some of them 'perhaps hoped to acquire on the cheap the halo of a hero, a fighter for the righteous cause, and to occupy prominent positions among the leaders of military operations. Most of them expected to become officers in the Boer troops without having the slightest idea about their organisation.'[28]

Burghers tended to distrust or even despise foreign volunteers, seeing them as a nuisance.[29] Nevertheless, several Russian volunteers received officers' ranks on commando. Maximov was elected *vecht-generaal* [fighting general] for his distinguished service. At least five Russian officers lost their lives fighting for the republican cause. Four of them were members of guerrilla units.[30]

Some Russians stayed with the burghers after June 1900, when most of the international volunteers left South Africa.

The total number of foreign volunteers with the Boer forces did not exceed 4 000. Most of them were immigrants who had settled in the republics before the war.[31] Their participation, as well as their articles, reports and diaries, helped to keep the South African War at the forefront of public consciousness in their home countries. The volunteer combatants and medical personnel represented Russia's only involvement in that conflict. Thanks to them, battles on the opposite side of the globe, outside the Russian sphere of influence, became a concern of the Russian public.

The republican armies did not gather statistics on foreign volunteers. Apollon Davidson and Irina Filatova, in their seminal study of the Russian participation in the war, were only able quote the figure from a book by Howard Clement Hillegas, a correspondent for the *New York World*. Citing the estimates by British and American reporters in South Africa, 'who had good opportunities of forming as nearly a correct idea as anyone', Hillegas stated that there were 225 Russian subjects in military units on the republican side.[32] It is not clear how the unnamed journalists arrived at that number. During the war, various estimates appeared in the British press. For instance, *The Times* of London reported in April 1900 that there were 300 Russians fighting with the Boers. Other British papers estimated that over 400 Russian volunteers were serving in burgher commandos.[33] These appraisals probably took into account not only the Russian combatants who arrived in South Africa during the war but also the personnel of the Russian ambulances, as well as at least some of the immigrants from the Russian Empire who resided in the republics before the outbreak of hostilities.[34] Besides, volunteers from other Slavic countries, particularly Bulgarians, were likely to be regarded as Russians.[35]

Several Russian volunteers made a name for themselves in their country after their return from the South African War. Alexander Guchkov became President of the Lower House of the Russian legislature and, later, War Minister. Vladimir Semyonov was the chief government architect of Moscow in the 1930s. Nicolai Popov, with his diploma from the Wright Brothers aviation school, was one of Russia's first pilots.

Then, there were Russian memoirists, who are best remembered for chronicling their participation in that war. Among the Russian combatants in the South African War, Second Lieutenant Yevgeny Avgustus was the most talented writer.

Yevgeny Avgustus with his scouts in Biysk, Siberia, on their return from a 4-month expedition to northern Mongolia (1908).

Yevgeny's career before the war

The historian Ēriks Jēkabsons of the University of Latvia in Riga discovered that although Yevgeny's surname had a Germanic root, he was not a German. After diligent research at the Latvian State Historical Archives, Jēkabsons established that he was a Latvian and that his original surname was Augusts. Yevgeny changed it to 'Avgustus' after he joined up to make it more manageable for his Russian colleagues. Moreover, his Christian name was also probably different: 'Yevgeny' is the Russian equivalent of 'Eugene'. The Latvian form would be 'Eižens', but this was too fancy, for Latvian peasants only started giving this name to their children decades later.[36]

From his record of service and other documents preserved by the Russian State Archive of Military History, we know that he was born to a peasant family in the Courland Governorate, which is now part of Latvia, on 17 December 1874.[37] But Jēkabsons also found a marriage record of Yevgeny's parents in the Lutheran parish of Bāta, a village in the western part of Courland, not far from the city of Libau (today Liepāja). Both his father, Kristaps, and his mother, Līna, were Latvian peasants working on leased land. By the time Yevgeny turned two, the family had moved to Dünaburg (the present Daugavpils), the second-largest city in the province and an industrial, commercial and railway hub of the Russian Empire. His father was employed by the railway, managing cargoes at the Dünaburg station.[38] Still, the family continued to be officially regarded as peasant because of their origin.

For five years, Avgustus studied at the Dünaburg Secondary School (*realnoye uchlishtshe*), which was the most prestigious educational institution in that part of Courland. It admitted pupils of all creeds and social classes, including Lutheran peasants such as Avgustus. What would proud parents not do to see their son in the school's grey, white-buttoned uniform? If the boy succeeded, he could enrol at a university to study physics, mathematics or medicine.

But Avgustus dropped out just before the final year. This could not be because he had decided to become a soldier: a qualification from his school would have given him advantages in military service, speeding his promotion and enabling him to matriculate at a military academy. Perhaps Yevgeny was dismissed for failure, or perhaps his father could no longer afford the high school fees.

In 1892, he enlisted as a volunteer and joined an infantry regiment stationed in Dvinsk. He wanted to be a commissioned officer, which was possible only after graduation from a military college. Avgustus went to Vilna (Vilnius, now the capital of Lithuania) to study at the local Infantry Cadet School. In 1896, he passed his final exams with distinction.[39]

Yet, before leaving, Avgustus took a step that could have far-reaching consequences for his career: he converted from Lutheranism to Orthodoxy, becoming a member of the established church of the Russian Empire. His Latvian name was changed to the Russian one, Yevgeny. In his published writings, he did not even hint at his Latvian ancestry, always presenting himself as a Russian nationalist, monarchist and imperialist.

Because of his excellent performance at the military college,

Avgustus was commissioned as a second lieutenant in the 189th Belgoray Infantry Reserve Regiment soon after his graduation. The unit was stationed in the Warsaw Military District in Poland, then part of the Russian Empire. The region was known as the 'Advanced Theatre' because of its proximity to the western border.[40] The district was meant to be at the forefront in a defensive war against Germany or Austria-Hungary.

This could sound exciting to a young officer, but Avgustus found out that none of those countries were of a mind to invade the Russian Empire. Avgustus recounted later how his 'grey, monotonous life of an army officer began: the drumming, the hoarse shouting of warrant officers on the parade grounds of the barracks, the evening dances, the cards and vodka at the officers' club, the drab guardhouse, the exercises and marches, and marches and exercises. A gloomy, tedious living, when my service was reduced to keeping my record unblemished.'[41]

From Warsaw to Pretoria

Three years went by, and the South African War started. Avgustus saw it as his chance to escape the routine and 'face the formidable, still unfamiliar phenomenon of war'.[42] He and another officer from his regiment, Second Lieutenant Leonid Pokrowsky, decided to travel to the Transvaal, enlist with the burgher forces and, for the first time in their lives, take part in combat.

According to Pokrowsky, Russian officers went to South Africa as volunteers 'to see action, experience grave danger, toughen themselves up to be ready when needed by their country, and, above all, learn through practice the work, the art which every soldier has devoted his life to'.[43] Pokrowsky accomplished more than that. He stayed with the Boers far longer than did other Russian volunteers. After fighting with Danie Theron's Reconnaissance Corps and Camillo Ricchiardi's Italian corps, he was promoted to captain. In an engagement at Utrecht, Pokrowsky was severely injured, and he died the next day, on 25 December 1900. (His name appears on a plaque at a memorial to the fallen members of the Utrecht Commando in the town's Dutch Reformed Church.)

The two young officers could not afford to pay for their passage

Second Lieutenant Leonid Pokrowsky,
a Russian volunteer and Avgustus's travelling companion.

from Warsaw to Pretoria and for their maintenance en route. They borrowed the money, took unpaid leave and departed from Warsaw in early December 1899, less than two months after the beginning of the hostilities in South Africa. The crowd who saw them off at the railway station staged an anti-British rally. The news of their departure even reached the English press.[44]

Both officers were commissioned by Russian papers to submit their reports from the voyage. Always a loyalist, the 25-year-old Avgustus contributed to the main government newspaper in Poland, the bilingual *Varshavsky Dnevnik/Dziennik Warszawski*, as well as to the *Novoye Vremya*, a popular Saint Petersburg broadsheet that was infamous for its anti-Semitic disposition and scathing criticism of the avant-garde. Avgustus sent his first articles to them from Brussels a few days after his departure. He wrote his last reports in Pretoria and dispatched them shortly before going to war.

They travelled overland to Marseilles where they boarded a French steamer, proceeding to Lourenço Marques (today Maputo). On the way, they were joined by other Russian volunteers, who became Avgustus's comrades-in-arms in South Africa: *Praporshchik* (warrant officer) Alexey Diatroptov, Lieutenant Fyodor Guchkov and Second Lieutenant Vasily Nikitin. Other compatriots travelling on the same ship included the personnel of the Russian Red Cross ambulance and the Russian attaché on the republican side, Lieutenant Colonel Vasily Gurko.

Avgustus and Pokrowsky were nearly destitute. They counted on remuneration for their articles, but most of all they hoped for command positions in the burgher units. In Brussels, they had an appointment with Willem Leyds, the South African Republic's consul general accredited in Russia. The two second lieutenants claimed that the diplomat had assured them that they would be made majors in the Transvaal.[45] It sounded reasonable because, during the Serbian Wars for Independence, Russian officer volunteers were often appointed commanders of battalions or companies on their arrival in the Balkans.

But it was not the case in South Africa. On 26 January 1900, Avgustus and his companions arrived in Pretoria, only to realise that they would not be offered an officer's rank.

'It was rather comical to see the long faces of some officers when they learnt that the Boers did not need their expertise in tactics, regulations, digging in and shooting techniques,' noted Avgustus in an article from Pretoria. 'Of course, the future did not seem bright when they had to take off their golden epaulettes, get a cartridge bag and a flask and join up as rank and file ... My compatriot [Pokrowsky?] was more disappointed than others when his last hope of serving in the headquarters burst like a soap bubble. I had to listen to a barrage of complaints about the misfortune that he had to leave his regiment, where he used to be an aide-de-camp and commander of a training team, while the Boers did not even care that he had taken a course in sapping and could build impassable artificial obstacles.'[46]

Not getting an officer's rank did not dampen Avgustus's enthusiasm or his willingness to participate in the war. The young Russian officer would eventually see how fortune favoured the Boers and how it abandoned them. Avgustus was sent to the Natal front towards the end of the conventional phase of the war, which was characterised by pitched battles. He took part in the Battle of the Tugela Heights (14–27 February). He also witnessed the transitional phase of the war, which began in March 1900 when burgher units tended to avoid direct confrontation with the numerically superior British troops and pursued tactical rather than strategic objectives.[47]

Avgustus first saw action as a member of the Krugersdorp Commando in Natal. The British managed to relieve Ladysmith on 28 February after a series of engagements that came to be known as the Battle of the Tugela Heights. The republican troops, including Avgustus and his Russian companions, retreated towards Glencoe.

Yevgeny Avgustus was a founding member of the Russian corps, witnessed the formation of General George de Villebois-Mareuil's international legion, conducted reconnaissance under General Philip Botha in the Free State and fought with the Johannesburg Police Commando until the fall of Pretoria in early June.

Why this memoir matters

Memoirs of foreign volunteers remind us of the link between the war and internationalism. Such accounts were written by strangers to South Africa who did not plan to make it their home and looked at the situation around them as outsiders. In the republican forces, they mostly served as rank and file, so their life on commando was similar to that of most burgher combatants.

Their views allow us to see the conflict from another angle and with a wider frame of reference. In other words, we can move from national to transnational history and recognise that the South African War offers insight into things that mattered to people around the world. These reminiscences give us a chance to read about the military side of life on commando as experienced by those who did not have to go to war and endure hardship without pay, and sometimes get crippled or spend years in British captivity, or even be killed. But they all did it for their own reasons.

Russian first-hand accounts can easily be overlooked in the historiography of the South African War. The contribution of Russian volunteers to the military effort was comparatively small. Most of them had returned to Russia by the time the British formally occupied the entire territory of today's South Africa and the guerrilla phase of the war began, which is why none of them wrote a memoir of such scope as Deneys Reitz's *Commando*.

But Russian memoirs set the war in a broader context. They reveal the perceptions of a nation that harboured no colonial ambitions in Africa. The discovery of diamond and gold deposits and the mass migration of Jews from the Russian Empire to the Cape and the Transvaal led to the establishment of diplomatic relations between Russia and the South African Republic. However, the Russian government did not seem to have clearly defined political or economic objectives in that part of the world. To Russian volunteers, it was a strange land, alluring but often hard to get used to.

While Russia had no direct political interest in South Africa, anti-British sentiment prevailed in the country. The Russian volunteers arrived in the Transvaal to support the Boer republics. Their strong prejudice against the British is evident in their reminiscences. Still, they were reluctant to vilify British soldiers. They recognised the flaws of the Boer military organisation despite their admiration for the defenders of republican independence. They also tended to criticise other foreign volunteers, even their own compatriots.

Comparatively few Russian accounts of the war have appeared in English. Such publications include abridged translations of reports by Russian military observers; memoirs by health professionals who worked for the Russian ambulances on the Boer side; and a possibly fictitious story of a woman who travelled to the Transvaal in men's clothes to find her husband, a Russian volunteer.[48] These accounts contribute to our knowledge of various aspects of this war, including the Russian involvement. However, by and large, their value is largely historical. They have an appeal for the scholar but not for the general reader.

The reminiscences of Yevgeny Avgustus are particularly lucid, engaging and evocative. Prominent South African journalist and historian RW Johnson calls him 'a gifted writer'.[49] Indeed, none of the other Russian witnesses to the war produced an account of such literary merit. His realistic portrayal of human frailty, courage and fortitude in the face of mortal danger also happens to be the longest record of the South African War by a Russian combatant.

'Augustus was in the unique position of relating the experiences of the usually silent category of "rank and file soldiers" in this war because he was in the Boer army as a soldier, not an officer, but at the same time was a man of letters, capable of relating his emotions and feelings,' note Apollon Davidson and Irina Filatova in their seminal study of the Russian involvement in the South African War.[50]

Even though Avgustus served with the rank and file, he was still a Russian officer. Unlike his fellow combatants, while he obeyed orders, he always tried to deduce the logic of his commanders' decisions. His comments on Boer objectives, manoeuvres and battle plans were based on the military education and training that he had received at home.

Unlike military leaders and government officials, whose war reminiscences were often stilted, Avgustus was not constrained by political considerations. He concealed the identity of his Russian brothers-in-arms behind initials, so that he could write about their actions and opinions without compromising their reputations at home. Apart from that, he does not seem to have obscured or intentionally distorted important facts.

Volunteer accounts are usually chronicles, descriptions of events in a chronological order. But Avgustus offers both keen observation and thoughtful introspection. His narrative is a series of paintings rather than snapshots. History comes alive as you immerse yourself in this memoir.

Avgustus takes us along on his journey from Europe to southern Africa. Thanks to the immediacy of his writing, we can almost feel his trepidation and excitement as he approaches the battlefield for the first time. His personal, sometimes even intimate, reminiscences demonstrate how an idealistic military officer who had never seen action became hardened, almost oblivious to the death and the gore.

His eyewitness account can be read also as a vivid depiction of the absurdities, trauma and evil attraction of any war. His stories, told in a simple, hard-headed, sometimes humorous manner, prompt the

'England's war with the Boers', a Russian poster (1900).

reader to ruminate on the nature of combat. In the best parts of his memoir, the events as interpreted by Avgustus acquire a universal character. It is a story of a man at war, one of the most terrifying situations that he can face.

His reminiscences reveal that armed conflict can appal and fascinate at the same time. We begin to understand why people are thrilled by the thought of standing up against an overwhelming force, like a surfer riding a wave in a raging storm. We begin to see why people crossed a hemisphere to fight in somebody else's war. This account rises above the chronicles and recounting of minutiae. Avgustus speaks to us through the years because his stories of wartime chaos pivot on the typical and the perennial.

Notes

[1] Nasson, B, 'The war for South Africa', in Giliomee, H and Mbenga, B (eds), *New History of South Africa*. Cape Town: Tafelberg, 2007, p 221.

[2] See, for example, Marks, M, 'War and Union, 1899–1910', in Ross, R, Mager, AK and Nasson, B (eds), *The Cambridge History of South Africa*, vol 2. Cambridge: Cambridge University Press, 2011, pp 157–164.

[3] Cuthbertson, G, Grundlingh, A and Suttie, M-L, 'Introduction', in Cuthbertson, G, Grundlingh, A and Suttie, M-L (eds), *Writing a Wider War: Rethinking Gender, Race, and Identity in the South African War, 1899–1902*. Athens: Ohio University Press, 2002, p xii.

[4] Van der Waag, I, 'Re-fighting the 2nd Anglo-Boer War: Historians in the trenches', *Scientia Militaria: South African Journal of Military Studies*, 2000, vol 30, no 1, p v.

[5] Nasson, B, 'The war one hundred years on', in Cuthbertson, G, Grundlingh, A and Suttie, M-L (eds), *Writing a Wider War: Rethinking Gender, Race, and Identity in the South African War, 1899–1902*. Athens: Ohio University Press, 2002, p 14.

[6] Maphalala, J, 'The African people and the Anglo-Boer War', in *A Century is a Short Time: New Perspectives on the Anglo-Boer War*. Clydesdale: Nexus, 2005, p 197.

[7] Van der Waag, 'Re-fighting the 2nd Anglo-Boer War', p iv.

[8] Lowry, D, '"The play of forces world-wide in their scope and revolutionary in their operation [J.A. Hobson]": The South African War as an international event', *South African Historical Journal*, 1999, vol 41, no 1, p 83.

[9] Omissi, D and Thompson, AS, 'Introduction: Investigating the impact of the war', in Omissi, D and Thompson, AS (eds), *The Impact of the South African War*. Basingstoke: Palgrave, 2002, p 10.

[10] Beckett, IFW, *The Victorians at War*. London: Hambledon and London, 2003, p 230.

[11] Cuthbertson, Grundlingh and Suttie, 'Introduction', p x.

[12] Lowry, D, '"The world's no bigger than a kraal": The South African War and international opinion in the first age of "globalization"', in Omissi, D and Thompson, AS (eds), *The Impact of the South African War*. Basingstoke: Palgrave, 2002, p 276.

[13] Alexey Vysheslavtsev, 1858. See Gorelik, B (ed), *'An Entirely Different World':*

Russian Visitors to the Cape, 1797–1870. Cape Town: Van Riebeeck Society, 2015, p 114.

[14] Lowry, "'The play of forces world-wide in their scope...'", p 92.

[15] Porter, A, 'The South African War and the historians', *African Affairs*, 2000, vol 99, no 397, October, p 647.

[16] Lowry, "'The play of forces world-wide in their scope...'", p 88.

[17] Katayev, V, *Razbitaya zhizn, ili Volshebny rog Oberona*, Katayev, V, *Sobraniye sochineniy*, vol 8. Moscow: Hudozhestvennaya literatura, 1985, p 407.

[18] Lowry, "'The world's no bigger than a kraal'", p 270.

[19] Petukhov, LA, 'Obraz Velikobritanii v rossiyskom obshestvennom mnenii v period anglo-burskoy voiny (1899–1902 gg.)', PhD thesis. State Academic University for the Humanities, Moscow, 2009, p 199.

[20] Mommsen, WJ, 'Introduction', in Wilson, K (ed), *The International Impact of the Boer War*. Abingdon: Routledge, 2014, pp 1, 6.

[21] Baskhanov, MK, 'U vorot angliyskogo moguschestva', in *AY Snesarev v Turkestane, 1899–1904*. Saint Petersburg: Nestor-Istoriya, 2015, p 104.

[22] Spring, D, 'Russian foreign policy and the Boer War', in Wilson, K (ed), *The International Impact of the Boer War*. Abingdon: Routledge, 2014, pp 48–58.

[23] *Anglo-burskaya voyna 1899–1902 godov glazami rossiyskih poddannyh*. V 13 tomah. Vol 9. Moscow: Izdatel I B Belyi, 2012, pp 6, 261–263.

[24] Okorokov, AV, *Russkiye dobrovoltsy*. Moscow: Yauza, Exmo, 2007, pp 20–25, 38.

[25] Ibid, p 35.

[26] Story, D, *The Campaign with Kuropatkin*. London: T Werner Laurie, 1904, p 255.

[27] Lowry, "'The world's no bigger than a kraal'", p 271.

[28] Romeiko-Gurko, VI, *Voyna Anglii s Yuzhno-Afrikanskimi respublikami 1899–1901 gg. Otchyot komandirovannogo po vysochaishemu poveleniyu k voyskam Yuzhno-Afrikanskhikh respublik Generalnogo Shtaba polkovnika Romeiko-Gurko*. Saint Petersburg: Voyenno-Uchetnyi Komitet Glavnogo Shtaba, 1901, pp 62–63.

[29] Pretorius, F, 'Welcome but not that welcome: The relations between foreign volunteers and the Boers in the Anglo-Boer War of 1899–1902', in Krüger CG and Levsen, S (eds), *War Volunteering in Modern Times*. London: Palgrave Macmillan, 2010, pp 127–128, 143.

[30] *Anglo-burskaya voyna 1899–1902 godov glazami rossiyskih poddannyh*. Vol 8, p 274.

[31] Pretorius, 'Welcome but not that welcome', p 122.

[32] Davidson, A and Filatova, I, *The Russians and the Anglo-Boer War, 1899–1902*. Cape Town: Human & Rousseau, 1998, p 40; Hillegas, HC, *With the Boer Forces*. London: Methuen & Co, 1900, p 257.

[33] '400 Russians with the Boers', *Lancashire Evening Post*, 20 March 1900, p 4; 'The Russian volunteers', *The Times*, 18 April 1900, p 3.

[34] On Russian Jewish immigrants in the burgher armies, see Saks, D, *Boerejode: Jews in the Boer Armed Forces, 1899–1902*. Johannesburg: Charlie Fine Printers, 2010.

[35] A Bulgarian volunteer wrote from Natal in December 1899: '[The Boers] cannot understand what a "Bulgar" means, they never heard of this people before; had I called myself a Russian they would understand at once ...' 'Letter from a Bulgarian officer with the Boers', *The Times*, 10 January 1900, p 11.

36 Ē Jēkabsons, personal communication with B Gorelik, 21 May 2020.

37 *Anglo-burskaya voyna 1899–1902 godov glazami rossiyskih poddannyh*. Vol 8, p 306; Jēkabsons, Ē, 'Zabytiy latysh anglo-burskoy voiny', *Otkrytyi Gorod*, 2019, no 7/8, p 102.

38 Ē Jēkabsons, personal communication with B Gorelik, 10 January 2022.

39 *Anglo-burskaya voyna 1899–1902 godov glazami rossiyskih poddannyh*. Vol 8, pp 306–310.

40 *Voyennaya entsiklopediya*, vol 5. Saint Petersburg: Tovaritshestvo ID Sytina, 1912, p 247.

41 Avgustus, Y, 'V gostyakh u turok. Puteviye ocherki i vpechatleniya', *Varshavsky Voyenny Zhurnal*, 1903, no 7, pp 633–634.

42 Avgustus, 'V gostyakh u turok', pp 633–634.

43 *Anglo-burskaya voyna 1899–1902 godov glazami rossiyskih poddannyh*. Vol 7, pp 241–242.

44 'Nos échos', *Le Journal*, 26 December 1899, p 1; *Sheffield Evening Telegraph*, 19 December 1899, p 2; Voropaeva, NG, Vyatkina, PP and Shubin, GV (comp and eds), *Anglo-burskaya voyna 1899–1902 gg. Po arkhivnym materialam i vosponiminaniyam ochevidtsev*. Moscow: Vostochnaya Literatura, 2001, pp 61–62.

45 *Anglo-burskaya voyna 1899–1902 godov glazami rossiyskih poddannyh*. Vol 9, pp 61–62; 'Nos échos'.

46 *Anglo-burskaya voyna 1899–1902 godov glazami rossiyskih poddannyh*. Vol 7, pp 122–123.

47 The term 'transitional phase' was proposed by Fransjohan Pretorius. See Pretorius, F, 'The Second Anglo-Boer War: An overview', *Scientia Militaria: South African Journal of Military Studies*, 2000, vol 30, no 2, p 111.

48 De Jong, C and Foxcroft, E (eds), 'Reports of neutral military observers during the Anglo-Boer War (The reports of two Russian military attachés, 1899–1900)', *Scientia Militaria: South African Journal of Military Studies*, 1975, vol 5, no 3, pp 1–21, and no 4, pp 49–61; [Ebergardt, AK], 'The Russian Red Cross in the Anglo-Boer War, 1899–1902: Report by a Russian doctor translated by C Moody', *Historia*, 1977, no 2, pp 112–129; Izedinova, SA, *A Few Months with the Boers: The War Reminiscences of a Russian Nursing Sister*. Translated and edited by HJ Moody. Johannesburg: Perskor Publications, 1977; Maria Z, 'How I was a volunteer in the Transvaal', *Hertzog-Annale van die Suid-Afrikaanse Akademie vir Wetenskap en Kuns*, 1964, vol 11, December, pp 112–122; Romeiko-Gurko, VI, 'England's war against the South African republics', *Scientia Militaria: South African Journal of Military Studies*, 1981, vol 11, no 4, pp 5–17, and 1982, vol 12, no 1, pp 44–57.

49 Johnson, RW, 'Rogue's paradise', *London Review of Books*, 1998, vol 20, no 14.

50 Davidson and Filatova, *The Russians and the Anglo-Boer War*, p 30.

Editor's note

The reminiscences of Yevgeny Avgustus were first introduced to South African readers by Elisaveta Kandyba-Foxcroft, the founder of the Department of Russian at the University of South Africa, in her book *Russia and the Anglo-Boer War* (1981). Apollon Davidson and Irina Filatova quoted long excerpts from Avgustus's account in *The Russians and the Anglo-Boer War* (1998). I translated an abridged version of the memoir that was brought out by the South African Military History Society in 2016.[1]

This edition is the first book of combat memoirs of the South African War by a Russian volunteer published outside Russia. It complements the research into Russian involvement in the South African War that has been carried out at the Institute for African Studies, Russian Academy of Sciences, since the 1990s.[2]

The text presented in this book is a reconstruction. It comprises accounts of the war by Yevgeny Avgustus which appeared in his book of 1902, as well as in Russian newspapers and magazines in 1899–1902.[3] The selections are arranged chronologically in a coherent narrative, from his departure for South Africa in December 1899 until the formation of the Russian corps and their departure for Natal in March 1900. The transitions between the sources (including sections appearing in subsequent issues of the same publication) are marked with the symbol ◆.

For this edition, which is aimed at a general readership, the editor has divided the memoir into chapters. The original instalments of the memoir published between 1900 and 1902 did not contain chapter titles; they were only numbered. However, for this edition the editor introduced chapter titles.

Several texts have been trimmed for inclusion in the present volume to eliminate repetitions and long passages unrelated to the South African War. Descriptions of military operations in which Avgustus did not participate as well as his tactical and strategic discussions based on information that he learnt from literature on his return from the war have also been omitted. For this reason, I have excluded his often-cited description of the Battle of Spion Kop, which could not be an eyewitness account because Avgustus joined the Boer troops after the battle had ended.[4] These deletions are indicated by an ellipsis (…) in the text.

Misspellings in place and personal names, and in foreign words in the original texts, have been corrected in the English translation whenever possible. The surnames of Avgustus's companions, which he concealed behind initials for original publication, have been spelt out in this edition (except one, which is still unidentified). The surnames were first revealed by Davidson and Filatova.[5]

In some instances, Avgustus uses racial and other terms that are now considered inappropriate or offensive. They have been retained in the translation for the sake of historical accuracy. The attitudes of Russian visitors to South Africa were often determined by colonial stereotypes, and the author refers to the peoples of South Africa as they were known to European settlers at the time. In the interests of authenticity, this volume retains passages that reveal his racial prejudices.

The original Russian text was translated into English by Lucas Venter especially for this edition.

The notes contain information on people, places and events referred to by the memoirist. Full bibliographical details of works mentioned in the notes are provided at the end of the volume.

Notes

[1] Avgustus, Y, *A Russian Fighting for the Boer Cause*. Translated and edited by B Gorelik. Johannesburg: South African Military History Society, 2016; Davidson and Filatova, *The Russians and the Anglo-Boer War*; Kandyba-Foxcroft, E. *Russia and the Anglo-Boer War 1899–1902*. Pretoria: CUM Books, 1981.
[2] Shubin, GV, *Rossiyskie dobrovoltsy v anglo-burskoy voyne (1899–1902) (po materialam Rossiyskogo gosudarstvennogo voenno-istoricheskogo arkhiva)*. Moscow: Institut Afriki RAN, 2000; Voropaeva, NG; Vyatkina, PP and

Shubin, GV (comp and eds). *Anglo-burskaya voyna 1899–1902 gg. Po arkhivnym materialam i vosponiminaniyam ochevidtsev.* Moscow: Vostochnaya Literatura, 2001; *Anglo-burskaya voyna 1899–1902 godov glazami rossiyskih poddannyh.* V 13 tomah. Moscow: Izdatel IB Belyi, 2012.

3   See the bibliography at the end of this volume.

4   Quoted at length in Davidson and Filatova, *The Russians and the Anglo-Boer War*, and fully reproduced in Avgustus, *A Russian Fighting for the Boer Cause.*

5   Davidson and Filatova, *The Russians and the Anglo-Boer War*, pp 27–29, 48.

Евгеній Августусъ

5834

Воспоминанія

участника англо-бурской войны

1899–1900

Типографія „БРИСТОЛЬ", Электоральная ул.
ВАРШАВА 1902 г.

YEVGENY AVGUSTUS

A combat memoir
of the Anglo-Boer War
1899–1900

– Kléber[1]

To Pavel Stakhovich[2]

CHAPTER 1

A farewell to Russia

In a brochure published abroad, Count Leo Tolstoy likens the Anglo-Boer War to a tavern brawl fought by drunken apprentices.[3] In the eyes of the staunch preacher of non-resistance to evil, the valiant Boer nation committed a grave offence when it fearlessly took up the challenge hurled at it by the mighty 'Mistress of the Seas' and resolved to defend to the last drop of blood its sacred principles and its historic right to exist.

Another Russian sage, Mr Menshikov, has adopted an even more unforgiving stance towards the Boer people.[4] 'The reason for the war', he writes in an article, 'is that the English asked the Boers for citizenship rights, nothing more. Yet it is written that if any man wishes to take away your coat, let him have your cloak also, and had the pious Boers but slightly possessed the wisdom of this law, we would not presently be witnessing the crime of suicide or the crime of murder being committed. Instead of war, they would still have had peace, the lives of all the fallen and at least some modicum of material power. Had the Boers, instead of fighting, made all the concessions required of them by Christian conscience, both republics would have been saved and poor old Kruger[5] could have lived out his old age in peace, free from all the hatred and curses showered upon him by the bereaved families of Boer and Brit alike. But no, old Kruger wanted war. Intoxicated by power and wealth, and ignorant of the forces at work in the world, the old man went and bought European instruments of death, cannons and cartridges in enormous quantities, proclaiming that to his best knowledge God was on the Boers' side; that war was a necessity. The result has been shame, despair, doom, ruin, captivity, craven retreat and a bloodstained conscience.'

Why did Mr Menshikov not ask himself why the British had laid their hands first on the Boers' coat and then on their cloak? Why should only the Boers be guided by the promptings of Christian conscience? What about the British, who are, incidentally, so proud of their notorious Bible Society? Mr Menshikov's attempt to portray President Kruger as the culprit for the war is not lacking in wit, and yet he completely ignores the existence of all the Chamberlains and Co, passes over in silence the true reasons behind this struggle for life and death between nations and, without the least embarrassment, attributes the war to the personal whims of a senile old man.

Similar opinions, characterised more by originality than by depth of thought, have been expressed about the support enjoyed by the Boers since the outbreak of war. We sympathise with the Boers, some say, not because their cause is just and law and justice are on their side, but merely because of the excitement, like at a bullfight, elicited by the breathtaking spectacle of war that has unfolded before us, and by the need to pick a side to support. The spectacle of war playing out before us is so excruciating, and yet so agreeable, that we fret and tremble as though experiencing the sensations of battle for ourselves. Indeed, the Boers knew full well that they were on centre stage and that the entire world was watching them as if they were gladiators from Ancient Rome, and this realisation encouraged them, spurred them on and ultimately led to their downfall.

But this does not explain the universal outpouring of heartfelt sympathy for the Boers. Rather, these feelings were born from the lofty and unshakeable courage with which this nation went to its death and destruction for the sake of freedom and independence. These astonishing exemplars of steadfastness and forbearance have had a striking impact on European society, and among our people too, as crushed and sullied as we have been by our petty interests and everyday concerns, the Boers have aroused the noblest human feelings: a sense of justice, a sense of indignation in the face of violence and a willingness for self-sacrifice. And thus it was that hundreds of volunteers from all countries and nations sealed this willingness with their own blood. They did not fight, suffer and die for honour, money or glory, and yet their pale bones now lie scattered in the mountains and plains of the Transvaal or rest beneath a layer of silt at the bottom of the turbid Tugela or the Modder River.

For six solid months I fought side by side with the Boers, lay with them in the trenches. Their blood and brains clotted my eyes when deadly shrapnel struck comrades close by. Together we endured all the deprivations and adversities of commando life; they shared their last rusks, their last sips of water with me, and I learnt to love and respect these stern and unfriendly looking, childishly good-natured, wholeheartedly courageous and profoundly religious men.

The personnel of the Russo-Dutch Ambulance with their patients in Kroonstad, March 1900.

When I returned to my homeland from English captivity, I often had to hear comments from some volunteers, and especially from the Red Cross doctors who had been in the Transvaal,[6] accusing the Boers of ingratitude and inhospitality to foreigners, and even of cowardice. Woe to the vanquished! For instance, some doctors reported that Boers had inflicted injuries upon themselves, even cut off their own fingers, in order that they might escape from their commandos, lie about in hospitals and wander back to their farms. These venerable adepts of Hippocrates take it upon themselves to judge an entire nation because of a handful of cowardly scoundrels. They forget the throng of unsung heroes who spent their days and nights in trenches to the sound of whistling bullets and screaming grenades, languishing from hunger and thirst, and dying from festering wounds far from any well-equipped hospitals.

As for the disgruntled foreign volunteers, these gentlemen forget that a nation writhing in the throes of death may have more on its mind than arranging galas and cheering crowds for its self-appointed saviours or decorating them with all sorts of ranks and medals. Frankly speaking, it is important to realise that not all the volunteers were idealists of the first water; many were simply drawn to the war by expectations of financial gain or a chance to give free rein to their ill-concealed instincts for thieving and looting. And so it was that men of sincere conviction, men of passion, laid down their lives, while the nimbler, more eagle-eyed ones filled their pockets with ringing Kruger and Victoria sovereigns and made it back to Europe in the nick of time, all resplendent in their tawdry laurels of 'Transvaal heroes'. ...

◆

December 1899, two months after the outbreak of war

Outside the carriage window, snowflakes flickered in a frantic dance. The sparks from the locomotive flared up and faded while the wheels of the carriages thumped and clattered rhythmically, as though drumming out the beat of some strange and unfamiliar melody. The carriage was warm and cosy inside. My frazzled nerves were gradually simmering down as fragmentary recollections of the last days before my departure rushed through my mind.

I had experienced and lived through much. There had been much hassle and fuss to obtain all the necessary papers and legal permits. I had to listen to ridicule, advice and entreaties not to leave for the ends of the earth, but to throw this mad idea out of my head, stay home and stick to faithful army service. Grey-haired, worldly-wise men shrugged ironically and told me that it would be unforgivable to put my life, my secure position and my future on the line for the sake of devotion to a romantic idea more worthy of a schoolboy whose head has been filled with the novels of Mayne Reid or Gustave Aimard.[7] I heard them out respectfully, agreed with them that my decision was truly unwise, even dangerous; and yet, since there was no law against it, why should I not go?

I travelled with a friend who fully shared my views.[8]

Why is it that any impulse, any passion for some abstraction is only good [illegible] or is met with condemnation, ridicule or incomprehension in our country? Why is the desire to join the Boers as they fight by force of arms for their freedom and very existence seen as strange, somehow quixotic?

Why is it strange for a man who cannot find any application for his energy at home to go off in search of another field of activity if the close confines of everyday life oppress him? Is it better if an excess of the exuberant force of youth, experienced only once in life, is spent on revelries, senseless orgies and the like? It is doubly commendable.

Finally, what soldier will not shiver like a war horse at the mere news that somewhere in the south of Africa cannons are thundering, bullets are whistling and blood is flowing like a river, that there is an opportunity to smell gunpowder not on the training ground, on the shooting range or on manoeuvres against a mock foe, but in the open field where valiant Boers struggle for their lives in mortal combat?

And now the hour of parting had arrived. Fellow officers from different regiments, family acquaintances and lady friends were gathered at the station.

Ordinary soldiers from my company stood bunched together on the platform to bid a last farewell to their commanding officer.

'Take us with you, sir!' a lean and handsome corporal asked me, with tears in his eyes.

And now, at last, we were on our way. We crossed the border late into the night. Instead of a friendly *'Proszę pana'* [Please, sir] we heard a menacing *'Bitte, Herr'*, and the blue-nosed face of a German conductor peered into the carriage.

Thorn, Bromberg, Schneidemühl and other stations flashed by as in a dream. Now and then, new passengers would enter or leave our carriage. It should be mentioned that in Prussia we exchanged second class for third, which was crowded and uncomfortable. Despite the steam heating, the cold was more tangible here. Frost covered the windows and formed intricate patterns of ice.

Nothing is as dull as travelling by night in a crowded railway carriage. There was little of interest about the other travellers: fat German townsmen with square faces, some shady-looking characters morosely reading the *Vorwärts*,[9] sharp-nosed German ladies who stared at us with fish-like eyes.

But the *Zugführer* [train driver] consoled us that we would soon be in Berlin, and, indeed, in the gloom of dawn we could make out the vague outlines of enormous buildings, factories and railway structures. From the towering viaduct on which our train was racing, a vista of endless rectilinear streets opened where dawn had already arrived courtesy of the many electric and gas streetlamps.

Every two minutes, trains from the Berlin City Railway rushed past our carriage's windows in the opposite direction with a deafening boom and whistle. One railway station flashed past, then another, but we chose to get off at the central station on Friedrichstrasse.

Despite the early hour, we left the enormous station building, under whose vaulted glass roof the piercing whistles of steam locomotives never grow quiet. We decided to go for a walk through the city.

Berlin's working people get up early: haggard labourers, skinny clerks with briefcases, kitchen maids and servant girls with groceries scurried along the streets shivering from the cold. A well-nourished *Schutzmann* [policeman] in traditional helmet and warm, fur-collared coat gazed indifferently at the crowd.

The shops gradually started opening up, their windows glittering with all manner of merchandise, and the traffic began to increase. Bulky, brightly painted wagons, jam-packed omnibuses and hand-drawn carts all crowded the streets. The whistles, rumbles and cries of the cabbies blended into a single stupefying buzz that had an unpleasant effect on our nerves, already worn out by the previous night's lack of sleep. Moreover, it was cold. A biting, fitful wind whipped up entire drifts of snow; the Berliners had not seen a winter like this in a long time, with temperatures around eight to nine below freezing point.

We entered the first restaurant we encountered along our way. Used to Warsaw's modest little *cukiernias* [cafés], we were astonished by the Café Victoria's vast halls, mirror-lined walls, crystal chandeliers and marble tables.

A group of students sat at one of the other tables, their bloated faces, dull eyes and drunken voices clearly signalling that these disciples of the Berlin alma mater had been making merry all night and were now trying to nurse their hangovers with the aid of countless glasses of wine. We must have caught their eye, for soon we overheard some feeble witticisms aimed in our direction. One of them, a blond youth with the muscles of an athlete, staggered over and, adopting a defiant pose, delivered a slurred speech to us. He said that as a theology student he was very pleased to see some Russian nihilists[10] who must clearly have fled their country after suffering for their ideology. He was amazed, however, that we preferred black coffee to Berlin's marvellous beer, and on behalf of his comrades invited us to join their company. We declined the invitation, wished him all the best and left the café in a hurry.

We now headed for Unter den Linden, which was already swarming with people: smug, well-fed bourgeois, army lieutenants with their invariable monocles and moustaches waxed *à l'empereur* [in the style of the Emperor], and soldiers from the Imperial Guard, who resembled the tin soldiers on display in toy-shop windows. Everywhere the military element clearly predominated. Incidentally, it is interesting to note that when we asked about Berlin's sights, we were mostly recommended to watch the changing of the palace guard, and only then advised to explore the museums, theatres and monuments.

We walked through an arcade where one of the shopfronts displayed a group of wax figures depicting the heroes of the day: Kruger, Joubert and two Boers armed to the teeth.

The shops in the arcade resembled an exhibition, such was the variety and richness of the merchandise on display in their mirrored windows. There were haberdashery items, jewellery and luxury goods that struck us with their fine workmanship and elegant trimmings.

We had to dine at Aschinger's,[11] and we astonished the waiters and patrons no end by declining any beer. The lunch was excellently served, splendidly cooked and very cheap, around two marks including the obligatory *Trinkgeld* [tip]. We were unpleasantly surprised by the Germans' patriotism, which could be inferred from the presence of Kaiser Wilhelm's portrait gracing all the beer mugs, crockery and advertisements for some new-fangled moustache wax.

We did not expect to stay long in Berlin, as we were in pursuit of a single goal, to reach Dr Leyds[12] in Brussels as soon as possible, and from there to travel to Marseilles or Naples, where we would embark on our sea journey to the Transvaal. The earliest tickets to Cologne were for the evening train at 10 pm, and therefore we took no hotel rooms but continued our aimless wanderings around the city.

We took a horse tram to the Tiergarten and admired the majestic Reichstag building, which was at the time a witness to fierce debates concerning the need for credits to increase the size of the German navy. This public issue was the subject of heated discussions in all cafés and restaurants, but opinions differed acutely among the public and various newspapers lining the political spectrum. The alluring picture conjured up by the fervent imagination of government supporters found no sympathy among liberals and socialists. They listened sceptically to Bülow's eloquent exhortations for Germany to have as many fearsome battleships as it has merchant vessels so that the German navy could be the equal of the British navy, and so forth.[13] But the German burgher skimps and scrounges; soon it would be Christmas and he would assuredly buy his tiny tot a paper helmet, a sword and toy soldiers, or even a sailor's suit, but he would not give any money to the navy.

Near the Reichstag, I saw a fenced-in square: our fellow passengers in the tram explained to us that the city was erecting a statue of Bismarck here. I struck up a conversation with a talkative Berliner and mentioned that Germany, and especially Prussia, is indebted to the Iron Chancellor for its might and grandeur and that the Berliners probably revere his memory. That is true, he replied, but before Bismarck tobacco, beer and everything else used to be better and cheaper; sooner or later Germany will have to pay dearly for the policies of its former rulers. Every year the working class, which is suffering heavily from the onerously high cost of living, grows visibly more dissatisfied with the belligerent policies of the Empire. The idolisation of militarism is gradually subsiding and has given way to an ironic attitude towards military service; officers of the Prussian Army speak disdainfully about the monotony of garrison service, the inadequate pay and the boredom of endlessly training recruits. Many of them spoke enviously to me of their comrades who had found employment as instructors in the armies of the South American republics or who are now fighting with the Boer forces, although I must note that for the right price, they would have joined the British just as willingly.

The soldiers were not particularly enthusiastic about the two-year length of military service or about soldiering in general. There was a stark difference between the conscripted soldiers, young beardless lads who look like frightened rabbits, and the *capitulante*, the long-service non-commissioned officers who make up the regular army. One could judge the soldiers' spirit by the peculiar jargon they use. For example, they called a steel helmet a '*Hurratute*' [literally, 'hurrah funnel'], and the standard, that holy relic of a regiment, was referred to as a '*Begeisterungknüppel*' [enthusiasm stick]. They have many other peculiar words that are untranslatable into Russian.

Unfortunately, the time we spent in Berlin visiting restaurants and cafés talking to whatever soldiers, warrant officers or policemen happened to cross our path was not enough for me to draw a more complete portrait.

It was already evening when we took one final stroll along Berlin's main street under the illumination of electric lights. Grey multi-storey buildings rose up on both sides of Unter den Linden. The statue of Elector Frederick William, the father of Prussian might, loomed like a menacing dark shape in the distance.[14]

Tomorrow we depart for Cologne, and from there to Brussels. Oh, I cannot wait to get to the Transvaal! What if they take Ladysmith and Kimberley without us?

◆

It was still too early to board the train, and so, whether we liked it or not, we had to wander aimlessly along the busy pavements of Unter den Linden, the main artery of Berlin street life.

Snowflakes swirled in the air, obscuring the light of the

Boer shoe polish, made in Russia during the war.

Boer chocolate.

streetlamps. The outlines of snow-covered buildings rose dimly from the semi-darkness while palaces and monuments loomed darkly in the distance. The pavement was as bright as day. In the colossal shop windows expensive jewellery glowed and glittered in the blinding light of the electric lamps.

I enjoyed looking through the window of a large toy shop. Beautiful tin soldiers stood on display, not the usual exact copies of the

Prussian Army, but British royal guardsmen in red uniforms and tall bearskin hats. All these toys, destined to decorate Berlin children's Christmas trees, had been given a caricature look, but the tin Boers in their wide-brimmed hats looked cheerful and dashing.

Here was another toy – a little devil whose features resemble Chamberlain's renowned face.[15] All this was testimony of the Germans' antipathy towards the British, but what do children's toys have to do with politics?

And here we were in a train carriage again, and again the dark night lay spread out before our window. From the sands of Brandenburg, the train carried us across the endless lowlands of Hanover, famous for its honey and fine-fleeced sheep, across the richest areas of the Prussian kingdom, Westphalia and the Rhineland, and on to Cologne, where we were to transfer to the Brussels train.

We endured the torments of the Holy Inquisition in our car: the seats in the third-class compartment were awfully hard, a jet of frozen air blew through the cracks, windows and doors, and our feet felt unbearably hot from the heated steam pipes. At one end sat a red-cheeked, snub-nosed German lady, a sister of mercy reeking of carbolic acid, and at the other end a fat merchant who gave off a smell of beer and cheap cigars.

Finally, at one of the stations some new passengers flocked in with whom I managed to strike up a conversation; one of them, a venerable grey-bearded old man, turned out to be a veteran of 1866, a former officer of the Hanoverian army who could still remember King George, who subsequently died in exile after Hanover's accession to Prussia.[16] He had taken part in the battle of Langensalza, where the Hanoverian troops had been utterly crushed by the Prussians;[17] he spoke with vitriol about the current regime and recalled the old days of Hanover's independence with regret.

He did not answer me when I asked him if there were still any separatist aspirations left.

'You know, in 1870 we were only waiting to hear about the first French victories in order to raise a general uprising. Our troops fought the French only out of necessity, just as Irish regiments are now fighting as part of the British troops.'

Another fellow, a handsome dark-haired man with a sunburnt,

manly face, told me that he was serving as second mate on a steamer belonging to the Krupp factories and was on his way to Antwerp, from where he would be taking a cargo to Japan.

When I asked him how Krupp's cannons and quick-firing guns end up in Pretoria, he gave a sly smile.

I saw fit to tell him of our plans and admitted to him that we were going to the Transvaal as volunteers, that we were Russian officers, and so on.

The gallant second mate perked up, and I learnt that a mere two years ago he himself had accompanied a consignment of cannons, siege weapons and quick-firing guns to Delagoa Bay, and from there to Pretoria.

The republic began to expect war against the British immediately after repelling the Jameson Raid. The government took measures to put Pretoria on a defensive footing, replenishing its military supplies and drawing up a war plan. Millions of Mannlicher rifles were kept in the arsenals.[18] A bullet from a Mannlicher can penetrate a two-inch-thick board from 4 000 yards.[19] The marksmanship of the Boers is astonishing: at the historic battle of Majuba, British General John Colley[20] was killed at 400 yards by a well-aimed shot from an old-model rifle.

Boers are avid wildlife hunters and use special bullets in their Mannlicher rifles, which they obtain by filing off the head of the nickel casing. Such a modified bullet inflicts a terrible wound and is as good as a dum-dum. At the start of war, however, President Kruger announced that the use of these bullets would be prohibited if the British renounced their use of the dum-dum.

The tough old sailor told me many other interesting things.

The climate of Natal is terrible in November and December, especially for the unaccustomed European; the heat is unbearable during the day and sometimes reaches forty degrees. Hurricanes can rise up unexpectedly and sweep whole clouds of hot sand from the Kalahari Desert. Sometimes these hurricanes burst into terrible tropical showers, only to grow silent and disappear at sunset. At night, however, the thermometer often falls below zero, and if you are sleeping in a tent, you have no choice but to cover yourself with a mass of blankets and animal hides.

He got off at one of the stations and, bidding us a hearty farewell, wished us the best of luck and safety.

We were approaching Cologne: factory chimneys rose on either side of the railway; the dense clouds of smoke, glow of blast furnaces and massive works proclaimed that we were now in the Rhineland's industrial centre.

The railway bridge spanning the Rhine's broad and muddy waters shook loudly beneath us. Tall buildings with abundant medieval-style gables and painted decoration gleamed white in the morning rays of the cold winter sun.

Advertisements of all kinds were plastered across the walls and on the red-tiled roofs. The ornate spires of the famous Cologne Cathedral, constructed in the austere Gothic style, towered above the labyrinth of buildings and streets.

Here, as in Berlin, the train passed along a high viaduct, until at last it stopped at the station, where, as it turned out, we would have to wait more than an hour for our train to Brussels.

We were utterly exhausted after our two sleepless nights, during which we had been unable to shut our eyes for even a minute, and so we preferred to enjoy a cup of tea in the vast, warm hall of the railway station rather than stroll through the streets of Cologne.

Foreign railway stations have no bells or whistles: had we not been warned in time by our efficient porter, we would have missed our train.

There was no third class on the nine o'clock express train and we reclined grandly in the threadbare velvet seats of the second-class compartment.

The landscape became more picturesque with every passing hour: bright little rivers snaked between the wooded slopes of the Ardennes mountains. There, atop a promontory, lay Aachen, the old German city with its ancient cathedral, where the emperors from the houses of Hohenstaufen and Habsburg used to be crowned.

The Belgian customs officials did not bother to inspect our luggage. On the whole, the dapper, light-limbed Walloons made a better impression on us than the self-important, puffed-up Germans, who had an air about them as if they had only yesterday signed the receipt for France's five-billion war indemnity.

Willem Johannes Leyds, the South African Republic's
special envoy in Brussels and Saint Petersburg.

And here we were in Brussels, but still far away from our goal.
In vain, our fellow travellers had assured us that finding Leyds, the
South African Republic's authorised agent, would be very easy: '*Il est
connu par tout le monde!* [Everybody knows him!] No one knew his
address, nor did his surname appear in any of the directories. In one
place we were told that he had recently left for Marseilles, in another
that he was dead. At last, we remembered that we had in our side
pocket a letter to Leyds on which his address was indicated. We had
to take a hired carriage, but within half an hour we were sitting in his
luxuriously furnished office.

A tall, dark-haired man with an expressive face, he seemed to be
a worthy representative of that valiant nation dying for its independence. After brilliantly graduating from the University of Leyden
in public law and jurisprudence, he enjoyed President Kruger's full

confidence from the start of the war and had been appointed to the important role of authorised agent of the South African Republic in Brussels.

We spent more than an hour in lively conversation with him, speaking both French and German.

He expressed his deepest gratitude to us for our willingness to serve this just cause, but subtly observed that we must be aware that he was not at liberty to recruit volunteers and that the republic had not provided him with any means to send foreign officers to the theatre of military operations.

I interrupted him, declaring that we were travelling at our own risk and peril and did not require any reimbursement, but, as our funds were somewhat limited, we were willing, as a last resort, to travel steerage, that we never counted on receiving any subsidy, and so on.

To this he remarked with a smile that, as he lived in Brussels, he was bound by the Belgian government's neutrality, but that it was his duty to provide all possible assistance to volunteers, and that if not he then the friends of the republic would never allow Russian volunteers to travel steerage, and that we would soon receive tickets, if not in first then at the very least second class.

'Gentlemen, you will not be able to depart from Europe earlier than the 25th. By that time, a French steamer will leave Marseilles and take you as far as Madagascar. From there another steamer will take you to the mainland.'

He asked us to drop by the legation office on a subsequent morning for final discussions.

Even before our visit to Leyds, we had rented a room in one of the hotels on the rue du Fossé aux Loups [Wolf Pit Street] in the city centre. Its owner turned out to be a Czech from Austria, and when he heard that we were going to the Transvaal as volunteers, he gave us a decent room with full board, lunch and coffee for 7 francs 75 centimes per day.

Despite the street's terrifying name, we lived close by the city's main thoroughfare, next to the post office and not far from the main train stations, the Gare du Nord and the Gare du Midi, which are connected by an extremely busy road.

Day and night, carts of all kinds rumbled past, drawn by heavy, towering dray horses. Every minute, one of the electric streetcars criss-crossing the city in all directions rushed by. The newspaper sellers shouted incessantly, deafening the passers-by with: '*L'Intransigeant! Le Soir!* [newspaper names] *Une défaite des Anglais! Une nouvelle de la guerre!* [An English defeat! The news of the war!]

The streets were partly paved with granite, partly with black tiles; there was no snow in the city, but everywhere the pavements were covered in sticky mud. Passers-by stopped unceremoniously to look us over from head to toe. Some suspicious-looking characters, recognising foreigners in front of them, whispered recommendations to us: the address of some '*Palais de Crystal, que le diable t'emporte!*' [Crystal Palace, damn you!]

A crowd of workers, with white clay pipes clenched between their teeth and clad in tattered cloaks, clattered loudly past us in clumsy wooden shoes.

'*Des russes, des russes*' [Russians], they jabbered and suddenly shouted, '*Vive la Russie!*' [Long live Russia!] and waved their hats.

The evening mist already hung over the street and innumerable gas lamps flickered on in the distance when we returned to our hotel, broken and exhausted. We were brought buttered rolls and coffee, but without touching a thing we dived into our snow-white feather beds and plunged into a deep sleep interspersed with the most chimeric dreams: over there was the Krakowskie Przedmieście[21] and some familiar faces; but now we were suddenly in the Transvaal, riding ostriches; and then – oh horrors! – we were put in the guardhouse for wearing non-uniform pince-nez;[22] and now we were in the train again, but neither the locomotive's whistle nor the clickety-clack of the wheels could be heard over the cry of the newspaper sellers: '*Le Soir!* Regimental orders! *Kurier Poranny!*'[23] Gentlemen! Officers!' But then we were back in the guardhouse again. Cannons thundered. Horses neighed and clattered. Someone groaned. I plummeted down a diamond mine shaft until, at last, I woke up …

◆

After adopting their constitution, the Belgians unanimously elected Leopold I, the Duke of Coburg,[24] as king. It was a happy choice. The revolutionary storms of the 1840s went unnoticed in Belgium; he maintained friendly neutral relations with the neighbouring nations, bequeathing the country in a stellar condition to his heir, Leopold II. Under his son, who successfully continued his father's policies, trade and industry reached new heights, and he organised an excellent army and a whole system of fortifications on the borders. It is to his artistic nature that Brussels owes the construction of entire new neighbourhoods, monuments, theatres, lavish museums, and so on. His successful colonial policies resulted in Belgium's acquisition of the Congo's largest and richest region.[25]

I was unpleasantly struck, however, by the abundance of all manner of *dégustation, distillerie* and other drinking establishments, which you literally run into on every corner of Brussels. Of course, it is hard to judge on first impressions to what extent systematic drunkenness has permeated the morals of the Belgians, but in all the eating establishments both waiters and patrons gave us dark, perplexed looks when we refused the Spatenbräu Bock [a popular German beer] offered to us and insisted on coffee instead. The restaurants and cabarets were filled not only with half-starved workers in torn smocks but also with a perfectly sophisticated public poisoning itself with absinthe in the company of dressed-up wives and even children. Lunch is always served with wine and invariably followed up with beer or strong liqueurs of all kinds.

One Sunday we went for a walk around the city. The boulevards were packed with people dressed to the nines, nannies in gaudy hats and ribbons pushing baby carriages with red-cheeked infants, and dashing *carabinieri* [policemen] strolling decorously with comely maidens. Automobiles puffed and graceful cabriolets and landaus raced along the avenues. Crowds of worshippers poured out of the churches. All the shops were closed, the shutters lowered, and peace and quiet reigned everywhere. Sundays were clearly observed quite strictly.

But with the approach of evening, we came across ever-growing numbers of revelling merrymakers: top hats flung back, drunken speech all about and the laughter, cries and squeals of dishevelled ladies and their unsteadily swaying companions. Over to one side stood a gentleman warmly embracing a lamppost with groans and moans – the result of the immoderate consumption of alcoholic beverages or, to put it more loftily, of the worship of Bacchus. One ran into sights such as these every hundred yards, but the crowd did not pay the slightest attention to them.

One evening we received an express letter by city mail from the *Secrétaire de Légation de la République Sud-Africaine* [secretary of the mission of the South African Republic] with an invitation to *prendre une tasse de russe chez moi* [to have a cup of Russian tea at my place].

We crossed half the city before we reached the remote Avenue Louise.

Jonkheer van der Hoeven[26] welcomed us warmly and led us into his study. ...

Van der Hoeven was much travelled and had moved in the highest aristocratic and literary circles of Saint Petersburg, Paris and Vienna. It should be noted that Van der Hoeven's mother is Russian, née Apreleva ...[27]

In the corner stood an Érard piano; the host played the Boers' national anthem for us, whose solemn and magnificent air was lost on my musical ear, raised as I had been on the trumpet calls of infantry signallers.

My comrade, on the other hand, drove our host, a great lover and connoisseur of the vocal arts and music, into a state of inexpressible delight when he sang a couple of romances in his sonorous baritone.

'Fare you well, my young man's life!'[28]

The host sat down to accompany him, and one song followed another.

'Oh how the mist has fallen on the blue sea ...'

'I heard your soldiers' songs in Krasnoye Selo,'[29] said Van der Hoeven. 'It was something completely spontaneous, and yet how much musicality it contained, how much spirit and at the same time how much wild energy! Sing something like that!'

My comrade began to sing:

> *Ahoy there over the Danube*
> *Over the Danube so still ...*

Van der Hoeven quickly picked up the accompaniment. His fingers ran over the keys and the strings came resoundingly to life:

The plains of the Transvaal
The graves of brave men.
Drakensberg Peaks,
Will I see you again?

This was a variation on a battle song that had once been sung far away, above the snow-capped Balkans, the Valley of the Roses and the Shipka Pass.[30]

We sat for a long time in friendly conversation, drinking tea and smoking real Russian *papirosy* [filterless cigarettes].

Although Van der Hoeven was born in Wiesbaden, graduated from the University of Göttingen and served two years in the Life Guard Dragoon Regiment in Karlsruhe, he had been to South Africa and even managed to serve his homeland by taking part as a private soldier in repelling the Jameson Raid. According to him, the conquest of the Transvaal had long been a part of England's calculations. This was why the British government so vehemently opposed the participation of a representative of the Transvaal and Orange Republic [Orange Free State] at the Hague Peace Conference.[31]

'It would be a blessing for the South African Republic if the Russian government were to establish a Consulate General in Pretoria or dispatch a chargé d'affaires with diplomatic powers there,' he said. 'There is a trade consul, Mr Von Gernet, but that is not the same thing.[32]

'Speaking of the Russians in the Transvaal: every year thousands of Jews with Russian passports come to us; these people who scorn no means of worming their way into a place and growing rich, have managed to earn the total dislike of the native population; they do not hesitate to call themselves Russians in the most shameless manner, and that is how they are also listed in court proceedings when they stand accused of all kinds of fraudulent scams.

'So, in the Transvaal the words Jew and Russian are presently synonymous; but as soon as your volunteers and ambulance units have arrived, my countrymen will change their views about the Russians ...'

◆

Time passed imperceptibly in Van der Hoeven's cosy office. The soft light of the gas lamp fell on the darkened landscapes and portraits by old Dutch painters, bounced against the bright trinkets that lay scattered in creative disorder across the writing table and sparkled on the gilded Chinese porcelain cups in which our tea had been served. The silver kettle bubbled and hissed softly. The charcoal in the fireplace blazed red-hot.

I resumed our previous conversation, drawing a parallel between the current war in the Transvaal, the Swiss struggle against Charles the Bold and the Spanish War of 1810.[33]

Van der Hoeven's friendly, open face brightened.

'Yes, the Boers are defending their motherland, their hearth and home. It is not uncommon among us to see a father going into battle with all his sons. These are all peaceful tillers of the soil, accustomed to guarding their homesteads and herds against predatory jackals with a rifle in the hand. Now they have armed themselves against people whose predatory instincts have flared up uncontrollably.'

He got up and began pacing the room nervously.

Van der Hoeven took from the table the issue of *Le Rire* that had caused such a stir, and continued: 'Look, messieurs, at the drawings of the talented Villette.[34] Look at the inhabitants of the world's richest country dying of hunger, groaning under the yoke of Albion; here is an ocean steamer mercilessly sinking flimsy little fishing boats: time is money. Here is Joan of Arc at the stake. This nation that invented the notion of the gentleman has provoked, and will continue to provoke, the antipathy of other nations thanks to the ugly face of its morality and its cold egotistical disposition.

'God is not in power but in truth, a Russian proverb says. The Englishmen will not be aided by their formidable fleet, or by all the infernal machines of their Woolwich arsenal.[35] The sons of Britain will die a pointless and inglorious death in the sands of the Kalahari and the radiant star of "Rule, Britannia!" will fade forever.

'You, gentlemen, are foreigners, and you are willing to sacrifice your lives. You do not fear the long journey, death from an English bullet or some fatal disease. But I, I am forced to languish here in idleness while at home the women and children have armed themselves to defend their fatherland.'

All told, Van der Hoeven but little resembled a phlegmatic Dutch-man: his round face with its somewhat prominent cheekbones, his slightly upturned nose and lively brown eyes – these all proved that Russian blood flowed in his veins.

We tried to comfort him by telling him that he would be of more use to his country through his endeavours in the diplomatic field than we who were only fit for cannon fodder.

He related much to us about the Transvaal and all the ways in which it exemplifies the terrible difficulties of war, especially in the light of the narrow-mindedness displayed by the English tacticians who have already suffered so many appreciable defeats.

The Drakensberg mountains, which form a natural border between the Transvaal and Natal, rise to a height of 10000 feet and are in-tersected by sheer precipices and deep ravines, through which any movement of regular troops with artillery and baggage trains is im-possible. A handful of daredevils perched behind rock ledges can delay and repel an offensive by the largest detachment. Even assuming that the English will cross the Drakensberg (did not the Russians cross the Balkans, after all, as the English gentlemen console themselves?[36]), they will have a difficult time of it on the vast plateaus where the most fearsome enemies – fire and hunger – await them. The most singular hallmark of these steppes, known as the veldt, is the absence of water. Even in Johannesburg water is sold in sealed bottles at a cost of two francs per litre. You will seldom find more than one or two wells in a vi-cinity of hundreds of miles. Farmers store water in specially excavated reservoirs during the hot season of the year.[37]

The Boers are exceedingly familiar with their country, which they have transformed through long endeavours into fruitful fields and gardens, and are able, with the aid of signs known only to them, to establish the presence of underground water. That is why the Boers are never without coffee, not even in the dry season, which lasts half the year. Coffee is their trademark, as well as biltong – meat dried in the sun or over a fire – and these make up the entire daily ration of these unfastidious warriors. Without supplies or provisions, they easily make crossings of 100 to 150 km on their sturdy horses.

When I recall what it cost us to conquer Turkmenistan under more or less similar conditions, I find it almost impossible to believe in a successful outcome of the war for England.[38]

The theatre of war has yet another unique feature: the vegetation, which dries out completely during the dry season, when even the earth cracks under the scorching rays of the midday sun, can catch fire from even the smallest spark, and then there is no salvation for the troops.

Troops fighting in southern Africa will have to contend with all these things. Just like Cambyses' hordes,[39] the English battalions will suffer inglorious death at the hands of starvation, let alone all the types of diseases now rampant in the active army. The number of wounded, killed or captured soldiers never gives an accurate picture of the victims of war.

Official reports and communiqués are always silent about the number of people who have been put out of action by disease, abandoned by the wayside and now lying somewhere along the army's path. And yet, every war is marked by the appearance of contagious epidemics, typhus, all kinds of fevers and dysentery. When adding up the number of casualties, it makes little difference whether a soldier dies with lead in his heart or departs this life from typhus.

It is interesting to recall that during the Crimean campaign, the French lost 20 000 men in military action and more than 75 000 men as a result of infectious diseases.[40] The ratio of soldiers killed on the battlefield to those who died in hospitals during the American Civil War of 1861–1864 is even more striking: 70 000 compared to 190 000.[41] In short, we can assume that the British will lose at least half of their army, even if one uses the most modest percentage of deaths from diseases, which have already taken on appalling proportions. And to think that the proud Englishmen have turned down any assistance from our Red Cross![42] ...

◆

On Leyds's instructions, passports with his signature and bearing the seal and coat of arms of the Republic were prepared for us by the appointed day. The coat of arms consisted of an oval shield divided into three fields: in the upper right a Boer in a wide-brimmed hat was depicted holding a rifle; on the left a lion; and in the lower half an ox-wagon, a symbol of the nomadic life of this free nation that now defended its independence by force of arms. The shield was surmounted by a single-headed eagle; at the bottom was a short motto, '*Eendracht maakt macht*' [Unity makes strength].

The assistant secretary toiled for a long time to complete the '*Signalement*' [physical description] fields on the passport, filling in the height in centimetres, colour of the eyes, hair, and so forth. Our special features were not neglected either: my near-sightedness and my comrade's goatee.

All *princes et états, amis et alliés de la dite République* [princes and states, friends and allies of the said Republic] were invited to render us assistance and succour, but we also knew that if we were caught with such passports in Lourenço Marques or some other landing point, the English would most certainly hang us without further ado.[43]

In addition to the passports, Leyds handed me letters to the Transvaal consul in Lourenço Marques and to the government of the Republic in Pretoria.

Finally, we said goodbye to Leyds.

The Transvaal legate's eyes glistened beneath his beetling brows and the muscles quivered on his impassive face when he reached out to shake our hands for the last time and wish us a happy journey. We had to return to the hotel to write our last letters, pack our things and pay the hotel owner, who at the last moment had transformed from an ally of *la dite République* into a most unscrupulous innkeeper.

The bill he handed us was three times higher than expected.

We were greatly upset by the maid, who started wailing like a Russian peasant woman seeing off a recruit: 'Ah … ah … ah … my dear, sweet boys! My precious ones! *À la guerre … où les dum-dum sifflent! Le sang coule en flots* [To the war … where the dum-dums whistle! Blood flows in torrents]. Ah … ah … ah.'

And she hadn't even received her tip yet.

At last, we were in the express train of the famous northern line, in second class for lack of a third; the coaches were dirty and impossibly cramped, and passengers had to sit in the narrow aisles on their suitcases. But the public was not despondent, and instead of protests we heard jokes and witticisms aimed at the railway administration everywhere.

Conversation did not cease for a minute. Just as everywhere else, people talked about the war, praised the valiant Boers, railed against *la perfide Albion* [perfidious Albion] for all they were worth, then moved on to other, no less interesting, topics: stories and innuendo-laden anecdotes concerning the latest scandalous gossip about Paris life alternated with serious discussions about Delcassé's policies[44] or analysis of the famous court case.[45] Words flowed in an uncontrollable stream and were accompanied by lively facial expressions and passionate gestures.

We arrived in Paris late into the night, at one o'clock, took a room in the first little hotel we came across – a miserable-looking place – and went wandering around the boulevards.

The life of Paris, that world centre, bubbled over like a volcano and engulfed us with the fretful breath of some fairy-tale monster. Despite the late hour, the pavements of the Boulevard de la Madeleine were swarming with cheerful, well-dressed crowds. The shops were closed, but in the windows, all-night cafés and restaurants, mirrors shone and shimmered from the reflection of countless chandeliers.

Gradually the crowd began at last to thin out here too. We too returned to our hotel, which was situated on one of the streets of the Faubourg-Montmartre. To be in Paris and not see all the wonders of this modern Babylon would be unforgivable to say the least.

When we turned into the Champs-Élysées, it seemed as if we had landed up in Paris at the height of the 1870 bombardment.[46]

The famous Palais de l'Industrie, which since 1855 has been the central point for all exhibitions, was a sorry sight; only the framework of the domes remained, the walls peered gloomily out from among heaps of timber and steam cranes.[47] Piles of rubbish and bricks lay all about and destruction reigned everywhere. The plan is to construct a broad avenue in its place from the Champs-Élysées to the Port de la Conférence, connected to the opposite [bank] by the Alexander III bridge.[48] …

The areas reserved for exhibitions were a hive of activity; as far as you could see there were timber and cranes, and everywhere thousands of toiling hands were busy dismantling and building all sorts of constructions that were quite striking in their architecture and dimensions.

The mountains of bricks and rubbish complicated access to the site, and it was impossible to get any sense out of the workers; every building you asked about was invariably called the highlight of the exhibition. Things got even worse when you directed your enquiries to the architects or engineers. They would either look you over with a haughty stare and disappear inside the galleries without bothering to reply, or grasp you by the collar and drag you around the piles of bricks, down some ladders and into some underground passages, bombarding you with whole flurries of technical terminology, arcane parlance and so many details that you could only twiddle your thumbs and roll your eyes wildly …

We wandered long around the Trocadéro and the Champs de Mars until we arrived at the Eiffel Tower, where we decided to climb to the summit of this ingenious but pointless creation of the French mind. 'No entry,' categorically declared a police sergeant, who wore a mantelet and was armed with a bladed weapon. As it turned out, the entire tower was closed for repairs while new lifts for a hundred people were being installed to replace the older ones.

We reasoned that we were first and foremost in a republic that represented complete individual freedom, and that the policeman's concern for our safety was entirely inappropriate, given that we had decided to risk life and limb for the Transvaal, a country unknown to us, and therefore we engaged in a heart-to-heart conversation with a young worker in a blue smock, parted with a couple of francs, and just a few minutes later found ourselves at the base of the tower.

There was chaos and disorder everywhere: the former restaurants, buffets and stalls were all boarded up, and the mighty arch lattices were bound with ropes and steel cords along which scaffolds with supplies were gliding up on pulleys. We began to climb higher. The weather was foul: a cold, gusty wind whistled through the steel beams and girders that formed a fanciful piece of latticework of curves and intersections. Looking up was terrifying; it seemed as if the apex, wrapped in slowly drifting clouds, disappeared into some infinite height.

The wind seemed to shake the tower, and the sound of beating hammers, rattling pulleys and the cries of the workers repairing the tower resounded in a sharp hum.

The handrails were covered in ice and the window ruffled and tore at the pitiful remnants of the leather that had previously covered the outside of the spiral staircase. In some spots, the stairs creaked and swayed plaintively.

On the platform of the first floor, we rested a bit and then continued our climb up the same spiral staircase, even though the workers discouraged us from doing this, warning us that the climb got harder the further you went up, and that they themselves only went up with pulleys.

We continued our ascent, nonetheless. On one of the steps, I almost lost my balance, frantically grabbed hold of the ice-covered wire, and glanced down at the magical picture of Paris spread out below my feet. The patterned flowerbeds of the Champs de Mars, the galleries, towers and domes of the Trocadéro, the Seine's dark ribbon, intersected by bridges, all beckoned to me with a terrible intensity. Some awful, intoxicating desire was pulling me down to the tiny figures of people bustling about, to the carriages, boats and a train scurrying around like toy models, to the smoke of the steam locomotives drifting up. But soon the whole picture grew dark, blurred and disappeared, red and purple circles appeared before my eyes and my temples began to pound.

It took some time for me to regain my composure and calm down. I smoked a cigarette of expensive but awful French tobacco and somehow made my way down again. Stumbling through the heaps of rubbish, logs and piles of bricks, I suddenly heard the sounds of my native speech. 'Aren't you fellows our lads, Russians?' The question was directed at me by the carpenters from our crews working on the pavilion of the exhibition's Russian section.

They are staying at a hotel. The food is good, and the city is cheerful …

◆

How are things at home right now? Frost and cold. Raging snowstorms and blizzards. Fields and forests covered in feathery snow. But here I can feel the breath of the south already. A warm, caressing breeze bursts through the open window. The shimmering stars seem somehow brighter in the dark sky.

Avignon flashed past. The lamps burned faintly in its narrow streets. The outlines of old buildings with quaint ledges and gables peered indistinctly from the surrounding gloom.

The city was dead asleep, and I recalled Avignon's distant past, its time of glory and splendour, when Pope Clement I entered the town to the jubilant cries of the people, here to establish his chosen capital of the Roman see.[49]

Life burgeoned in the small, hitherto unknown town. Monumental palaces and churches sprang up; the splendour and luxury of Catholic court life attracted throngs of nobles, scientists and troubadours: incidentally, the illustrious Petrarch[50] lived here at one time, and in his resonant sonnets he immortalised his love not only for Laura but also for Avignon's wonderful countryside, the blazing southern sun, its shady olive groves and its cliffs and mountains that reach into the blue firmament.

But the lights of this city also disappeared, and the only brightness came from the blue and red semaphore lanterns above the station, until at length they too grew faint and vanished in the dark of night.

An oncoming train approached us with a deafening whistle and rumble. The lights of the locomotive and the brightly lit windows of its carriages flew past in an unbroken ribbon of light, and then before me lay the dark mountains again, and the forest, which came right up to the railway bed.

Before eight o'clock we were in Marseilles already.

We made our way along some poplar-lined boulevards to La Cannebière, Marseilles's main street, where all the business offices, agencies, brokerages, largest stores and offices of the shipping companies are located.

At one of these companies (there are five of them in Marseilles) I received the tickets for passage to Diego-Suarez[51] in Madagascar. I had to pay 1 350 francs for two second-class tickets.

Marseilles is France's leading maritime trading city. It houses the offices of the five transatlantic shipping companies, massive docks, convenient promenades and workshops of all sorts.

The fast deep-draft ocean steamers have their own wharfs in a special bay. A set of railway tracks goes right up to the warehouses and stores of the shipping companies, so that freight can be loaded or unloaded right on the spot. Port workers swarm around like ants, carrying bales and barrels of overseas goods. Steam crane pulleys creak and screech; the piercing locomotive whistles are drowned out by the mighty boom of the ships' horns. The air is filled with the din of constant shouting by pedlars selling oranges, pistachios or halva, and the roars of blue-jacketed sailors. Everywhere one hears the laughter and joking of carefree Provençals. But all these sounds are dominated by the hollow booming of the deep blue sea, as the bright midday sun gilds the domes and crosses of the cathedral, whose peculiar Byzantine style reminded me of my distant motherland, which perhaps I would never see again.

I was unable to get any money, because it was Christmas, Noël, and all the businesses were tightly boarded up.

There was an unprecedented amount of excitement on the streets: greasy, fat bankers were riding in spring-landaus, while the pavements were bursting with crowds of dressed-up clerks, officers, sergeants and sailors in new hats and bright ties. Tables had been placed in front of the restaurants, where respectable bourgeois with *Légion d'honneur* ribbons in their buttonholes and decked-out ladies accompanied by their children and wet-nurses were drinking coffee and cocoa. The crowd was in a very festive mood, and I followed the advice of Mr Pomorsky:[52] I left him a cheque and a statement on the official letterhead of the consulate, requesting him to wire money to Port Said.

By four o'clock we were already on board the steamer *Natal*. It was a long, fast vessel with a 4 000-ton capacity.[53]

We settled into our assigned cabin near the engine room and went on deck to admire the scene of goods being loaded onto the steamer from the warehouse. The deck was cluttered with bales, barrels, bundles of tackle and heaps of tarred rope, and passengers swarmed about in search of their quarters and shouted at their porters.

There were merchants or plantation owners in bright tropical suits wearing small, light hats, officers and lower ranks of French troops being shipped to Madagascar…A lady in a travelling dress was soothing and caressing her red-cheeked little Cupid, who had taken fright at a swarthy, grinning Negro.

Then a jet of steam burst with a piercing whistle from the vents;

smoke poured from the funnels and a rumble broke from the capstan around which the anchor chain is wrapped. Somewhere, inside the very hull of the steamship, something gave out a dull groan and a hiss, and suddenly the ship, now free of the last mooring ropes and gangways, began to move smoothly and steadily.

The people on the quay waved their handkerchiefs and the passengers flocked to the side railings to say a last farewell to Marseilles. The first lights were already burning and the colossal warehouses, tall commercial buildings and majestic cathedral were shrouded in haze and gradually disappeared in the gloom of the fast-approaching evening.

Here and there, long ribbons of gas lamps flared up. The lights from the lighthouses burned brightly, casting reflections on the gentle swell of the waves. In the distance, the red and blue lights of other ships bobbed up and down, but they too soon disappeared. All around us was endless sea, and above us the dark blue sky. It sparkled with a myriad of stars, whose soft light fell with a strange gleam on the black enamel of the waves. I stood leaning against the side railing of the stern and filled my lungs with the fresh sea air …

Notes

[1] Jean-Baptiste Kléber (1753–1800) was a French general in the French Revolutionary Wars and Napoleon's Egyptian campaign.

[2] Colonel Pavel Stakhovich (1865–after 1917) was the official Russian attaché with the British armed forces in South Africa in 1899–1900.

[3] Tolstoy likened the South African War to a drunken fight over a game of cards in a tavern. The Russian novelist condemned both sides, because as in any war, neither had the moral right to commit violence and murder; see Tolstoy, L, *Sobraniye sochineniy v 22 tomakh*. Vol 19. Moscow: Khudozhestvennaya literatura, 1984, p 454.

[4] Mikhail Menshikov (1859–1918), a conservative Russian journalist.

[5] Stephanus Johannes Paulus (Paul) Kruger (1825–1904), President of the South African Republic.

[6] The Russian Red Cross ambulance operated on the republican side of the front in the first half of 1900.

[7] Thomas Mayne Reid (1818–1883) and Gustave Aimard (1818–1883) were European writers who produced best-selling adventure novels set in the American frontier, Latin America and South Africa. Reid's *The Young Yagers, or, A Narrative of Hunting Adventures in Southern Africa* (1857) was translated into Russian as 'Adventures of Young Boers' and published in several editions in the Russian Empire.

[8] Second Lieutenant (*podporuchik*) Leo (Leonid) Pokrowsky (?–1900) had

served with Avgustus in the same regiment in Warsaw. In South Africa, he fought with various Boer commandos, including Danie Theron's Reconnaissance Corps, as well as with Camillo Ricchiardi's Italian corps. Promoted to captain, he was severely wounded in an engagement at Utrecht and died the next day, 25 December 1900. *Anglo-burskaya voyna 1899–1902 godov*...(2012), vol 7, pp 211–215, 368; vol 8, pp 280, 299–303.

9 *Vorwärts* was the central mouthpiece of the Social Democratic Party of Germany, the largest Marxist party in Europe.

10 The Russian nihilist movement was associated with radical activism. As a monarchist and conservative, Avgustus did not share their political persuasions.

11 The largest chain of beer halls in Germany.

12 Willem Johannes Leyds (1859–1940), the South African Republic's special envoy and minister plenipotentiary in Brussels, was accredited in various European states, including Russia. Before the war, he had served as state attorney and state secretary of the South African Republic.

13 Bernhard Heinrich Karl Martin von Bülow (1849–1929), the German Foreign Secretary.

14 Frederick William (1620–1688), Elector of Brandenburg and Duke of Prussia, whose rule led to the elevation of Prussia from duchy to kingdom.

15 Joseph Chamberlain (1836–1914), the British Secretary of State for the Colonies.

16 George V (1819–1878), the last King of Hanover.

17 The Battle of Langensalza (1866), during the Austro-Prussian War, was won by King George's troops, who eventually had to surrender to the Prussians. Hanover was annexed by Prussia as part of the unification of Germany.

18 The Boer republics are known to have bought Mauser, not Mannlicher, rifles.

19 3658 metres.

20 Avgustus refers to Major General Sir George Pomeroy Colley (1835–1881), governor and commander-in-chief of Natal, who was killed at the Battle of Majuba Hill in February 1881.

21 An important street in central Warsaw.

22 In 1898, when Avgustus was 23 years old, he was granted permission to wear glasses in his regiment. *Anglo-burskaya voyna 1899–1902 godov*...Vol 8 (2012), pp 306–310.

23 A Polish daily newspaper.

24 Leopold was the youngest son of the Duke of Saxe-Coburg-Saalfeld.

25 Leopold II of Belgium privately owned the Congo Free State in Central Africa from 1885. It covered the total area of the present Democratic Republic of Congo. In 1908, the state was annexed by Belgium and became its colony.

26 Frederik Adriaan Alexander van der Hoeven (1869–?), a member of a noble Dutch family.

27 Nadine van der Hoeven, née Aprelev (1843–1869).

28 Russian folk song.

29 A village southeast of Saint Petersburg, where annual military manoeuvres took place in the presence of the Tsar.

30 Sites of important battles of the Russo-Turkish War of 1877–1878, in which the Russian Empire, in coalition with Bulgaria, Romania, Serbia and

Montenegro, fought to liberate these Balkan nations from the Ottoman Empire.

31 The First Hague Conference was convened at the suggestion of Tsar Nicholas II. The documents that the delegates adopted are known as the Hague Convention of 1899.

32 Richard Adolf von Gernet (1863–1942), a mining engineer and entrepreneur, was appointed honorary Vice Consul in Pretoria after the establishment of diplomatic relations between the Russian Empire and the South African Republic. He fell ill in May 1899 and left the Transvaal before the country declared war against the British Empire.

33 References to the Battle of Grandson (1476) in which Charles the Bold, Duke of Burgundy, was defeated by the Swiss, and to the Peninsular War, also known as the Spanish War of Independence (1807–1814), with its large-scale guerrilla warfare.

34 Adolphe Léon Willette (1857–1926), a French artist and cartoonist. Avgustus refers to a special issue of *Le Rire* (no 264), which came out on 23 November 1899.

35 The Royal Arsenal in Woolwich, England.

36 During the Russo-Turkish War of 1877–1878, a Russian army crossed the Stara Planina (Balkan) mountains by a high pass in winter, launched a surprise attack on the Ottoman troops and captured Sofia.

37 This description is partly wrong and reflects Avgustus's ideas before his arrival in South Africa.

38 The Russian conquest of Turkmenistan in Central Asia, mostly covered by the Karakum Desert, took place in 1879–1885.

39 Cambyses II ruled the Achaemenid Empire in 530–522 BC. During his reign, he conquered Egypt and Cyrenaica.

40 Russia lost the Crimean War (1853–1856) to a coalition that included France, the Ottoman Empire, the British Empire and Sardinia.

41 Avgustus underestimates the number of soldier deaths in the American Civil War (at least 620 000). However, he is right to assume that approximately two-thirds of deaths were caused by disease.

42 The Russian Red Cross offered a fully equipped ambulance, staffed with Russian medical personnel, to attend to the wounded on the British side. The offer was officially declined, which is why a Russian Red Cross ambulance was only sent to the republican forces.

43 In 1899, the British renewed their guarantee of Portuguese possessions in southern Africa with the Treaty of Windsor. The British needed the cooperation of Portugal during the war with the Boer republics. Mommsen, WJ, 'Introduction', in K Wilson (ed), *The International Impact of the Boer War*, p 4.

44 Théophile Delcassé (1852–1923) was the French Foreign Minister.

45 A reference to the Dreyfus affair (1894–1906). Captain Alfred Dreyfus, an officer of Jewish descent, was wrongly convicted of treason and sentenced to life imprisonment. The case was reopened after new evidence of his innocence was found, and a popular movement in support of Dreyfus started to grow. A new trial, which divided French society, began in 1899. Eventually, Dreyfus was exonerated and reinstated in the army.

46 A reference to the siege of Paris (1870–1871) during the Franco-Prussian War, which led to the capture of the city by Prussian troops.

[47] The Palais de l'Industrie (Palace of Industry), an exhibition venue between the Seine River and the Champs-Élysées, which was demolished in 1897. In 1900, the Grand Palais of the World's Fair was built and opened in its place.

[48] The street is currently known as Avenue Winston-Churchill.

[49] Pope Clement V moved the papal court from Rome to Avignon in 1309.

[50] Francesco Petrarca (1304–1374), or Petrarch, an Italian Renaissance poet.

[51] A port city in Madagascar, known today as Antsiranana.

[52] An attaché of the Russian consulate in Marseilles.

[53] The Messageries Maritimes liner *Natal* was put into service in 1882 and plied routes from Marseilles to Australia, China and Madagascar. It had a displacement of 6 150 tonnes.

CHAPTER 2

First sightings of Africa

The days dragged on, one after the other: endless cups of coffee in the morning, breakfast and yet again breakfast. At six in the evening the bell would ring for dinner, which usually lasted for around an hour and a half. They served fancy sauces, fancy sides, spicy salads and other delicacies of French cuisine, finishing with desserts and coffee.

The public usually went out onto the deck during the intervals between second breakfast and dinner, resting in the rows of deck chairs or decorously wandering back and forth on deck. Among the passengers I should note the various government emissaries: Colonel Gurko of the General Staff, sent by our government as agent to the theatre of military operations;[1] the Dutch agents Captain Thomson and Lieutenant Ram;[2] French volunteers, some of whom were being sent at the expense of the special committees formed in almost all the large French cities, and others who were travelling, like yours truly, at their own expense; the former numbered about 15 men, under the command of a former naval lieutenant; of the latter, only two were travelling at their own expense – officers of the Chasseurs d'Afrique,[3] both reservists.

I also made the acquaintance of some French officials who had been transferred to serve in Madagascar. They were a young, merry bunch and every evening the whole company sang boisterously to the accompaniment of the grand piano.

We mostly sang risqué ballads with a salacious or political slant from the Parisian *café-chantants*, such as these:

En Franc' nous avons depuis longtemps
Des députés épatants pour vingt-cinq francs,
Mais les Anglais, des malins comm' tout,
Achètent des soldats, dans les prix d'vingt-cinq sous.[4]

[In France we have, for a long time, / Got
amazing deputies for twenty-five francs a day, /
But the English, cleverer than everybody else, /
Buy soldiers for twenty-five cents.]

The chorus would join in the refrain, clapping their hands and
banging their heels:

Qu'est-ce qu'est fait prisonnier d'guerre
Qui s'en fout pas mal
Et joue au Foot-ball?
C'est le soldat d'Angleterre
Dougle-digle-dum
Et ling a ling, dum-dum!

[Who's that prisoner of war / Who doesn't give
a damn / And plays football? / It's the English
soldier / Dougle-digle-dum / and ling a ling,
dum-dum!]

They also sang some other songs, which never failed to raise a laugh
from the audience with their ruthless humour and ambiguous innu-
endos. We also had some English passengers on board, but they kept
to themselves and treated the barbed songs with true British coolness.

Paul Déroulède's famous song 'Le Clairon'[5] always brought down
the house. The contrast between the song's mournful motif and the
wild calls of the chorus, in imitation of an infantry's signal to attack,
made a strong impression on me too:

L'air est pur, la route est large,
Le clairon sonne la charge,
Les zouaves vont chantant,
Et là-haut sur la colline,

Dans la forêt qui domine
Le Prussien les attend.
Tra-ta-ta, tra-ta-ta, ta-ta-ta ... et cetera.
Le clairon est un vieux brave,
Et, lorsque la lutte est grave,
C'est un rude compagnon.
Ta-ta-ta, ta-ta-ta ...

[The air is clean, the road is wide, / The bugle
sounds the charge, / The Zouaves are walking
and singing, / And up there on the hill /
Overgrown with the forest / The Prussian awaits
them ... The bugle player is a good brave man,
/ And, when the struggle gets rough / He is a
tough companion.]

There was a kind of passion and energy in their voices, and their
eyes burned with a glow of fervour. Clearly, the blood of those moustachioed grenadiers who sleep in the plains of the rushing Elbe,
under the snows of freezing Russia or beneath the burning sands of
the Pyramids, still stirred and seethed in these peaceful officials and
plantation merchants.

Every Frenchman, even the most humdrum bourgeois, is a soldier
at heart, capable of understanding and getting carried away by the
aesthetics of war. The smell of gunpowder, standards fluttering in
the wind and the thundering of cannons utterly intoxicate him, and
commanders such as Napoleon, capable of tapping into this impetuous nature, will always lead French troops to victory ...

Regarding our Russian volunteers, I shall mention a Cossack officer, a *sotnik* of the Kuban Cossack Army,[6] who joined us in Port Said.
He was a sickly man and suffered from a heart defect, and yet he had
decided to go to the Transvaal.

Another one was a reserve *praporshchik* who had worked as a railway engineer but abandoned his family and his lucrative position
out of a desire to aid the true cause and join the ranks of freedom
fighters.[7]

On the night of our sixth day at sea, at four o'clock in the morning, our steamer anchored in the Port Said roadstead.

The Russian Red Cross ambulance, brought to Port Said by the Russian steamer *Olga*, came on board here. The unit consisted of five doctors, eight nurses, four medical assistants and 12 orderlies. The eldest of the nurses, Tikhomirova, had participated in the Serbian war of 1876 and in the last Russo-Turkish campaign.[8]

Among the passengers taken aboard in Port Said, there was also a blond German fellow from Riga, pursuing his dream of settling down somewhere in the Transvaal gold fields as an accountant or agent.[9] There was an interesting couple too: a thin young man with a pimply face accompanied by a lady playing the role of a pretty damsel and with a look as sweet as a nightingale's. They first introduced themselves to me as brother and sister, but later admitted to being bride and groom. Why, and for what purpose, they were heading to the Transvaal remained a mystery to me.

While the ship was standing at anchor, I went into town to collect my money from the consulate and buy myself some light cotton suits for my further travel. Despite the early hour, the shops and cafés and various places of entertainment were already open. Ragged fellahin danced and shrieked around us, trying to coax us into their shops and cafés and inviting us to feast our eyes on the dancing girls. They thrust postcards and photographs of a certain kind into our hands.

I took a seat on the terrace of a Greek coffee shop, and for the first time in my life slowly sipped a real fragrant mocha. For the first time I was admiring the sight of an Eastern city: the graceful, strange outlines of the Moorish-style houses with their terraces, their gables decorated with arabesques and carvings, their flat roofs and their vaulted, narrow windows and doors, before which sat Arabs swathed in dirty yet picturesque cloaks and turbans. It was exactly as if a scene from *One Thousand and One Nights* had risen up before me, and I relived the dreams of my distant childhood as I gazed in admiration at the slender minarets, already set ablaze by the golden rays of the sunrise. A fresh morning breeze rustled the fronds of a lonely palm; in the distance the desert, menacing in its silence, menacing in its infinity, stretched out around us.

While I was in Port Said, I also remembered to pay my respects to the statue of the famous Frenchman De Lesseps, the creator of the famous channel, through which our ship was quietly steaming for an advance fee of 36 000 francs.[10]

◆

It was eight o'clock in the morning when our steamer entered the shallow roadstead of Djibouti, the capital city of the French possessions on the Somali shore. Mountains loomed around the bay, and around their peaks the morning mists floated slowly and dissolved.

Before us, at a distance of two kilometres, the buildings of the city's European section gleamed white; beyond, the mud huts and reed tents of the natives lay huddled like an ant hill. Not a single palm tree or shrub was to be seen in the vicinity; the entire shore was strewn with limestone boulders and fragments of some kind of sulphurous stone, apparently of volcanic origin, that glittered brilliantly in the sun.

As soon as the *Natal* dropped anchor, it was besieged from all quarters by natives in boats and canoes who, with deafening screams and bothersome shouts, offered us oranges, dates, ostrich feathers, many-hued seashells and leopard skins. Naked children bounced and splashed about in the water searching for copper centimes, which they hid in their mouths.

For a franc we were taken to shore, where we climbed onto the stone quay and headed towards town, accompanied by an entire crowd of Somalis begging for baksheesh and foisting upon us reed wicker baskets, coins and postage stamps depicting Menelik.[11]

The arrival of the ocean liner brought excitement to Djibouti's monotonous life. The passengers scattered across the square. A crowd of colonists, eager for news from distant France, flocked around the post office. Some spring-carriages drawn by donkeys or mules appeared, in which sat perched the ladies of the local aristocracy.

The houses in the European part of town were all built of limestone slabs in which fossilised coral shells and the like were visible.

But I was not in the mood for any geological research. I had experienced no seasickness or sunstroke during the voyage, but ever since Marseilles I had begun to have intermittent bouts of fever, and now a host of copper-faced Somalis with bulging eyes, the flat-roofed buildings with their patterned terraces, coloured fans, circles of fire and sparks began to dance before my eyes.

I woke up in semi-darkness. I was lying in the large, cool room of a local pharmacist. He was busy stuffing all sorts of pills and drops into me. Half an hour later I had regained my senses completely and was in a condition to get up and leave. I bade a heartfelt goodbye to the esteemed pharmacist and his spouse, who was dressed in a light, translucent dressing gown.

Out in the street, the bothersome boys besieged me again, and I was forced to buy an ebony stick decorated with copper wire in order to keep them away from me. Swinging the stick, I cleared myself a pathway to the nearest café, above whose veranda, in two-feet-high golden letters, a sign read 'Grand Hôtel des Arcades'. Suddenly, my attention was arrested by the extraordinary sight of a tall Cossack in a brown Circassian coat and an Astrakhan hat with a crimson top. I thought at first that I was hallucinating.

'What brings you to these parts, brother? Which unit do you belong to?' He wore some or other decorations and medals, including, incidentally, a bronze medal bearing the inscription 'Not unto us, not unto us, but unto thy name' in commemoration of the war of 1877–1878.[12]

The Cossack narrowed his eyes, then broke into a grin and asked: 'And you? Where are you from and why have you come here?'

I explained to him who I was, and where and to what end I was travelling.

The Cossack's face shone, and he snapped a dashing salute.

'You should have said so, Your Nobleness. As for me, I'm in the escort of His Excellency, Count Leontiev.'[13]

When I learnt that Leontiev was here in Djibouti, I decided to make use of the opportunity, and asked the Cossack to tell me his whereabouts. Half an hour later I was seated in a vast room at the head of the Governor General of the Equatorial Province's bed.[14]

Although Leontiev was himself ill with a bout of a local fever on that day, he kindly received me, gave me tea and breakfast, and after enquiring of me what was happening in Russia, what plans I had, how I intended to get into the Transvaal, and so on, told me that this was already his third week in Djibouti and that he would soon be leaving for Europe. Mr Leontiev is well known in Europe and especially in Russia, even though he is the subject of the most contradictory, and sometimes even absurd, rumours. As for myself, I can say that Mr Leontiev made the most favourable impression on me. As I admired his strong, sturdy frame, his intelligent, intense face, and his bright eyes that glowed with gritty energy, I could not help but think of the Novgorod river pirates, those daring companions of Yermak Timofeyevich, the famous Cossack.[15] Their home had become too small for them, their youthful energy had flared up, and off they went over the hills and far away, beyond the sleeping woods and mountains to uncharted lands …

This is what I can recall from my three-hour conversation with Leontiev: 'When I was appointed Governor General of the Equatorial Province, an area generously endowed with natural resources, I wanted to involve Russia in the colonisation and development of the country's mines, seeing that the Negus had entrusted unlimited control to me.

'But everywhere in Moscow and Saint Petersburg I encountered total mistrust, an absence of any enterprising spirit, and I realised I had no chance of persuading our Russian capitalists, so I gave it up as hopeless and turned to the financiers in Brussels, and in less than a week an anonymous joint-stock company was set up with a fixed capital of 18 million francs. The company's immediate goal was trade, the building of roads, setting up coffee and sugar plantations, and so on. There is inexhaustible wealth in those impenetrable rain forests. Enormous salt, copper, zinc and iron deposits are still waiting to be developed. Lord Cavendish, the British traveller who explored the shores of Lake Rudolf, already spoke about coal deposits.[16] There are also gold deposits. I granted the company extensive privileges and advantages but reserved the right for myself to exercise final control and oversight over the progress of both the industrial and trade enterprises.

'But, I repeat, it pains me that it is not Russian people who are destined to bring the light of culture and civilisation to this country. They mocked Ashinov[17] but worship Mamontov.'[18]

As Leontiev was unable to stand up, he asked me to fetch some photographic views and reconnaissance surveys of the area that had been made by his officers during the last expedition.

'In Russia they say that I begged the Negus to give me the post of governor general of a non-existent province, the Equatorial Province. Meanwhile, this territory has been under the command of Menelik for a long time, albeit under a different name, and has been governed according to the laws and customs of Abyssinia. The last governor was Tessema, the son of Ras Dlargue and a relative of the Negus himself.[19]

'On 7 June 1899 I received the staff of the *Dedjas*,[20] the highest rank of general in the Abyssinian army. This is the last step in the chain of command, and it places me on an equal footing with those who carry the title of Ras and the Emperor's relatives, and it places me in a vassal relationship with the Negus, bestowing upon me the right to command an army.

'In July of this year, I undertook an expedition into the interior of the country to quell some riots and to familiarise myself with unexplored country that is completely unfamiliar to European travellers.

'I organised a unit of 2 000 Somalis and Abyssinians under the command of French and Russian instructors, of whom I now have 12. With them I travelled all over the country. I punished the rebels, revised the tax collection system, appointed rulers in the remote districts, and so forth.

'By then the agents of the joint-stock company had also begun their activities; they chose Bako, the province's main city, as their residence.

'Here you can see snapshots of our skirmishes with the natives.'

I shuddered at the thought that such expeditions by white men were actually no more than a massacre of the hapless black population, armed with spears and arrows. They calmly allow the locals to get within 400 paces, they aim their deadly quick-firing guns, the latest thing in British technology, and then they immortalise the scene on a photographic plate.

'Here's another view of the Omo River: it flows into Lake Rudolf, taking many tributaries and streams with it along the way. And here you can see us wading through such a river. The disassembled volley guns[21] and the baggage are carried by bearers. A whole chain of marksmen under the command of Lieutenant Babichev[22] has spread out on the other bank to secure the crossing.

'The country is located on a mountainous plateau that rises up to a level of 2 500 metres, so that the climate is hot and the vegetation quite tropical in the valleys, while on the mountain slopes the temperature drops the closer you get to the peaks and the climate resembles the south of France or the Crimea.

'In general, the average annual temperature is not subject to any sharp fluctuations, and therefore European visitors easily get used to living conditions, without the need for any special acclimatisation. For this very reason it is possible to cultivate the main crops of southern and even central Europe in this country.

'The population is divided into a multitude of smaller tribes, each of which speaks a different dialect. Here, take a look at some examples of the Uba, the Bao, the Karoro and the Bashada ...'[23] Photographs of all conceivable kinds of black people flashed before me – with or without feathers, in leopard or antelope hides, armed with spears, painted shields and ancient flintlocks, and so on.

I asked Mr Leontiev about his wound.

'I was wounded in Harar in May 1898 while I was testing a new quick-firing volley gun. I was standing sideways in front of the muzzle of the gun, when a shot accidentally went off, through the negligence of an Abyssinian officer, and it pinned both legs together just below the pelvis, causing four perforated wounds.

'The Negus Menelik displayed the utmost concern for me. He immediately telephoned Vlasov, the head of the Russian mission in Addis Ababa,[24] and requested him to send a doctor to provide me with the necessary medical care.

'I waited in vain for the doctor, however. Russians have the bad habit of always treating each other with hostility when abroad, and I cannot boast of being in good relations with our diplomatic mission.'

At that moment, a Russian servant approached us. The man, who had already been in Leontiev's service for over 14 years, spoke something in the guttural Abyssinian tongue.

Dismissing the orderly, Leontiev continued: 'Two of my Cossacks are asking permission to travel by steamer to meet up with the orderlies from the medical unit. I let my boys go. Personally, however, I have no urge to see my dear fellow countrymen, especially those dispatched on official business with travel allowances; I have too painful a memory of 1896.[25] Just before your arrival I refused to receive some member of your Red Cross, Lord bless them. Tell me, how are the doctors and the sisters of mercy treating you? Have you managed to get to know them any better?'

I confessed that the official Russian envoys also treated us as if we were fortune-seekers in search of who-knows-what, in accordance with instruction number something-or-other, and were clearly afraid that we officers might somehow wheedle our way into the medical unit as orderlies or hide in an empty lint box, in case we were caught by the English off the Mozambican coast.

Leontiev told me many other things about his sorties and excursions into the interior of the country.

'As for the widespread rumours in Europe that Negus Menelik wants to use the opportunity to move an army into the Sudan, that is unfortunately not true. At present Menelik is concerned about the rebellion of Ras Mengesha.[26] Because of its feudal system, internal unrest and internecine strife never cease in Abyssinia. Menelik will not any time soon succeed in consolidating his power, creating a centralised government and subduing the discontented. At one stage there was even talk about a secret conspiracy between the princes and the Egyptian Khedive, President Kruger and the Negus. But this rumour too is entirely unfounded. Relations between Egypt and Abyssinia have always been extremely friendly. Only recently, the Khedive received an Abyssinian delegation, and the Bishop of Gojjam presented him with a handwritten letter from Menelik. The friendly relations between these neighbouring countries are also strengthened by the fact that the Abyssinians and the Copts in Egypt share the same Christian confession and the Coptic Patriarch ordains and appoints Abyssinian bishops.

'You have probably had time to notice the construction work at the port and the new railway line that will eventually reach Addis Ababa.[27] Ninety kilometres of rail has already been laid, the work is actively going on, and once everything is complete, Djibouti will gain significant importance as a seaport linked by rail to the centre of Abyssinia. Djibouti is the place from which I usually undertake my trips to Europe; it is also the destination for caravans from Abyssinia and Central Africa.'

For lack of space and time, I have not quoted even half of what I learnt in this lively, fascinating conversation with a man who turned from a modest cavalry lieutenant into a confidant of the mighty Negus and became the absolute ruler of an immensely rich province.

At length, I left Leontiev and rejoined my companions, who had been wandering aimlessly around the city. As it transpired, they had encountered an officer of Leontiev's, one Babichev, a former cornet of the Kazan Dragoon Regiment, who, apparently at the behest of his master, had told everyone that Leontiev had already departed from Djibouti the previous day.

Regarding my impressions of [the next stopover, at] Aden, I will only report the following: as I was handing in registered letters with my news reports to Warsaw and Saint Petersburg at the post office, I was quite surprised when the postal official copied an address on one of the letters without any difficulty, and then addressed me in comprehensible Russian, asking if I was heading for the Transvaal.

I politely replied to the goggle-eyed Englishman that I was for the time being only going to Mozambique, and that I was enlarging my entomological collection along the way. As proof, I produced from my pocket two beautiful carabid beetles with gold-tinted velvet wings I had captured just before.

'Allow me to present one to you as a gift, sir,' I continued. 'I trust that you will not open my letters?'

'Oh no, sir, we are gentlemen!' the clerk replied, handing me the postal receipt. What do you think, dear reader? Did he open my letter?

◆

The French were actively reinforcing their coastal defences at all of Madagascar's main harbours: batteries were being raised for huge 42 cm cannons. Muscular, sunburnt soldiers drenched in sweat were burrowing in the clay earth, creating mounds and setting up heavy artillery. Batteries such as these were going up all around the bay. The French intended beefing up the garrison at Diego-Suarez considerably. Up to now it had consisted of four naval artillery battalions, one regiment of the Infanterie de Marine and one company of the penal battalion, but it was their intention to increase the garrison to 8 000 men.

The French government's efforts at strengthening Diego-Suarez are quite understandable when one takes into account that it is one of the best harbours on Madagascar after Tamatave.[28] The shipping lines connecting the Cape Colony with India and Indochina cross here; German and British steamers also call here on their way from Zanzibar to Mozambique, Beira or Natal.

On 15 January we parted ways with the *Natal* and went on board the *Gironde*.[29] Everything was better: the halls were bigger, it had a double deck with a covered top, and its engine was said to be faster than the *Natal's* – 15 knots. It was not without a measure of sadness that we left the old steamboat: during our 20 days aboard her she had become almost family, and we had grown fond of her for the way in which – almost like a well-worn posthorse – she had brought us safely to our destination without enduring any storms, cyclones or any of the other terrors of sea travel. Some of my fellow passengers complained about the fact that we had not been battered along the way by that species of storm that snaps masts, blows up boilers and tosses ships around on waves as if they were splinters of wood. But on this occasion the capricious sea had decided not to treat us to one of those classic storms, the hair-raising tales of which cause goose bumps all over your body. God forbid that anyone should experience the horrors of a storm and a shipwreck; if all the inveterate braggarts and bigmouths grow green, or pale, or go into hiding at the slightest pitching of the ship, what would happen to them if the voice of an all-destroying storm boomed out and the grey waves turned the vessel into a powerless toy? In Diego-Suarez harbour we saw the *Djemnah*, a ship of the same French transatlantic line, which fell into such an altercation while rounding Cap d'Ambre,[30] lost all its dinghies, masts and rigging, was cast ashore and barely rescued by German steamers that had arrived just in the nick of time.[31] Of the numerous passengers who had to man the pumps for two nights in a row, one drowned and the other went mad, unable to bear the shock to his nerves. The ship was already safe and standing anchored in Diego-Suarez, but the poor fellow still imagined seeing the horrors of that stormy night, until he finally plunged unnoticed into the sea, where he was immediately torn to pieces by the sharks.

What profound meaning there is in the Russian saying, 'You've never truly prayed to God until you've been at sea!'

At one o'clock the next day, the engine raised steam. We set off, rounded Cap d'Ambre and found ourselves in the open sea again.

It is a horrible feeling to be in the tropics for the first time: the unfamiliar heat weakens the body, and a kind of lethargy, a sleepiness, passes over you, numbing any energy left in you, until your book and your quill fall from your hands; you move your pith helmet over your eyes and that is how you fall asleep until a sharply rung bell wakes you up for dinner.

By now, French cuisine had become terribly boring: watery soups and sauces, boiled meat and poultry, beans, peas and something resembling thistles, seasoned with olive oil.

The only consolation was that things would be worse among the Boers, and one would have to live off dried meat and hard biscuits.

It was pleasant on deck in the evenings. The ship's enormous hull shuddered rhythmically, the dull thuds of the engine resembling the choppy breathing of some fairy-tale monster. Now was the season of monsoons that blew from the northwest. The sky was mostly covered with clouds and only occasionally the full disc of the moon would roll out or a tiny star flash briefly. A wide jet of water stretched behind the stern, marking the trail of our moving ship. The water boiled and bubbled, and the seething waves burned and shimmered with green phosphorescent lights. This interesting phenomenon is caused by a myriad of tiny sea creatures, and in places the water blazes like molten lava, one moment lighting up with bright flashes and the next disappearing into the impenetrable darkness of night.

In Mozambique, where our steamer arrived on the third day, the first news that awaited us was that the German steamship *Bundesrath* had been intercepted by a British cruiser and diverted to Durban. The cargo, destined for the Transvaal – saddles, tents and other military supplies – had all been confiscated by the English;[32] no one knew what fate awaited the passengers, who included Colonel Braun of the German Army and the famous Lieutenant Brausewitz, who had achieved notoriety the previous year for stabbing a peaceful German burgher in a restaurant. He was forced to resign and leave for the

Transvaal, where his belligerent inclinations could be put to more worthwhile use. Apart from the officers, there were also 150 volunteers on board, and they had probably all been arrested. It would be sad if the same fate awaited us. The British consul in Mozambique boarded our ship, presumably to enquire about the aims and intentions of the passengers. We often gathered on the foredeck in the evenings and made the most fantastic plans, discussing what to do if a British cruiser inspected the cargo and passengers. Each of the 50 volunteers possessed a passport or cover documents in the name of a merchant, a press correspondent, and so forth, but we understood perfectly well that the British would not be fooled by our spurious papers, and that in spite of all our outcries and protestations, we would be towed to Durban; some said that we should take a rowboat 30 km from Lourenço Marques and put ashore separately from the *Gironde*; others even proposed that we throw the British officer and the consul overboard, as they were duty-bound to turn us over to the British government.

In the morning a French cruiser appeared in the bay, the *tricolore* fluttering from its mast, and it fired a salute that boomed far across the waves. In response, 21 shots were fired from an ancient fort, probably dating back to the times of Vasco da Gama; an immense number of pigeons, alarmed by the shooting, circled above its towers and battlements, from where the rusty muzzles of ancient cannons stared.

The Island of Mozambique is separated from the mainland by a wide strait in which the white sails of native fishing boats scamper about like seagulls.

I will not soon forget my stroll down the town's clean, cemented roads: the huge leaves of coconut palm trees overhanging the houses with their lattice shutters, flat roofs and cosy balconies; fiery-red oleander flowers that peeped from behind the trellised gardens and boulevards and the large, multicoloured butterflies of the *Vanessa* and *Sphinx* genera fluttering above them. Every now and then I almost stepped on a lizard, its metal scales glinting in the sun.

The old church exuded an air of medieval tradition, and brave seafarers sprang to mind with their berets and swords, those men in flimsy ships who entrusted their lives to the threatening elements and sailed round the southern tip of Africa, opening the sea route to fabulous India.

The grateful descendants of those brave navigators were now armed with Snider rifles, whose rusty bayonets dangled at their side. Officers, proudly smoking *pajitos* [corn-husk cigarettes], paraded about in snow-white uniforms and immaculate gloves, but treated us with much kindness and courtesy.

I was shown an art school and taken to the post office, where I was charged 250 Portuguese coins for a registered letter. Then I was taken to an ancient fort from whose bastions a wonderful view opened up of the town as it lay shrouded in bright tropical greenery.[33] I admired the soldiers guarding the fortress for their bearing and the gallant way in which they saluted the officer accompanying me. I asked the sentry to perform some rifle drills, which he smirkingly did in a fairly distinct and clean manner; when I offered him a rupee he grinned and refused with an energetic shake of the head, but he took some cigarettes and hid them in his uniform pocket. When I tried to take his rifle, he protested and stepped back. It is a pity that the Portuguese government does not have the money to strengthen its ports and organise its colonial troops in a better way. Regardless of who emerges victorious from the present war, England or the South African Republic, its outcome will affect the fate of Portuguese colonies, and at least some of them will go to the victor.

◆

Beira belongs to the Portuguese in name only; were it not for the occasional encounters with officers and soldiers of the Portuguese garrison sporting the House of Braganza's crown on their cockades, buttons and buckles, one would be forgiven for thinking that fate had carried us off to some industrial town in Cornwall or Queensland: you hear English everywhere – all the buildings, roofs and fences, sport signs, announcements and advertisements are in English.

English shops with enormous mirrored storefronts, English banks, money exchanges and agencies – everywhere there were clear signs that all commerce is in the hands of this nation, whose main attributes are insatiable greed and repulsive egoism, but the kind of egoism that, thanks to its ability to insinuate itself into every nook and cranny, can only provoke involuntary astonishment.

A few years ago, nobody knew about the existence of Beira, an abandoned Portuguese settlement at the mouth of an insignificant little river. Sharp-toothed crocodiles used to bask here on the scorching sand; lions and hyenas sauntered around the huts of the natives and yellow-faced half-castes, filling the surrounding air with their drawn-out roars.

But then news spread about the discovery of gold deposits to the west of the Portuguese colonies, in what later became known as Rhodesia. Fortune-seekers from all over the world came flooding in, followed by merchants, artisans and a rag-tag crowd of bottom-feeders. Locomotives began to blare and trains to rattle as they traversed first thickets of tropical forest, then mountain rivers on boldly placed iron bridges and viaducts. Beira, as the starting point of the railway line linking Rhodesia and the Portuguese possessions with the Cape Colony, the southern extremity of Africa, has become the most important and the most flourishing city along the entire Mozambican coast.

European buildings constructed out of tinplate or softwood on a foundation of porous bricks rose quickly one after the other. Factories, shops, banks and agencies alternated with hotels where blond, tanned Englishmen drank enormous quantities of whisky and soda water; and somewhere close by you stumbled upon a caricature of a Parisian nightclub: the bright light of electric lamps was obscured by a haze of tobacco smoke, while on the stage *chansonette* singers flashed their lace-trimmed stockings as they capered about to the harsh sounds of an Ariston organ or a broken piano. Even the most emancipated Hottentot woman would be horrified by the lurid songs and equally lurid body movements of the gaudily rouged singer, but the public sipped their brandy, unbuttoned their greasy shirt collars, and listened with delight as hoarse cries of 'All right!' and 'Hip hip hurrah!' erupted every now and again.

The war with the Transvaal severed communication with the Cape Colony; in Rhodesia, gold mining came to a halt, as did any trade or industry. If any mines were operational, it was only in those districts farthest from the border, which was guarded day and night by armed volunteer units. The English feared a raid by the Boers, who might move far inland on their sturdy horses and blow up bridges and railway buildings, thus putting a complete stop to the railway line, which would undoubtedly affect Beira's commercial life. After all, the town was filled with Englishmen who had abandoned their affairs in Rhodesia. These were either gold-diggers, suspicious-looking characters in wide-brimmed hats, or the former owners of various boarding houses or drinking establishments of the sit-down or take-away variety. They all struck me as prime candidates for the gallows, with their small, permanently darting eyes that could be cloudy and colourless the one moment and flash bright green the next, as well as their sharp, sparse teeth. In a word, they looked as if they had stepped out of some famous Mayne Reid novel.

I could imagine it. A couple of sinister-looking diggers are snoring under the wooden awning of some boarding house after a hard day's work in the gold fields. They have drunk a couple of bottles of Scotch whisky with the owner until their ears started ringing. That is how they ended up sleeping there for the night. But that wouldn't be the end of the story. It is a dark and stormy night, the jackals are howling and the owner, clutching a sharp knife in his hairy hand, cold-heartedly chooses one victim after the next. He thrusts his knife neatly in between the fifth and sixth ribs. As the poor diggers convulse in the throes of death, gold nuggets and bags of gold dust come tumbling out of their pockets …

In reality, these men turned out not to be the villains and gallows birds I had taken them for. Quite the opposite. After I got to know them more closely, I spent several pleasant moments in the company of these gentlemen, who had lived through all manner of trials and tribulations.

I should note, first, that apart from Englishmen I also encountered Germans, Italians and other nationalities. But they all had in common an insatiable passion for profit, and all of them were blinded by the lustre of gold. Each one of them was trying, often at the price of incredible effort, labour and deprivation, to grow rich at any cost. Not all of them would achieve this goal. Many would perish in the struggle against weather, disease and exhaustion. I was sitting in one of the rooms of a wooden barracks that bore the fancy name of the

Imperial Hotel. My companions had turned down the pleasure of joining me as I loitered about the kind of pubs and dens of iniquity where one might run into the devil alone knows who.

Sharing my table were several men wearing the kind of outfits usually worn in Africa: light trousers, jackets made of faded cotton and wide-brimmed hats. Massive gold rings shone on their calloused fingers, and one of them was sorting bundles of British banknotes and stuffing them into special pockets in his broad leather waistband.

I was drinking vile coffee, diluted with even viler condensed milk, and leafing through a copy of *The Graphic*,[34] admiring an etching depicting the incredible feats of bravery, self-sacrifice and humanity of the English, when my neighbour, who had just poured himself an enormous glass of whisky, turned to me with an utterly charming smile: 'If you please, sir!'

I shook my head vigorously and explained that as a result of an incurable disease I could drink nothing except coffee or milk, and that I was now on my way to the Transvaal to receive treatment for consumption.

My neighbour smirked: 'I know, I know. I can certainly see you're in the last stages of consumption. But goddamn, I'm willing to bet my soul the English won't let you into Lourenço Marques!'

'Why, sir?'

'Because all communication with the Transvaal has been cut off; the German ship *Bundesrath* was captured by a British cruiser the other day. Their cargo's been confiscated, and all the passengers have been taken to Cape Town where they'll be thrown in jail for filibustering. They probably had all sorts of excuses and explanations, but nothing helped. Did you arrive on the *Gironde*? Mark my word. You can kiss Lourenço Marques goodbye!'

My neighbour turned out to be from Alsace, and as he knew both the country and the people well, he advised me to make my way into the Transvaal by land: to disembark here in Beira and put together a caravan with native guides who could take me along the coastline to the border.

'You're probably not alone, so speak to your companions and believe me when I tell you that there's nothing special about a trip like that. A supply of quinine will protect you against the fever, and at night you'll make a fire to protect you against the lions and the jackals. Mules for the transport of your provisions cost a couple of shillings here, and most importantly, you'll be guaranteed against all accidents. The English wouldn't dare capture you on Portuguese territory. A glass of whisky if you please!'

'Thank you, *mais c'est impossible* [but it's impossible].'

'Strange,' interjected another character with a copper-red complexion and a nose resembling the beak of a bird of prey. 'What possessed you to go to the Transvaal and fight for the Boers? You'll get knocked, and all for nothing, or even worse – get crippled, and what then? Will you go begging on the streets of Pretoria? I can understand how someone can die for his country, for his people, but with this business I don't get you … My brother was also stupid enough to go fighting for the Boers as a volunteer, and now I got his last letter in which he says that the Boers give the foreigners the cold shoulder, look down upon them, that's how dizzy their recent victories have made them. You have to pay out of your own pocket for your kit, shoes, clothes and provisions, and I doubt if you have a lot of money left after your *partie de plaisir*' [pleasure cruise].

All this time the man from Alsace was nodding approvingly.

'So you would advise me to join the British? Am I right?'

The copper-red face smiled: 'The British put a high price on cannon fodder. But you're a consumptive, and, what's more, you want to fight for an idea, for the weak and the oppressed. First of all, I'm not an Englishman, and the German that you and I are speaking is my native tongue. I was born in Darmstadt. Remember never to believe the newspapers when they accuse the British of everything and depict the Boers as some Old Testament patriarchs. Once you get there, you'll understand things better and change your convictions. You'll realise that this war was caused by the Boers' hatred of all other nations and their fear of losing their oligarchic form of government in their struggle against new and alien elements. On both sides you'll see the most unbridled greed and narrow-minded egoism conceivable. But in any case, my sympathies are with the English, because they and they alone brought the light of culture and civilisation to these shepherds, who spend all their time singing psalms and reading the Bible … I feel sorry for you, young man, so take my sincere advice: go home before it's too late, before you're struck down by an English bullet and become carrion for the hyenas and the vultures. Do you know that whole flocks of vultures, hyenas and jackals have migrated from all across Rhodesia and apparently even from the Kalahari to this new kingdom of death and destruction? I feel sorry for you because I lost my son when he was your age. Maybe you also left behind family, a father, a mother ...'

His eyes sparkled with a kind of gleam, and he shook my hand firmly, fitfully.

But I only had to look at that copper-red nose, and all the charm of his heartfelt speech disappeared.

'Your words, *mein geehrter Herr* [my dear sir], have affected me more deeply than a glass of the best, strongest whisky, but I won't abandon my original purpose, come what may. *Leben Sie wohl!* [Farewell!]

As a parting gift, these judicious fortune-seekers wanted to thrust a passport signed by the British consul into my hands, stating that it would help me reach the Transvaal. But I wanted to play my role as a knight without fear and beyond reproach to the very end, and so I was stupid enough to refuse it. I had already returned to the ship when mature deliberation caused me to realise that such a document would have carried more weight than a passport issued by some police chief in the name of Lieutenant so-and-so.

In the evening, around 80 Englishmen came on board our ship. They were all evacuees from Rhodesia. With their usual British lack of inhibition, these gentlemen spread out across the entire deck, taking other people's chairs, and soon the first-class halls resounded with disorderly, drunken voices: 'The queen is over!' The keys of the grand piano tinkled and rattled under the pianist's clumsy fingers, and a whole crowd of singers gathered around him with bottles and glasses in their hands. After each verse a thunderous 'Hip hip hurrah!' or ' For he is a jolly good fellow ...' rang out, and then, with a wave of his arms and a tap of his feet, the broken tenor would start again.

On the upper deck, a group of French volunteers gathered around the open hatch, and they welcomed each number of this improvised concert with deafening whistles and catcalls.

This did not discourage the Englishmen, however, and they went on singing one song after the other, until at last they roared: 'God save the Queen!'

This was answered by the sounds of 'La Marseillaise' and boisterous cries of '*À bas les anglais! Vivent les boers!* [Down with the English! Long live the Boers!] Goddamn the Queen!' and so on.

This was more than the Englishmen could endure: with faces twisted in anger and foaming at the mouth, they rushed to the exit in order to give the protestors a proper thrashing. It took the captain and ship's officers much effort to restore order and calm the fighting audience.

We should give the English captain his dues for pacifying the brawlers. Previously, he had graciously declined his compatriots' offer of a glass or two of gin, and only made his appearance when the altercation threatened to grow into a bloody brawl and some revolvers and knives had already made their appearance in the crowd. Eventually, both the Englishmen and the volunteers calmed down, the conflicting passions subsided, and the rest of the night passed quietly.

◆

What made me throw caution to the winds, abandon my homeland and my military service and – forgetting the wise Russian proverb, 'Jerome, Jerome, why stayed you not at home?' – head for the Transvaal, to war, to fight for a foreign nation and a foreign cause? I will not try to answer that question. Was it a spasm of self-sacrifice à la Karamazov[35] or simply a desire for danger and risk, a desire to experience the extreme pleasure of putting your life at stake? Whatever it was, here I was, on the last day of my sea voyage; tomorrow I would be in Lourenço Marques.

Except for us five Russians, there were another 40 to 50 volunteers on board. Most of them were Frenchmen, a spunky, merry, vivacious bunch, but there were also Germans and Dutch. Along the way we had got to know each other and established the friendliest of relations.

We spent the last night on deck, expecting a watchful British warship to appear at any moment and stop the *Gironde* in the open sea, and for British officers to start inspecting the cargo and the passengers' passports.

Our fears were not groundless: when we called at Aden, we had seen the German steamer *Herzog*, confiscated by order of the British authorities, and we knew that all the harbours of southern Africa were closely guarded by British cruisers.[36]

The volunteers stood huddled together in small groups, only rarely exchanging half-sentences and casting occasional glances into the distance, waiting anxiously for the appearance of the beacon lights illuminating the entrance to the bay. But everything was covered in impenetrable darkness. A strong gusty wind rattled and tore at the rigging and the tarpaulin covering the deck. The *Gironde*, steaming at full speed, was tossed about like a splinter of wood. The wind grew stronger and stronger and threated to turn into an actual gale.

Every now and then, waves lashed over the side, drenching the men with sprays of bitter salt water as they clutched at railings and tackle.

Gradually, the menacing waves subsided, and the sombre clouds parted, grew brighter and lit up with a crimson fire. Soon the first rays of the rising sun glittered over the foam-flecked sea.

Before us lay the steep shore of the bright-green island of Inhaca, and we steamed at full speed into the no-man's land of Delagoa. The volunteers relaxed and speculated as to why the British cruisers had missed us.

The captain's choice of making an arc and entering the bay from the south led some to suppose that this had been a trick on his part to slip in unnoticed. Others said that the British cruisers were unable to approach us because of the extreme choppiness of the water. Several other theories, no less fantastical, were offered.

◆

Avgustus arrived in Lourenço Marques, Mozambique, on 23 January 1900

The picturesque clusters of houses stood huddled high above the sea, buried in green. The roadstead stretched out along the steep shoreline, and above it flew the flags of Dutch and German cruisers; amid the large merchant ships was silhouetted a strange vessel with an armoured deck and closed hatches: it was a British torpedo boat.

When we reduced speed and manoeuvred between the ships, a

horde of gallant sailors in white jackets poured onto the deck of a Dutch cruiser. They stood on both sides of the ship waving their handkerchiefs and caps, and a 'Hurrah' rang out that did not subside for a long time.

We had breakfast on the *Gironde* for the last time, took leave of our courteous captain and his officers, and then collected our meagre belongings and pushed off from the side of the ship.

As we sat in the rowboat, a gust of wind blew off my pith helmet, which spun and danced away over the waves. Seized by the rapid current, it would have been carried out to sea, back to the verdant shores of Madagascar, had it not been spotted by a British steam launch. Its helmsman, a fine fellow, fished out the helmet and deftly tossed it straight at me into our boat. 'Thank you, my brave!' I cried. 'All right!' answered the Englishman, and the launch disappeared from sight. I was greatly disconcerted by the courtesy of the gallant English sailor. 'I will have to kill these people, even though they did not cause me the slightest harm!' I thought unwillingly as I slapped the soaking helmet back onto my head.

At last we stepped ashore, and for a moment it seemed as if all our misfortunes were now at and end, but that was not to be. First, the swarthy Portuguese rummaged through our luggage at customs. Next, I will mention the following curious event: when our military agent, Colonel Gurko, unlocked his trunks, the customs officials were horrified to see the uniform and medals of a Russian officer, deemed it military contraband and confiscated it on the double. Despite all the colonel's protestations, the stubborn Portuguese stood their ground and only later returned his luggage to him by special order of the governor.

The Portuguese authorities were even less ceremonious with the foreign volunteers. We had to do much running between all sorts of consulates, embassies, chancelleries, municipalities, and so on. *Caramba! Caracho!* [Dammit].

In fact, under pressure from England, the Portuguese government placed all sorts of obstacles in the way of the volunteers, of which around 50 to 100 arrived with each ship. On the streets and boulevards they openly walked about in droves; all the hotel rooms were occupied by 'merchants' and 'tourists' with a distinct military

Lieutenant Colonel Vasily Gurko (in a white cap) with other foreign military attaches, Orange Free State, March 1900.

bearing; in all the restaurants and bars one could hear loud, self-assured German, interspersed with French laughter and the guttural dialect of the Dutch.

The Portuguese authorities discovered a new source of income, forcing the volunteers to pay a hefty price for passports granting right of entry to the Transvaal. The trains ran only once a day, and tickets were only issued upon presentation of a passport signed by the governor.

To complete all the formalities necessary to endorse the passports and receive a certificate of upstanding behaviour from the local police, one had to be in possession not only of a fat wallet but also vigorous health and angelic forbearance. Exhausted from the heat, I ran through the streets in search of the *governo do distrito* [district government], and all kinds of *câmaras* [municipal chambers] and consuls. Even though I bore a letter to him from Leyds, the Dutch consul, who was also the Transvaal consul, did not render us the slightest assistance, explaining that 'the Chamberlains' were following his every step with watchful eyes. Moreover, his secretary, a thin, spiderlike Hollander, fleeced us to the tune of ten shillings and sixpence each for the endorsement of our passports.

We were no less kindly met by the Russian consul, an elderly Frenchman, who, despite the fact that he was an agent of the French shipping company Chargeurs Réunis, refused to exchange our francs for pounds or réis. I was rescued by a Jew from Vilna who had lived in Lourenço Marques for nearly 15 years, had spawned a dozen black children and through righteous works had earned himself a bamboo house on a wooden foundation.

He alone greeted us with utter kindness, found us a hotel room, and refused to charge us anything for the currency exchange, but was only endlessly surprised at our decision to go to the Transvaal to fight in the war. 'But what do you think will happen to you?' he kept saying as he shook his grizzled sidelocks. 'The Boers won't pay you any wages, and the English will kill you for free.'

The esteemed merchant did not confine himself to mere platonic sympathy either, but continuously invited us over to his house and brought us bananas and pineapples by the basketful. It should be noted that in Lourenço Marques, as in all tropical seaside towns where commerce pulsates feverishly, everything is fabulously expensive: fruit, matches, cigarettes, buns and lemonade are all paid for in sterling shillings. And yet we barely persuaded our benefactor to accept a few roubles as a keepsake.

The following day, we managed to finish all the necessary paperwork for our passports. After slipping the secretary a gold coin, we received our passports and proudly stepped out of the doors decorated with a sign stating, '*É proibida a entrada*' [no entry]. The day thereafter we would board a train, and two days later we each would receive a rifle, 200 bullets and a black horse, and off we would go on commando.

Notes

[1]   Lieutenant Colonel Vasily Gurko (1864–1937).

[2]   Avgustus confuses the agents' military ranks. They were Lieutenant Lodewijk Willem Johan Karel Thomson (1869–1914) and Captain Johan Hendrik Ram (1861–1913).

[3] A light cavalry corps in the French Army of Africa, recruited mostly from French volunteers and French colonists in North Africa.

[4] 'Dougle, Digle, Dum', an Anglo-African song, by Félix Mortreuil and Henri Christiné.

[5] Paul Déroulède (1846–1914) was a French poet and politician, whose poem 'Le Clairon' (The Bugle) was set to music in 1875 and became popular in France.

[6] Fyodor Guchkov (1860–1913) was a retired Cossack lieutenant (*poruchik*). Before the South African War, he had served in Manchuria, protecting the Chinese Eastern Railway. With his brother Alexander, another Russian veteran of the South African War, he was among the founding members of the Octobrist Party, which formed the largest faction in the Russian parliament in 1907–1912. NG Voropaeva et al (comp and eds) (2001), p 237; *Anglo-burskaya voyna 1899–1902 godov…* Vol 8 (2012), pp 277–282.

[7] Alexey Diatroptov, aged 30, was a retired military railway engineer. *Anglo-burskaya voyna 1899–1902 godov …* Vol 8 (2012), pp 277–282.

[8] The Russo-Turkish War of 1877–1878.

[9] Vasily Rückert, a Polytechnic School student in Riga. He enlisted in the Boer forces, and was wounded and captured by the British. He spent two years as a prisoner of war in Ceylon. *Anglo-burskaya voyna 1899–1902 godov…* Vol 8 (2012), pp 72–73, 129.

[10] Ferdinand Marie, Vicomte de Lesseps (1805–1894) was the developer of the Suez Canal. His ten-metre bronze statue had been erected less than two months before Avgustus saw it. The statue was removed in 1956.

[11] Menelik II (1844–1913), Emperor of Ethiopia.

[12] 'Not unto us, O Lord, not unto us, but unto thy name give glory, for thy mercy, and for thy truth's sake' (Psalms 115:1). Avgustus refers to the Russo-Turkish War of 1877–1878.

[13] Nikolay Leontiev (1862–1910) was a Russian military officer who entered the service of Emperor Menelik II.

[14] In 1898, Leontiev was appointed governor of Ethiopia's southwestern region. See Henze, P, *The Horn of Africa: From War to Peace*. Basingstoke: Macmillan, 1991, p 71.

[15] Yermak Timofeyevich (?–1585) was a Cossack *ataman* (commander) who began the Russian conquest of Siberia.

[16] Henry Sheppard Hart Cavendish, 6th Baron Waterpark (1876–1948), a prominent British hunter and explorer, visited the western side of Lake Turkana (then known as Lake Rudolf) in East Central Africa and made notes for the Royal Geographical Society of London.

[17] Nikolay Ashinov (1856–1902), a Russian adventurer who tried to establish a Cossack village in French Somaliland (Djibouti).

[18] Savva Mamontov (1841–1918), a prominent Russian industrialist and patron of the arts.

[19] Ras Tessema Nadew (?–1911), governor of Illubabor Province and a son of Dejazmach Nadew Abba Baher, Menelik II's tutor.

[20] *Dejazmach*, a commander of the central body of a traditional Ethiopian armed force. This title was bestowed on Leontiev by Menelik II; see Henze, *The Horn of Africa*, p 71.

[21] Guns with several barrels for shooting projectiles in volley fire.

[22] Ivan Babichev (1872–1952), a Russian lieutenant who served under Leontiev in Ethiopia.

[23] These may be corrupted names of Ethiopian ethnic groups: Opo, Karo and Basketo.

[24] Pyotr Vlasov (1850–1904), the head of the Russian diplomatic mission to Ethiopia in 1897–1900.

[25] In 1895, Leontiev accompanied the Ethiopian delegation, headed by the Emperor's brother, to Russia. He also took part in the First Italo-Ethiopian War (1895–1896).

[26] Ras Mengesha Yohannes (1868–1906) was governor of Tigray. In 1899, Mengesha Yohannes rebelled against the Emperor and was eventually put under house arrest.

[27] The Ethio-Djibouti Railway was built in 1894–1917 to connect Addis Ababa and Djibouti.

[28] The present Toamasina, on the east coast, the main seaport of Madagascar.

[29] *La Gironde* was a Messageries Maritimes liner with a displacement of 4 023 tonnes and a maximum speed of 14 knots.

[30] The cape at the northern tip of Madagascar.

[31] On 16 December 1899, *Le Djemnah*, a Messageries Maritimes steamer, was caught in a cyclone and had to be towed by the French Chargeurs Réunis steamer *Caravellas*.

[32] As part of the British sea blockade, the cruiser HMS *Magicienne* intercepted the German imperial mail steamer *Bundesrath* in Delagoa Bay on 29 December 1899 and escorted her to Durban. When no contraband ammunition was found on board, the ship was released. See Atherley-Jones, LA, *Commerce in War*. New York: Appleton, 1907, p 309.

[33] The 16th-century Fort of São Sebastião on the Island of Mozambique.

[34] A British illustrated weekly.

[35] *The Brothers Karamazov* (first published in 1879–1880) is a philosophical novel by Fyodor Dostoevsky. Avgustus refers to the youngest brother, Alyosha Karamazov, a kind and highly moral character.

[36] The German mail steamer *Herzog*, with Dutch and German officers on board, was captured by the cruiser HMS *Thetis* and escorted to Durban on 6 January 1900. The ship was released because no contraband of war was found. See Atherley-Jones, *Commerce in War*, p 309.

CHAPTER 3

From Pretoria to the Natal front

Carrying our tickets, we arrived at the station at the crack of dawn the next day, and took our places in the carriages of the 'Zuid-Afrikaansche Maatschappij'.[1] The train flew at an astonishing speed; the rails rang under the wheels, spraying gravel from the track ballast in all directions. As lowlands and swamps rushed swiftly by, the sea disappeared forever in a haze of steamboats and white sails. The tropical landscape stretched out before us. Pardon me – not tropical, but the South African bush with which we had grown up from the novels of Mayne Reid. This, then, was where the intrepid Boers lived and hunted, chased swift-footed antelope, hid at elephant watering holes and roamed through the mountains and plains in their heavy ox-wagons.

This was not a forest in the Russian sense of the word, but rather an immense park where individual groups of strange trees rose from among the tall grass. Here and there we could also see large specimens of cacti and palm trees. Broad-leaved creepers with large bright flowers overgrew the dead tree stumps.

The train was now climbing up a hill. We were approaching the elevation marking the end of Portuguese territory. To the north of the railway line, the wide valley of the Crocodile River appeared; here and there, mountain massifs came right up to the riverbanks, and streams broke through the cliffs of red sandstone and fell down in pretty cascades. The mountains grew higher and more inaccessible, steep cliffs alternated with deep hollows, and at times the train ascended the steep slopes at a snail's pace, only to rush down from the summit at a dizzying speed.

At the border, all the passengers were asked for their passports. A couple of the French volunteers did not have any, and no matter how hard they tried to hide under the benches or behind the backs of their companions, they were shown out of the train and detained.

At the next station, Komatipoort,[2] we were met by Boers – and very unkindly, to tell the truth. Our passports and luggage were carefully checked, and some revolvers found in the possession of French officers were confiscated despite the protests of their owners.

Here, for the first time, we saw the famed fighters for freedom and the independence of their country: tall, able-bodied men with bandoliers across their shoulders and a Mauser rifle in the hand. They all wore their ordinary working outfits, and their wide-brimmed hats were decorated with a metal Transvaal badge and a four-coloured national ribbon.

These people, who had risen as one to wage war against the Uitlanders, made a strange, even terrifying, impression on us. To us Europeans, accustomed to seeing the members of that distinctive military caste all dressed up and decorated in bright buttons and gold braid, it seemed incomprehensible that these fighters, torn from the plough and without any visible organisation or proper structure, were gaining victory after victory against one of Europe's leading nations.[3]

We were now rolling through Transvaal territory. The train was racing with the same speed along breakneck curves, steep descents and slopes. I was already halfway feeling myself the free citizen of a free republic, and, noticing the absence of any impeding warning signs, instructions or preachings, I clambered onto the roof of the wagon where I somehow managed to find a perching spot.

A vista of a vast plateau intersected by mountain ridges opened up before me. Gigantic table-shaped mountains lay in an unbroken chain along the horizon. At every station, new panoramas opened up, each fascinating in its wild beauty. The woods disappeared. Here and there among the swaying green grass, there appeared mighty granite cliffs, gloomy in their darkness, or red patches of earth wholly devoid of vegetation.

Along the banks of the winding Nkomati River, I would sometimes see green cornfields, as well as cone-shaped African huts made of brushwood and reeds that stuck out here and there like gigantic ant hills. Occasionally, groups of natives appeared with animal skins engirdling their loins. Some of them wore crumpled hats and tattered trousers. There were few guard posts, and yet the railway tracks were in quite good condition; there were even fewer stations. The bridges and the most important sections of the track were guarded by small units of armed Boers, seeing that British agents were generously offering gold and promises to incite the warlike Swazi tribe to open rebellion against the Transvaal.

At one of the large stations, Middelburg, we visited the buffet, where we each had a cup of watery coffee and a couple of juicy apricots. Many burghers from town had come there in light two-wheeled cabs or bicycles. Veils of mourning hung over the hats of the women and children. They looked at the volunteers with curiosity but little enthusiasm. I struck up a long conversation with my dear countrymen, some Russian Jews, who flaunted elegant outfits and massive gold rings and chains decorated with trinkets fashioned out of gold nuggets. They generously treated me to atrocious cigars made from stinking local tobacco, and told me, among other things, that two Russian volunteers in full officer's uniform had passed through two weeks before, that they were extremely glad to meet some fellow countrymen, and that business was going well despite the war.

◆

In Waterval Boven, the train halted for the night. In the buffet we had a hearty lunch of milk porridge and a deliciously prepared hot sweet pudding. After overnighting in the carriage, I rose early the next morning to go for a walk in the hills around the railway station. There was a sanatorium for consumptives here, which before the war had been frequented by merchants from Cape Town and Natal, as the area is famous for its splendid healing climate, the best in all southern Africa. It was at this station that a disagreement arose between the conductor and me, and I was forced to speak to the stationmaster. The issue was that we had decided not to trust the rumours that the government of the republic issued free tickets to volunteers at the first station and paid in full for second-class tickets to Pretoria in Lourenço Marques, at a cost of around three and a half pounds. The French, on the other hand, had only paid their way up to the first Transvaal station, and they were in fact given free tickets, which saved them each a whole three pounds. The station-master in Komatipoort had expressed regret about the unnecessary expense and kindly placed a first-class compartment at our disposal, without, however, replacing our tickets. In Waterval Boven, we were confronted by the conductor, a large red-cheeked Boer in a long coat with light buttons; explanations were fruitless, and I was forced to approach the stationmaster, who took a further eight shillings from each of us but comforted us with the promise that we would be refunded in full in Pretoria if we approached the director of the railway line.

The closer we came to Pretoria, the more red-roofed farms drowning in lush green gardens we could see in the distance. We also began to catch sight of bulky wagons drawn by eight or nine pairs of large oxen. Coal mines, where active work continued, were pointed out to us. The gold and diamond mines were now aban-doned, as they belonged to foreigners who had left the area after the declaration of war.

In the evening we turned off into Pretoria. The passengers were let out of the carriages one at a time after a thorough passport check. There were a lot of people at the station: Boers armed to the teeth, officials in red caps, policemen and the ever-present agents. I took a hotel next to the train station (which turned out to be owned by a fat Russian Jew), and immediately set off for the railway director. He received us quite kindly in his luxurious office but declared that our money could only be refunded by order of the government and that thus far there was no issuing of free tickets.

◆

At the Komatipoort border post, where we had first seen armed Boers in wide-brimmed hats, the Transvaal customs officers had unceremo-niously rummaged through the passengers' luggage and confiscated the weapons that some volunteers had managed to conceal from the Portuguese authorities.

After all these ordeals, I was not in the least surprised when in

Pretoria Station during the war.

Pretoria, instead of ovations from the public, we were met at the train doors by moustached policemen in white helmets. They let us out of the coaches one by one after carefully examining our passports.

In the pouring rain, splashing through puddles and bumping into wire entanglements in the dark, we made our way from the railway station to the red lantern of a hotel shimmering in the distance, where the smell of onion and garlic revealed the presence of a Berdichev countryman.[4] The host welcomed us warmly and gave us supper and the best rooms.[5]

I listened for a long time to the large raindrops pattering on the window glass. The lights of the railway station burned in the distance. The harmonious sounds of a folk song were coming from there, drowning out both the noise of the rain and the howling of the wind:

> *Dat vrije volk,*
> *Dat vrije volk…* [that free people][6]

A Boer commando was apparently leaving for the border.

For a long time still, I was kept from falling asleep by the thought that I would soon be there, where 'the fatal battlefield thunders, blazes …'.[7] In my imagination I saw a series of fantastical images of future combat life, filled with dangers, worries and adventures…

The next day, as soon as the sun began to shine over the mountains, which were topped by a chain of forts, I was already up, had breakfast and took a stroll around town, inhaling the fresh morning air deep into my lungs.

Far, far beyond the Transvaal, cannons thundered and blood flowed, but even here, in Pretoria, one could already feel the noxious effects of war.

The main streets of the city, which used to be all hustle and bustle, with the imposing buildings of banks, trading companies and large shops speckled with gilded signs, now looked astonishingly deserted. Shop windows and doors were boarded up, offices no longer open. In the streets, instead of the elegant carriages of businessmen, African two-wheeled carts clattered and farmers' wagons squeaked by, drawn by ten to twelve pairs of oxen with long, spreading horns. The sale of alcoholic beverages had been completely halted, and all remaining commerce was now concentrated in the hands of a few German and American stores where the price of all the merchandise reached unheard-of heights.

Other Pretoria streets exuded peace and quiet: among the dense leaves of magnolias and orange trees one could see ornate balconies and the gables of elegant villas or the red roofs of small one-storey houses surrounded by flower gardens, dappled with red and white geraniums against a background of dark green oleanders and *Thuja orientalis*.[8] The vast orchards, together with uncultivated patches between blocks of houses, would have been more reminiscent of a village than a capital city, were it not for the network of telegraph wires entwined in all directions overhead.

By midday, I was at the parliament building where the government offices are concentrated.[9] Volunteers loitered around the monumental entrance, in the vast corridors and staircases and elsewhere. Some of them had already put on, in place of traveller's pith helmets, the wide-brimmed Boer hats adorned with the four-colour ribbon of the Transvaal.

I also hurried to register my wish to join the ranks of the valorous Boers as a volunteer. The procedure was essentially very simple. There was no order, no system: those who wanted to, presented themselves to State Secretary Reitz,[10] a venerable and courteous old man; those who did not want to wait their turn at the reception room headed straight to the Commandant-General's department, where De Souza, a dark-haired Portuguese who was acting War Minister, administered the oath to the volunteers[11] while his secretaries prepared the vouchers for the issuing of horses, clothing and equipment, and the letters assigning you to a specific unit. In a hurried, faltering voice, he read to us the pledge in Dutch: to defend the independence of the republic and obey the orders of our commanding officers.

We repeated after him the concluding words of the oath: '*Zo waarlijk helpe mij God*' [So truly help me, God]. Then we signed our names in a large bound register. Despite the commotion, despite the fact that some secretaries were scurrying about and shouting at the next table, one could glimpse in the volunteers' faces an awareness of the solemnity of the moment. I remembered a warm day in May, the quiet rustling of the battle-worn regimental colours, and the murmur of a hundred voices repeating after the priest: 'cold and hunger … all the duties of a soldier … selflessly … as behoves a brave and competent soldier …'[12]

Next door, in another 'ministry' room, lay heaps of rifles, mostly of the old single-shot Martini-Henry type[13] without bayonets, as well as cartridges, saddles, bridles and stirrups. The commotion was terrible: the officials and De Souza himself, not understanding any other languages except Dutch and English, frantically searched for interpreters and explained to the discontented volunteers that Mauser rifles were no longer available, and that the old saddles and bridles were being issued because the stocks had been depleted.

I realised that I would not need either a rapid-firing rifle or a new saddle on the way to the battlefield and that I should procure both once I got there; with this I left the department, having persuaded my comrades to calm down too. Their saddles were old British ones and not particularly good, yet they were armed better than others: with Mauser carbines. We still had to receive our horses and I still had to get some clothes, as mine had been stolen in Lourenço Marques and I had arrived with just a grammar of the Dutch language in my pocket.

We learnt that the state would pay our hotel bills, and that our choice of unit and time of departure was entirely up to us. Due to such delicate courtesy on the part of the government, some volunteers stayed in first-class hotels for months while they 'formed their units'. In fact, they preferred sitting at the table d'hôte to endangering their precious lives on the battlefield.[14]

Incidentally, I had the honour of meeting a lieutenant of the Chasseurs d'Afrique, who described his participation in the bloody fighting on the Tugela[15] and near Colenso[16] meticulously and in great depth in reports for a Paris newspaper,[17] while mostly spending his time in the halls of the Grand Hotel.[18] At least that gentleman went to the front once in a while to observe the 'tactical situation'. But there were others who, spurs all clanking, reported to the Commandant-General's department several times with only a change of hairstyle, and demanded horses, weapons and provisions for themselves and for their 'five comrades'; they were invariably given all that, which they then secretly auctioned off in close cooperation with the sons of Israel.

Adventurers and rogues abusing the government's trust were free to do what they liked: just look sharp and do not miss the Kruger sovereigns flying around.

I was roaming confused in the corridors of the parliament buildings among volunteers, red-cheeked artillerists in embroidered uniforms and French kepis, bald members of the Volksraad[19] and Jewish agents holding animated conversations with officials. Suddenly, I heard a whisper, 'Look, there is the President! Make way!' The President, the patriarch, preacher and leader of his people, passed by with his old-man shuffle, his head hanging down, as if he were unaware of the crowd around him. Several people unfamiliar to me accompanied him. What strong spirit, what unshakeable conviction in the justness of his cause must that old man have! How deeply must he, the one who had stirred his people to battle against the formidable 'Mistress of the Seas', believe that 'God is not with the strong but with the just'![20]

Among the people who accompanied him, I was shown a tall, thick-set man with restless, shifty eyes. That was his eldest son, the chief of the secret police.[21] This I found slightly jarring: a patriarchal republic, and out of the blue the President's first-born plays the role of Goron.[22]

It was then that I also had a chance to see the hero of the 15th of December, Vecht-Generaal Botha;[23] taller than average, red-cheeked, with quick, clever eyes, a loud voice and self-assured movements, he

President Paul Kruger.

stood apart from the sedentary, phlegmatic Boers and, by all accounts, enjoyed both popularity and authority among them.

◆

The next day, I received horses for myself and my companions: not stately but sturdy and hardy ones, branded 'Z. A. R.' (Zuid-Afrikaansche Republiek). For each of us there was also a waterproof

70

raincoat, a blanket, a pair of canvas saddlebags, a water flask, 120 cartridges, etc. We still had to get railway passes, stock up on tobacco and smoking pipes, and set off on our journey.

After long consideration, I decided to join the Boers fighting on the Tugela against Buller's army.[24] Other volunteers were, however, in no hurry to depart. They were preparing to leave for their commandos based near Ladysmith, Colesberg and Kimberley. Three Russians and one German, my travelling companions on the steamship, wanted to go with me.

My dashing comrades were Diatroptov, a *praporshchik*[25] transferred to the reserve, who had undertaken this journey in order 'to learn how people die for freedom', and Lieutenant Nikitin,[26] who brought with him all the infantry combat guidelines and instructions. We took the last opportunity to send farewell letters home, and that same evening we were at the station. We loaded our horses on the train, gave them fodder and smoked our last cigarettes awaiting our departure.

At last, our third companion, a certain R,[27] arrived. He was a frivolous but pleasant young man, and he was accompanied by his ladylove, who had travelled with him from Russia. Her tearful eyes demonstrated more eloquently than any avowal the sacrifice she was making for her new fatherland at this moment of parting, perhaps forever, with her beloved. She had already put on the Red Cross headscarf and bandage, which, incidentally, became her very much. In fact, she did not join either the Russian Red Cross ambulance,[28] where the doctors were secretly infatuated with her and the sisters of mercy unmercifully condemned her dissolute behaviour, or the Dutch one, where there were already nearly five nursing sisters for every wounded or diseased man.[29]

At the station, we met several cultured Jews who spoke good Russian. They were sincerely happy to see their former countrymen and wished us to return with victory. When we boarded the train, we found baskets with juicy peaches, bananas and oranges and several boxes of fine cigars on our seats.

The train began to move. I stepped out onto the carriage platform and the sparks from the engine darted past me in a fantastic dance, flashing, fading and vanishing in the impenetrable darkness of the night.

At the stations I noticed crowds of armed Boers returning home on leave from Ladysmith and other places. They were all in a cheerful mood, laughing and jubilant, though I do not know whether it was because of their new victories over the British or because they had managed to get furlough for two weeks.

From the commissioners at the stations, we received sheaves of oats for the horses, and soft white bread and round tins of corned beef and pilchards for ourselves. We were well provided with provisions for the road.

In general, the Boer support units, which are a weakness in many regular armies, are remarkably well organised, and, as I later became convinced, much better than the British ones.

As we approached the Drakensberg mountains, which form the Natal border, the terrain became more picturesque and at times even inhospitable. The sheer cliffs of stone colossi rising into the blue sky sometimes approached right up to the rails, only to disappear after a sharp turn, revealing a vast valley amid whose green radiance a silver mountain stream sparkled.

Far below us, so small as to resemble toys, we could make out round African huts. The train was barely crawling as it climbed up the railway snaking around the mountain, but the next minute it rushed down at a dizzying, breathtaking speed. It felt as if we would be derailed at any moment and our wagons plummet down the abyss, but…

But all was well. The locomotive took a deep breath and gradually began to slow down as it pulled up at Prospect Station, which offered a marvellous view of the forked peak of Majuba reaching into the clouds…

◆

Once we left Majuba, we were already in Natal, which was British territory occupied by the victorious Boer hordes. Deserted farms and derelict coal mines flashed past the carriage window; tall chimney stacks loomed black amid the ruins of charred walls. Newcastle, a picturesque, fairly large town, seemed completely lifeless. Everything around us bore the signs of ruthless, senseless destruction: the ruins, the heaps of rubbish and bricks, the oppressive silence of the deserted streets and squares, recalled the darkness of the Middle Ages, when wars were characterised by savage hostility between peoples, when it was considered inadequate merely to rout the enemy in an open field and every victory was accompanied by looting, destruction and the wreaking of violence upon peaceful, unarmed civilians.

Is it possible that even now, in our age of civilisation and progress, the demon of enmity and mutual hatred between peoples is still alive? Is it possible that modern war will trigger ethnic conflict?

The British prisoners of war that I first saw at the Glencoe railway station did not ask themselves this question; they were engaged in lively conversation with the Boers crowded around them and were howling with laughter; they appeared to be quite satisfied with their fate and – more importantly – with the merits of the whisky generously served to them by a gentleman in a uniform cap.

I was intrigued by these young chaps dressed in their dirty-yellow-hued khaki uniforms, with trousers of the same kind, and wearing boots entirely wrapped to the knees in khaki-coloured cloth. The copper buckles of their white buckskin waistbands were adorned with the terse but significant motto of the ancient Normans: '*Dieu et mon droit*' [God and my right].

It is hard to tell where this 'right' lies: Kruger declared that the Lord himself determined the path of Boer bullets, while the British War Office, without the slightest embarrassment, decorated their soldiers' gear with the name of God.

I walked up to the prisoners and asked one of them: 'What is the name of your regiment, my brave?' With this question I exhausted almost all my knowledge of English.

'My brave,' a snub-nosed lad with short-sighted little eyes, the spitting image of some Mikhryudkin of the seventh company,[30] called out, 'Royal Dublin Fusiliers', and pointed to the hat of the red-haired Boer escort guard. The brass letters RDF, taken from the Englishman's shoulder strap as a war trophy, were pinned to the hat.

'Tobacco please, sir,' the poor soldier piped. I sacrificed one of my last cigars to him and began searching for some words or phrases to continue the conversation, mindful that the military manual recommends questioning prisoners and locals as a way to gather intelligence about the enemy – an enemy I would be facing in the next day or two – when the senior guard, with an umbrella in his hand and a Mauser on his back, blared out, '*Terug kêrels!* [Step back, fellows!], waved menacingly and separated us from the prisoners. They were assigned to wagons and the train resumed its journey to Pretoria.

Once again, I was astonished by the large number of Boers on furlough: the first- and second-class passenger wagons were jam-packed with burghers sporting tanned, bearded faces. They leaned out of the windows, jostled on the platform and waved their hats, shouting something at us in parting.

Although we were only a few stations away from the end of the line at Modderspruit, it transpired that our train would remain in Glencoe till the morning, and the five of us began to settle in so as to somehow spend the night in the cramped compartment. My comrade Diatroptov settled in cosiest; he turned out to have cotton blankets, a warm plaid rug and a down pillow in a snow-white pillowcase, whose corners were embroidered in multicoloured silk thread with arabesques and some mysterious initials.

'The ladies from N presented these to me on the day of my departure,' he announced, not without some pride. 'This is the Transvaal coat of arms, and here is a couplet:

> *Who sleeps on this at night*
> *Should have no fright*
> *Of dum-dums or lyddite*

'Here in the corner they embroidered the French words '*Fraternité* and '*Egalité* [fraternity, equality] in Gothic letters, and in Russian the word for 'brotherhood' on top. They didn't know what the French was for that. Isn't that very sweet? I'm going to cherish this pillow as a precious keepsake, as a talisman.'

'Surely you're not thinking of taking it with you to the battlefield?'

'Of course I am. Just look how many possessions the Boers in this train are taking with them: crockery, mattresses, chickens in cages … They have wagons and spare horses in the baggage wagons, for heaven's sake! Peculiar notions of camp supplies and equipment, wouldn't you say?'

We would still have discussed the pillow and camp supplies for a long time, but the door of our compartment opened, and a tall old Boer, pipe unfailingly clenched in his toothless mouth, stumbled in. Without saying a word, he sat down on Diatroptov's seat, propped himself up with his pillow and soon fell into the sleep of the just.

We were somewhat indignant over such lack of ceremony on the part of the old man, who carried 200 bullets in his two bandoliers and 120 more in special little pockets on his corduroy waistcoat. The owner of the pillow, however, rushed to declare that he had no objections, and took up position on his trunk.

'I undertook to sacrifice my life, if necessary, for this freedom-fighting people. Why shouldn't I offer up my pillow for this distinguished old man who is carrying an entire ammunition box on his body, unlike us with our 50 bullets apiece?'

'Russian ammo boxes carry more bullets,' Lieutenant Nikitin muttered, half-asleep. 'It says in the War Department's order of 1891, number …'

'And your ladies, the ones who embroidered this pillow with their own hands? What would they say if they knew that an old Boer in greasy riding pants was sleeping on it?'

'In our town of N, they would have carried him in their arms as the defender of an independent republic. And in any case, private property is theft,' Diatroptov objected vehemently.

◆

The next morning, as the first rays of the sun appeared over the horizon, we were already up, having watered our horses and fed them some of the hay that lay scattered near the station. Our provisions, bread and tinned food, had run out the day before, and we smoked our pipes, consoling ourselves with the hope that soon we should reach our destination and appease our hunger adequately at some Boer camp.

About two hours later we were at the Modderspruit station, a few miles from besieged Ladysmith.[31] The station buildings were barely visible behind the piled-up boxes, barrels and sacks of flour, rice and other provisions. Bulky wagons, as big as railway goods wagons, drove up ceaselessly one after the other. The air was filled with a moaning that came from the bellowing of the harnessed mules and oxen and the hoarse shouting of the black drivers cracking their long whips in the air. With amazing dexterity, the black labourers carried enormous bales of fodder and sacks of provisions and loaded them onto the wagons. The Boers, meanwhile, stood aside and calmly smoked their pipes.

Working together, we led our horses, exhausted by the two-day journey, off the train, took them away and, laying claim to the first sack of maize we found, poured out some fodder for them. We cast envious glances at a group of Boers sitting round a fire and sipping coffee from large mugs, while a black boy in a British soldier's jacket roasted succulent pieces of meat with onion in a frying pan. Starving from hunger, I resolutely walked up to a respectable-looking Boer in large blue glasses and explained to him, in a mixture of German, English and Dutch, that we had just arrived and had had nothing to eat since the previous day. We asked, first, where to get food and then where to find General Joubert.[32]

The Boer, still holding his cup, waved vaguely towards a heap of sacks and then in the opposite direction, *'Daar is die kommissaris, daar is die Hooflaer!'* [The commissariat is there; the main encampment is there!] It made little sense, so we decided to saddle our horses and set off without wasting time. The camp was clearly not far away: through our binoculars we could see groups of white tents gleaming on the mountain slopes. Moreover, it was better to ride in the morning because the day promised to be hot.

With much effort I managed to bridle and saddle my horse and strapped my rolled-up coat, the saddlebags, various sacks and a flask to the saddle. Having always served in an infantry regiment, I was completely unprepared for my new role as a guerrilla cavalryman and mounted my Bucephalus[33] with fear and trepidation.

During these fumblings, my four-legged comrade had stood in silence, dolefully hanging his head as if he could sense that an infantryman was straddling him. I remembered the saying by the infamous Dolokhov in *War and Peace*: 'Just like a dog sitting on a fence!'[34]

But I had no choice. I grudgingly worked with my hands and legs to start moving and caught up with my comrades, who were already prancing off into the distance in clouds of reddish dust.

With my right hand I held the bridle, and with the left I convulsively clasped in turn the pommel of the saddle and the butt of my rifle, whose bolt was mercilessly striking against my back. My horse strode on, shaking his head, and now and then wilfully broke into a gallop. Oh, how sincerely I repented the sins of my youth and my dissolute behaviour in the regiment, which had prevented me from earning the favour of my superiors and the aiguillettes of a battalion adjutant.[35] At least then I would have acquired some smattering of the art of horseback riding!

I somehow managed to catch up with my companions, who showed me in the authoritative tone of hussars on jury duty how to hold the reins without tightening or relaxing them. They spoke much about the inside of your legs, about gaits and about fixed and movable axes... But everything I did was wrong.

During one of our halts a party of mounted Boers caught up with us. '*Goeiemôre, goeiemôre!*' [Good morning, good morning!] they greeted us, and looked us over with some curiosity. One of them, a young Boer with an open and pleasant face who had been an unintentional witness to my equestrian acrobatics, separated from the party, pulled up to me and without saying a word resaddled the horse, tightened the stirrups and adjusted my rifle sling.

'All right,' he said, and upon learning that we were on our way to Joubert, pointed towards a low hillock, behind which was located the so-called *Hooflaer*, the headquarters of the commander-in-chief of the troops of the allied republics.

The heat was unbearable. The sweat poured down like a river and, mingling with the acrid dust, covered our faces in a layer of wet mud. We had sucked the last drops of water from our flasks, our throats were parched and, for as far as we could see around us, there was not a single little tree or bush under which we could rest and find shelter from the searing rays of the midday sun.

Here and there we rode past the rocky hollows of dried-up streams; sometimes we also encountered puddles of turbid green water. A few paces from the path lay the ugly, bloated carcasses of horses and oxen, with clouds of big, fat flies hovering above them. And then there were the large African vultures, their sharp beaks and the white feathers of their long necks stained with blood and entrails. Upon hearing the ringing clatter of our hooves, they slowly spread their powerful wings and with heavy flaps took off into the cloudless sky of war, from where to look out for new prey.

The unbearable stench of ever-increasing heaps of carrion infected the air for a great distance about us, and we began to inhale our strong Transvaal tobacco as deeply as possible. But although the smoke stifled the stench to some extent, it did not save us from the annoying flies buzzing around our faces, landing on our hats and clothes, and never giving us a moment's peace.

Notes

1   A reference to the Netherlands-South African Railway Company, which constructed and operated a line between Pretoria and Lourenço Marques.
2   A town on the Mozambique border.
3   In the early stages of the war, the republican forces triumphed at Colenso, Magersfontein and Stormberg. They also besieged Kimberley, Ladysmith and Mafeking.
4   Berdichev, a town in the present-day Ukraine. Its population was largely Jewish.
5   Jacob Joffe, owner of the Hollandia Hotel, across the square from the Pretoria railway station. After the British occupation, it was renamed the Victoria Hotel; see *Longland's Pretoria Directory for 1899*. Pretoria: The State Library, 1979, p 192; Allen, V, *Kruger's Pretoria: Buildings and Personalities of the City in the Nineteenth Century*. Pretoria: Protea Book House, 2007, p 131.
6   A line from 'Die Volkslied van Transvaal', the national anthem of the South African Republic.
7   A quote from Alexander Pushkin's long poem 'Poltava' (1828).
8   Oriental thuja (*Platycladus orientalis*), an evergreen tree of the cypress family.
9   The Ou Raadsaal, on the south side of Church Square. This was the council chamber where the Volksraad, the republican legislative assembly, held its sessions.
10 Francis William Reitz (1844–1934), formerly State President of the Orange Free State.
11 Louis Francisco de Souza (1865–1900), secretary to the Commandant-General. After his superior, Petrus Jacobus (Piet) Joubert, had left for the Natal front, De Souza unofficially became 'acting Commandant-General' in Pretoria; see De Souza, FLH, *A Question of Treason*. Durban: Kiaat Creations, 2004, pp 16, 56, 59.
12 Words from the oath of allegiance of the Russian Imperial Army.
13 The Martini-Henry rifle had been adopted by the British Army and produced until the late 1880s. By the beginning of the South African War, it was already obsolete.

14 The volunteers waiting for dispatch to the front stayed in Pretoria hotels at government expense. However, alcohol was only served for the volunteers' account.

15 The largest river in the present province of KwaZulu-Natal. The modern spelling is Thukela.

16 A town in Natal. The Battle of Colenso took place on 15 December 1899.

17 Avgustus refers to Lieutenant Ernest Galopaud (?–1917), a veteran of colonial wars in Sudan and Madagascar. Galopaud reported on the war for *Le Matin*, a popular Paris daily. He took part in the Battle of Colenso as aide-de-camp to his famous compatriot, Count Georges de Villebois-Mareuil; see Macnab, R, *French Colonel: Villebois-Mareuil and the Boers 1899–1900*. Cape Town: Oxford University Press, 1975, pp 96–7; Lugan, B, *Ces Français qui ont fait l'Afrique du Sud*. [Étrépilly]: Bartillat, 1996, p 310.

18 A designated hotel for volunteers. It was situated on the southeast corner of Church Square; see Theron, B, *Pretoria at War, 1899–1900*. Pretoria: Protea Book House, 2000, p 60.

19 The Transvaal parliament.

20 An expression attributed to Prince Alexander Nevsky (1220–1263), a Russian military leader.

21 President Paul Kruger's youngest son, Tjaart, was the chief of the Transvaal secret service; see Gooch, J, *The Boer War: Direction, Experience, and Image*. London: Frank Cass, 2000, p 81.

22 Marie-François Goron (1847–1933), a famous French detective and author.

23 Louis Botha (1862–1919), future Commandant-General. On 15 December 1899, he led the Boers to victory at the Battle of Colenso. In 1910, Botha became the first Prime Minister of the Union of South Africa.

24 General Sir Redvers Henry Buller (1839–1908), commander-in-chief of British forces in South Africa in the early stages of the South African War.

25 A Russian military rank given to senior non-commissioned officers, similar to warrant officer.

26 Second Lieutenant (*podporuchik*) Vasily Nikitin, formerly of an infantry regiment in Russia. Nikitin spent more than four months with the republican troops and was wounded. Soon after his return to Russia, he left for China where he took part in the crushing of the Boxer Rebellion in Manchuria. *Anglo-burskaya voyna 1899–1902 godov*... Vol 8 (2012), pp 277–282.

27 Pavel R, a Russian volunteer. His surname remains unidentified.

28 The Russian Red Cross Ambulance reached Pretoria on 26 January 1900. During their stay in South Africa, the Russian medical personnel treated nearly 7 000 sick and wounded; see Shubin, *Rossiyskie dobrovoltsy*, pp 140, 174.

29 A reference to the Russo-Dutch Ambulance.

30 A typical Russian soldier.

31 The Boers laid siege to the town of Ladysmith on 2 November 1899.

32 Commandant-General Piet Joubert (1831–1900) had left Pretoria and remained in Natal, directing his troops in the field.

33 Bucephalus (c. 355–326 BC) was Alexander the Great's horse.

34 A reference to the following passage from Leo Tolstoy's *War and Peace*: 'A dog astwide a fence! A weal dog astwide a fence!' shouted [Hussar] Denisov ... the most insulting expression a cavalryman can address to a

mounted infantryman ...' (translated by Aylmer and Louise Maude).

[35] In the Russian Imperial Army, each infantry battalion had a mounted junior officer, assistant to the chief of the battalion.

CHAPTER 4

With the Krugersdorp Commando

Like distant peals of thunder, the sound of cannon fire rumbled, then faded gradually in the air. There it was! My heart sank painfully as if in foreboding at the realisation that something terrible was happening on the other side of those mountains, beyond that dark blue horizon. Perhaps at this very moment in the trenches, people maimed by lethal shrapnel were writhing in the throes of death, and the last echoes of that discharge had been drowned by moans and screams. Then another boom rang, and another, and yet one more!

I was entirely gripped by an ineffable feeling – the awareness that I should face at last that dreaded and yet unfamiliar phenomenon of war made me forget my hunger, thirst and exhaustion after the two-day journey by train, and I rode on as if being lured forward by some strange and fatal power. Massive table-like mountains towered in front of us; beyond them lay entrenched the troops under the command of White,[1] who had turned Ladysmith into a new Plevna.[2]

To the side of the road, in a valley through which there wound a small river, we noticed white tents. We had reached our destination.

We had arrived, as we learnt later, at the camp of the Pretoria District; General Joubert's headquarters was also here.

Tents and marquees of different shapes and sizes were pitched across the slopes of the small mountains that bordered the valley with its winding river. Bulky covered wagons loomed in the spaces between the tents; pyramids of sacks filled with maize and rusks were kept under tarpaulin shelters; the entrails of slaughtered cattle and empty tins were scattered everywhere.

The Boers had just finished their lunch; blacks squatted round the smouldering fires licking clean the pans and pots in which their masters' food had been cooked.[3] The sleepy, sunburnt faces of the bearded Boers glanced at us from the tents.

Commandant General Piet Joubert.

It took us quite a while to get some sense out of them and establish the whereabouts of Joubert's tent. Finally, at a spot in the middle of the camp, we saw a large green marquee crowned by the four-colour flag of the republic. In the tent, at a table buried under papers, sat the *Kommandant-Generaal*, commander-in-chief of the allied armies of the Transvaal and the Orange Free State, Piet Joubert. He was alone.

The five of us entered the tent, and I, with some agitation, began a speech I had prepared earlier in my head, explaining that we had just arrived, that we would like to join a commando on the Tugela, and that we were 'at his command'.

Joubert raised his head slightly, moved the papers aside, took his glasses off and surveyed us with his penetrating gaze. He enquired where we came from and why we did not wish to remain at Ladysmith.

We answered that the siege was of no interest to us. After the unsuccessful attempt of 6 January, it seemed unlikely that the Boers would attempt another assault.[4]

'*Jammer om de mannen te slachten!* [It would be a shame to sacrifice the men!] The British will surrender anyhow,' Joubert replied.[5]

While he was writing a letter to General Lucas Meyer[6] for us, I had time to study the interior of the tent, which probably served as a venue for meetings of the *Krijgsraad* [military council].

A telephone attached to the middle pole, a dozen bentwood chairs and a large table with papers heaped on it in great disorder: these were all the furnishings. Among the papers I noticed a blue large-scale map of Natal, reports by field-cornets[7] with many pencil markings, and copies of the English-language *Cape Times* and of the *Volksstem*, published in Pretoria.

Handing us the letter and shaking our hands, Joubert said, '*Alles van de beste!*' [All the best!] The audience was over.

'That general headquarters is something!' Nikitin grumbled. 'They don't even have any adjutants or orderlies!'

'Such spartan simplicity!' Diatroptov gushed.

We began looking for our horses, but at that moment a gentleman in spectacles and a yellow British jacket came up to us and explained that he had ordered the horses to be unsaddled and allowed to graze. He introduced himself as a former lieutenant of the Prussian Army. We were delighted to accept his kind invitation and followed him into the tent, where we found about six other volunteers. Our welcoming hosts, who had already been under fire, fully supported our decision to join a commando near Colenso and gave us food and drink, and one of them even volunteered to guide us to Lombardskop.[8]

It was hard to imagine that this volunteer, with his worn jacket, tanned face and bristly beard, had formerly been a wasp-waisted *premier-lieutenant* [platoon leader].[9] The lieutenant and his comrade, an artillery captain, approved of my choice of unit.

'In the foreign commandos there is always quarrelling, scheming and disagreements; their superiors, elected by the volunteers from their own ranks by a majority of votes, command no respect; the German corps, which is the largest, has been completely discredited among the Boers, and the Italian and the French commandos are in fact just looting under the pretext of conducting reconnaissance that is of no need to anyone.'

The German corps near Ladysmith (1900).

I told him about our conversation with Joubert.

'"*Jammer om de mannen te slachten!*" is the cornerstone of his tactics; quite rational, however, as you will realise later. The Boers have splendidly implemented the principle of saving men while inflicting the biggest possible losses on the enemy. Just try not to show off when under fire; the Boers regard any unnecessary bravado as rashness and only laugh at it.'[10]

It turned out that the Tugela was about six hours' riding away and that we could leave that very afternoon for the camp of the German corps, where we would find our fellow countryman, a Russian officer by the name of Shulzhenko.[11] The camp was located to the southeast of the Platrand, and from there it was only a three-hour ride to Meyer's headquarters. Two Germans volunteered to be our guides. We agreed, saddled up our horses, took leave of our gracious hosts and set off, hoping to sleep over at the camp of the German corps.

One of our new companions taught me the necessary rules of riding, and in particular how to control Boer horses, strong and hardy Basotho ponies. At one of our rest halts, he adjusted the straps of my flasks and saddlebags and proved to be cheerful and witty company.

'You're going to be in the front position, face to face with the khakis. Don't even think of getting bored if things don't get serious in the beginning. Remember that the two most important things in war are patience and good digestion.'

I couldn't help but recall the half-forgotten pages of Mayne Reid's novels about the lives of the first settlers in the region. So here they were – the thorny acacia shrubs of the South African bush with their small, feathery leaves and sharp thorns. One moment the horses' hooves would ring loudly on the layers of hardened red clay, devoid of any vegetation, and the next moment they would sink into a soft carpet of bright-green grass dotted with red and white geranium flowers.

Field partridges, as well as some sort of long-tailed bird with plumage that glittered in the sun, would fly up from under the horses' hooves, flapping their wings and emitting piercing cries.

Occasionally, the graceful silhouette of a springbok would appear on the hills, only to take fright at the clatter of our hooves and disappear in a few jumps into the thicket of sprawling acacia.

But nowadays one no longer encounters the massive herds of giraffes and antelopes of former days; the distant plains no longer resound with the mighty roar of the king of the animals or the lingering howl of jackal. In half a century of persistent labour, man has conquered this land; ploughed fields now mark the mountain slopes and riverbanks. Vast pastures lie hedged in by barbed-wire fences, and poplars and fruit trees from Europe have proliferated around the farms.

But now the walls of ruined farmhouses, abandoned by their inhabitants, stand ashen and forlorn. More and more we came across pits dug in the earth by grenades, tatters of rotting uniforms, shell fragments and rifle casings – a battle had taken place here on 30 October.[12] ...

Along the way we met a black man wrapped in a colourful fleece blanket with copper bracelets on his arms and legs; our German companion considered it his duty to get off his horse and search the man.

'Why are you doing this?' I asked him. 'Surely the English don't use blacks as spies?'

'Oh, of course they do!' he replied. 'Despite all the vigilance of our sentries, Buller and White communicate splendidly with each other through these black devils with their greed for British gold. Mind you, we also occasionally make use of their services.'[13]

He lit his pipe and drew in the strong Transvaal tobacco. 'I've been in this country for eight years already and know the blacks very well: they have a lot of expectations from this war. It's said that when hostilities were announced, their elders, the descendants of their former kings and high priests, gathered in the impregnable valleys of the Drakensberg and sacrificed three bulls, a black one, a red one and a white one, to their idol. The red bull bit the dust first, then the white one, but the black bull kicked about the longest. Based on this oracle, the priests decided that the Boers would defeat the red-haired ones, that is, the English. But then the [Xhosa], Zulu, Basotho, Swazi and other black nations will rise and free themselves from the foreigners' yoke. But now we only have the Klip River Valley to pass and over there, behind that mountain where the sun is setting, is the camp of the German corps. *Vorwärts!* [Forward!]

We crossed the Klip River through a fairly deep ford that reached up to the horses' chests. The current was swift and the crossing not without incident: one of my comrades was swept 20 paces or so to the side; his horse stepped into a pit and capsized, and the rider would have become food for the fish had not some Boers appeared on the other bank right at this moment, jumped into the water and fished him and his horse out.

After this little adventure, which provoked general laughter, we took off at a gallop to reach the camp before nightfall. In the south, day quickly gives way to night: as soon as the last rays of sunset were extinguished in the west, the constellation of the Southern Cross sparkled in the dark-blue sky and everything around us sank into impenetrable gloom.

Our guides dismounted and led their horses by the reins; we followed suit. We stumbled over rocks, scratching our faces and hands in the thorny acacia branches, until we had all climbed to the top of the hill, and at last could see a little light burning somewhere in the distance.

'Just another half an hour!' the Germans consoled us.

Another half an hour! My legs were burning, my back hurt from the heavy Martini-Henry rifle, and my horse held its head down and was barely moving. The unwelcome cold bath and the cool evening air forced us to spur our horses on so that we could reach the camp before dark. ...

They led us straight into the tent of Commandant Krantz.[14] A German who had lived about ten years in the Transvaal, he was elected the commander of the German volunteers on the strength of his reputation as a well-known lion hunter; in his lifetime, he had killed exactly 68.

'And my wife ... Oh, wait until I introduce you to my wife! She's personally shot a whole 86!'[15]

He managed to tell us all this while attending to his duties as a host. He was a short, restless man with a big, well-groomed moustache, and bustled around us, carrying in crockery, pouring each of us a cup of hot coffee and serving us meatballs and flat ash cakes. All the while he talked incessantly, telling us about his participation in the assault of 6 January, that it had been his idea to build a dam and flood the besieged town, and about his determination to storm Ladysmith again if given 500 men.[16]

We listened to him reverently, drinking cup after cup, and devoured an enormous pan of delicious meatballs.

Meanwhile, news of the arrival of new volunteers had spread over the camp, and Prussian *Premier-Lieutenants* and Austrian *Rittmeisters*[17] entered the tent one by one. Krantz introduced us to a captain of the Swedish General Staff, who immediately considered himself duty-bound to switch the subject of conversation to the Battle of Narva[18] and the Finnish issue.[19]

I had to remind him of the Battle of Poltava[20] and of the arming of the Norwegians.[21]

But R kindly helped me out of my trouble: 'Tell me, is it true that the restaurants in Stockholm serve the world's best vodka and hors d'oeuvres free of charge?'

At the mere recollection of his distant fatherland, the Swede rolled his blue eyes and let out a deep sigh as an answer.

Commandant Paul Krantz of the German corps.

'And here is your fellow countryman!' Krantz announced, introducing us to a young man in a dashingly cocked hat with an ostrich feather. 'Dr Siegel of the University of Derpt.'[22]

Dr Siegel, his hat adorned by a fluttering feather and sporting a round beard à la Henry IV,[23] bore a greater resemblance to some musketeer from Dumas's famous novel than to a peaceful surgeon, even more so because, instead of a band with a red cross, he wore a bandolier over his shoulder. We learnt that the doctor had grown bored with his work at the hospital, and without giving it a second thought had exchanged his lancet and probe for a rifle and bandolier and now shot people in bloodthirsty ecstasy, just like the artist Vereshchagin had once done near Geok Tepe.[24]

'Gentlemen! What brought you here?' a voice exclaimed in Russian, and we found ourselves in the embrace of a tall gentleman with a tousled jet-black beard. 'Come to my tent! We'll chat, and you can spend the night there.'

We were forced to thank our gracious hosts and from there headed to the tent of our countryman, almost groping our way as we stumbled over tent pegs.

He turned out to be a staff captain from a sapper company at a fort in the Odessa district who had used his six-month leave to study the artillery and engineering aspects of the Ladysmith siege. Now he regretted it: he was dissatisfied with the primitive way in which the blockade was being maintained; he was extremely annoyed by the Boers' inaction and by the fact that he had been stupid enough to join the German corps.

'Almost half of the gentlemen you have seen are fortune-seekers drawn here by their instincts for pillage and plunder or by some sordid affair that forced them to leave their country. Krantz himself is a first-rate little coward, windbag and schemer.[25] If he still hasn't been relieved of his commandant's rank, it's only because of his beautiful wife, who rides and shoots better than he does. She often comes to the camp, always with a box of whisky or cognac, chases her husband from the tent and …'

'You know what? I'm staying here!' none other than R burst out. 'So tell me … When is Mrs Krantz coming?'

We spent the night in the second captain's tent. In the morning, we found our horses, which had become mixed with the herd, after much effort, and rode on, this time without a guide.

The road ran entirely over the mountains: the Boers we encountered merrily exchanged nods with us and explained in detail how and where to find General Meyer. From time to time we heard dull rifle shots being fired somewhere.

We were still under the impression of the splendid manner in

Martha Catherina Krantz, the wife of Commandant Krantz.

which we had passed the previous evening, as well as of the unexpected meeting with our fellow countrymen. It was a glorious morning, of the kind wholly unknown to Europe, with a cloudless azure sky that rained a sea of blinding bright light down, and the mountains and valleys decked in velvet green. This lulled us into a state of good humour, and we decided – without the usual disagreements and differences of opinion – to forget any thoughts of joining a foreign corps, and to invite the second captain, who seemed a very affable fellow, to transfer over to us on the Tugela.

'We'll form a separate corporal's guard and elect him our corporal. He is older than us and has been at war for more than a month,'

Nikitin said. 'We need to set the Boers an example of proper organisation.'

'No, gentlemen. No superiors please,' the free-thinking Diatroptov protested. 'We didn't come here to obey any corporals.'

Along the road we began to see fragments of shells, copper shrapnel tubes, even entire bombs, with only the head crumpled and the bottom torn off.

Enormous pits, almost two arshins[26] in width, testified to the force of the lyddite shells. The sight of these sharp, twisted pieces of hardened steel was not exactly pleasant.

'Gentlemen, if I am killed by such a bomb, write her a letter; I will leave you her address!' R, the seducer of women's hearts, said melancholically.

'He is right. Who knows what might happen?' Nikitin joined in and proposed that we exchange addresses and promise to notify each other's relatives if someone were to die. We halted our horses and started gravely writing down our comrades' addresses. In the cloudless sky, high, high above our heads, the vultures hung in motionless flight, their mighty wings outspread …

◆

Lucas Meyer received us in his tent on the northern slope of Grobler's Kloof.

'So, gentlemen, have you come here to admire the war or to work?' he asked us bluntly.

'It would not be particularly safe to admire the war near you, General!'

He was clearly happy with our reply and treated us to a proper general's dinner: leg of mutton with rice, as well as prunes, biscuits, whisky and coffee. We met Meyer's aide, Assistant-General Kock, and learnt that he was a graduate of the Leiden and Oxford universities and spoke two languages very well.[27] He expressed a very grim view of the situation and had harsh words for Joubert, accusing him of timidity; his view of Cronjé[28] was not much better.

'But you will see everything for yourselves later, and now help yourselves, messieurs; you will not have these comforts at the front line!'

Generals Lucas Meyer and Louis Botha.

He told us that his father and brother had been killed near Elands-laagte;[29] he had participated in the crushing of Jameson's gang and he showed us an elegant rifle with the initials of that modern filibuster, which had belonged to Jameson himself.[30]

Then he explained to me the command structure, showed daily reports of his subordinate field-cornets and took us to the telephone station and the heliograph, used for transmitting orders.

◆

We had to decide which unit to join. I recalled the Jews who had seen us off at the station recommending Field-Cornet Ben Viljoen of the Johannesburg Commando as a cultured commander who was very well disposed towards foreigners.

'Gentlemen,' Kock objected, 'fighting is currently in full swing on the right flank, which is where the Johannesburg district finds itself; nobody will have time for you right now; you will immediately find yourselves in an unfamiliar environment. I recommend that you join the Krugersdorpers near Colenso. They are probably going to attempt a sabotage action in Chieveley, where Buller left only one brigade. Taking the offensive is more to our liking, I think, than this endless hiding behind rocks as bullets and grenades whistle past. And there is the field-cornet himself …'

A group of horsemen rode up to the tents; the ones in the rear were dragging a black man bound with a rope behind them. A tall Boer with a grey beard riding in front jumped deftly from his horse and, walking up to the general, began to tell him something, gesticulating and pointing at the black man.

'They caught a kaffir spy from Ladysmith,' Kock explained and started questioning the black man, who only spun the whites of his eyes around in terror. A naked bronze body, muscular and sinewy, stuck out from beneath his tattered clothes. Fear had turned his face, which bore traces of cuts and bruises, into a greyish shade of brown, so that it took on something of a dirty-yellow hue, like the skin of his palms.

His teeth chattered as though he had a fever, and to all the questions he replied with some incomprehensible guttural sounds: 'Baas! Baas!'

'So when are you going to tell us at last, *allakragtie* [by Jove], if you had any papers with you?' the field-cornet bellowed and kicked the wretch in the stomach. The man only groaned, and his white pupils raced around faster than ever.

'Did you search him properly?' Kock interjected. 'Didn't he have anything with him?'

'We nabbed him in a kraal where he apparently wanted to spend the night; we gave the devil a right hard time, but there was nothing with him except for this stick. He's clearly a spy, no two ways about it. He couldn't mention a single burgher by name.'

'Confess, goddam!' he said and let loose on the black man again;

to drive the point home he clobbered the man over the head with the stick. It shattered and a rolled-up piece of paper fell out. Everybody dashed to grab the paper and unroll it, and with a triumphant smile Kock showed us a clearly drawn contour map, with scale attached, of the Boer dispositions at End Hill and Lancer's Hill; the map indicated all the Boer cannons and the location of barbed-wire obstacles.

'This is not the first time,' Kock told us, 'that we catch a kaffir spy delivering highly accurate information of our positions to the English. These follows have set up a real postal service between Buller and White. Shoot him!' he said to the Boers.

'The death penalty! The death penalty in a republic!' our free-thinker Diatroptov, distressed by this scene, repeated over and over again. The ill-fated black man stood there wide-eyed, as if hypnotised by the glittering rifle sight aimed at him. We could see his knees shaking, his fingers twitching convulsively, and his grey-brown face had by now grown almost white.

'Baas, baas!'

The dry crack of a shot went off. The Boer fidgeted impatiently with the bolt of his rifle as he pushed out the bullet casing; the horses only twitched their ears for a moment and then continued nibbling the green grass; a mere couple of paces from us the black man lay flat on the ground. The bullet had gone right through his eyebrow and his bare feet dug into the earth. At the back of his head, instead of woolly hair, was a huge scarlet stain of blood and brains. A feeling of unease came over us.

'I'm curious to see the effect of a modern small-calibre bullet,' Nikitin mumbled and wanted to walk over to the corpse.

'Gentlemen, if you want to leave, the field-cornet will take you,' Kock reminded us, and said with the kindest of smiles: 'Have a good trip! If you get bored in the camp, you are welcome to visit me; I receive magazines and newspapers.'

'Are you going to continue shooting poor blacks?'

He frowned. 'The English killed my father and two of my brothers; surely we aren't going to beat around the bush with these scoundrels who've been bribed with English gold?'

◆

We rode on to catch up with the Boers, who were already heading for their camp.

The road crossed a railway embankment with blown-up rails and a dismantled wire fence. The green valley of the Tugela lay spread out in front of us; the evening mist was already rising over the river. Here and there we saw deep holes torn out by British shells; jagged shards, copper percussion fuses and pieces of shrapnel lay scattered everywhere; sometimes we came across horse carcasses with swollen abdomens and protruding legs. The picture was depressing, and we made our horses break into a gallop so as not to choke at the unbearable stench.

The Krugersdorp district commando had set up its dugouts and pitched its tents and marquees on the slope of a small mountain.[31] We unsaddled our horses, and the field-cornet led us to a respectable, powerfully built old man, Commandant Van Wyk.[32] He greeted us with an emotional speech, from which we gathered that he and the burghers welcomed us, travellers from distant lands who wished to fight for the right cause.

'You will carry out your service like burghers. And whatever is given to the burghers will be given to you as well.'

Then he invited us to sleep over in his tent, firmly shook our hands and handed us over, for the time being, to the care of the volunteers, of whom there were about 20 in the Krugersdorp Commando.

The volunteers welcomed us like comrades: they tethered our horses to a post and gave them fodder, and treated us to hot pancakes and coffee, but without sugar, which they had finished a week before. We soon struck up a lively conversation.

There were Hungarians from the Honved,[33] who looked terribly brave.

'We won't forgive you for 1849!'[34] Rittmeister Illich declaimed.[35] 'And now let us drink a cup of coffee like brothers!'

Baron Luzsénszky, a former Austrian hussar and veteran of the Bosnian campaign of 1880–1881, seemed like a very pleasant fellow.[36]

Our German companion found his countrymen, Prussian lieutenants and warrant officers. Among the volunteers there was a Swiss from Geneva, a young red-cheeked student who had given up his studies at the school of law to defend *les droits de l'homme*

Krugersdorp Commando.

[human rights] under arms. There were two brothers from Styria, modest and helpful.[37] There was a lieutenant of the Bulgarian Army, Buzukov, an ardent nihilist who dreamt of establishing a federation of Balkan states with a democratic government. He told us many things about his adventures in the mountains of Macedonia, where he had led a gang of robbers and fought against Turkish gendarmes. When the gang was dispersed, he was condemned to death in absentia by the Turkish authorities, after which he fled to Odessa and then to South Africa.[38]

A man entered our tent. '*Habe die Ehre*' [I have the honour], he said in a falsetto. '*Premier-Lieutenant* Wagner of the Royal Bavarian Horse Artillery!'[39]

We introduced ourselves and studied the esteemed artilleryman with some curiosity. What had brought him from the beer halls of the glorious city of Munich to the distant, sweltering Transvaal? His unimaginably dirty jacket hung loosely like a sack on his thin body; the brim of his frayed hat covered an angular skull with short-cropped hair. He felt somewhat awkward among these robust, sunburnt freedom fighters; you could see it from his guilty smile and clumsy movements. The appearance on the scene of Wagner, who indeed strongly resembled *Le chevalier de la Triste Figure*

96

[Knight of the Sad Face],[40] immediately aroused excitement among all present.

'Herr Wagner, Herr Wagner!' they called him, 'Did you find your Rocinante today?[41] Have you finally written your report to President Kruger on changing the Boer tactics? How is your digestion?'

It went on and on.

Wagner started to blink and, almost sobbing, said, in French for some reason: '*Vous vous moquez de moi!*' [You are teasing me!]

His heavy dry coughing interrupted his words. He rose and headed for the exit, his long legs stumbling over the saddles and stirrups lying about, overturning cups and teapots. It caused another roar of laughter. The Hungarian *Rittmeister*'s rather heavy belly even started to shake.

I felt sorry for poor Herr Wagner. Perhaps he alone of these latter-day *Landsknechts*[42] thirsting for blood and booty carried more honest and sincere convictions.

I went out after him. After the stuffy, heavy air of the small tent, full of tobacco smoke and the soot from tallow candles, the gentle freshness of the warm southern night felt like an embrace.

The dark silhouette of the Bavarian artilleryman loomed over a heap of stones. I sat down next to him and thought of a subject to strike up a conversation.

'You're not related to the famous composer Richard Wagner, that king of enchanting sounds and mighty chords?'

'*Vous vous moquez!*' he spluttered again and wanted to get up. I managed to stop him only by force.

'Oh!' Wagner sighed and an unceasing stream of words started flowing from him: there was no country more beautiful in the world than Bavaria with its mountains, woods and waterfalls, no city better than Munich with its Pinakothek, Gothic churches and beers.

Then I started talking of Bavarian beer, translucent as amber, of all that was beautiful in his fatherland, where wooded mountains cast reflections in emerald lakes … and there had been no king as brave and brilliant as Ludwig II.[43] Prussia's iron hegemony now hung over Bavaria, but …

He was a retired lieutenant. He had lived for many years in California, where he had a farm. He had gone to the Transvaal immediately after the declaration of war. He had wanted to join the artillery, but these uncultured Boers did not group their guns into batteries – they did not even have range tables – so he had ended up with the Krugersdorpers. He had caught a cold during a rain shower, when they had to live in the mountains for weeks without tents or fire. He was very glad of our arrival: those Hungarians were such vandals.

Measuredly rocking his body, he talked and talked without end. His quiet voice was putting me to sleep. From the river came the murmur of waves, indistinct as if stifled by the grandeur of the silent, starry night. The dark mountains in the distance, the camp and everything around us was sleeping peacefully. Then cannon shots thundered far in the distance. A horse's hooves clattered loudly on the rocks. I came to my senses.

'Tell me, do you know if the Boers are planning anything for tomorrow?'

'Oh, only the field-cornet knows that. As for us volunteers, we are keeping watch tomorrow.' ...

Notes

1   General Sir George Stuart White (1835–1912) commanded the British garrison at the siege of Ladysmith.

2   During the Russo-Turkish War of 1877–1878, troops of the Ottoman army besieged the town of Plevna for five months.

3   The *agterryers*, black Africans and coloureds who did menial tasks as mounted personal servants and, on a few occasions, performed combat duties on the Boer side. Up to 12 000 *agterryers* accompanied commandos to the front; see Nasson, B, 'The war for South Africa', p 218.

4   The Battle of the Platrand (6 January 1900) was the only major attempt by the Boers to break through the British lines during the siege of Ladysmith.

5   Elsewhere in his memoir, Avgustus notes: 'By the way, Joubert was said to disallow heavy shelling of Ladysmith not only because it was "*jammer om de mannen te slachten*", but also because he did not want to ruin his own houses in the town. And on the day of his intimate funeral in Pretoria, it was openly said that he had been poisoned because the republican government was wary of his undesirable interference in decision making regarding a continuation of the war.'

6   General Lucas Meyer (1846–1902) commanded the Boer troops on the Tugela River until early February 1900, when General Louis Botha took over.

7   A rank in the Boer armies comparable to a major. A district had a commando (for example, the Krugersdorp Commando) with a commandant; the

district was divided into three to five wards, with a field-cornet at the head of each ward.

8 A hill near Ladysmith that dominated many siege positions. From the beginning of the siege, the British tried to regain it.

9 One of the lowest commissioned ranks in the German armed forces. It was renamed *Oberleutnant* in 1899.

10 The Boers developed their tactics of 'saving lives to fight another day' in conflicts with the African societies within their republics in the second half of the 19th century. Boer military leaders relied on protracted sieges to avoid heavy casualties among their own, relatively small troops when attacking enemy strongholds; see Pretorius 'The Second Anglo-Boer War: An overview', p 112.

11 Second Captain (*shtabs-kapitan*) Alexander Shulzhenko, aged 30, formerly of the Kerch Miner Company. One of the last Russian volunteers to remain with the Boer troops, he surrendered to the British in April 1901 and was imprisoned by them in Bombay. *Anglo-burskaya voyna 1899–1902 godov …* Vol 8 (2012), pp 277–282.

12 On 30 October 1899, British troops tried to break out of besieged Ladysmith.

13 Black African spies and dispatch runners supplied the British military authorities with intelligence about Boer commandos. When captured by the Boers, many of these agents were shot; see Nasson 'The war for South Africa', p 218.

14 Commandant Paul Adolph Krantz (1862–1939) had settled in the Transvaal before the war. He was elected the commanding officer of the German corps by his fellow volunteers in December 1899; see Van Niekerk, M, 'Adolf Schiel en die Duitse Kommando. (M.A.-tesis – Universiteit van Pretoria)', *Archives Year Book for South African History*, vol II. Cape Town, 1951, p 173.

15 Krantz's wife, Martha Catherina, née Botha, aged 24, accompanied him on commando throughout the Natal campaign.

16 The German corps took part in many engagements on the Natal front. They distinguished themselves during the battles of Platrand and Spion Kop in January 1900.

17 *Rittmeister* was a cavalry captain's rank in the army of Austria-Hungary.

18 At the Battle of Narva (1700), Swedish troops defeated a Russian siege force several times its size.

19 In February 1899, the autonomy of Finland within the Russian Empire was restricted.

20 The Russian victory at the Battle of Poltava (1709) marked the end of Sweden's dominance of northeastern Europe.

21 The people of Norway wanted to dissolve their union with Sweden. The country achieved independence in 1905.

22 The present University of Tartu in Estonia.

23 A reference to Henry IV (1553–1610), King of France from the House of Bourbon.

24 Russian war artist Vasily Vereshchagin (1842–1904) did not participate in the siege of Geok Tepe (1880), in the present Turkmenistan. It was his brother General Alexander Vereshchagin (1850–1909). After the capture of Geok Tepe, the general was appointed its temporary commandant.

25 Though initially popular with the members of the corps, Krantz was

overshadowed by his field-cornet, Richard Runck. After an appeal to General Joubert, Krantz managed to get rid of the rival, but his authority had been subverted. Many volunteers grew dissatisfied with his leadership and transferred to Boer commandos; see Van Niekerk, 'Adolf Schiel', pp 173–174.

[26] The arshin was a Russian unit of measurement equal to 71 centimetres.

[27] Antonie (Antoine) François Kock (1869–1948) did not have a military rank. Neither was he a Leiden and Oxford graduate. He studied in Rotterdam, Edinburgh and London and was admitted to the Middle Temple. Before the war, he was a lawyer and, later, judge in Pretoria; see Uys, IS, *South African Military Who's Who 1452–1992*. Germiston: Fortress, 1992, pp 123–124.

[28] General Pieter Arnoldus Cronjé (1836–1911), commandant of the Boer forces in the western front. After his defeat at the Battle of Paardeberg, he surrendered on 27 February 1900 with over 4 000 of his men. This undermined the morale of republican forces and led to further humiliating defeats.

[29] Antonie François had served as head of staff with his father, General JHM Kock, who was fatally wounded at the Battle of Elandslaagte (October 1899).

[30] Sir Leander Starr Jameson (1853–1917) studied medicine at the University College Hospital, London. In December 1895, Jameson and his companions attempted a military invasion of the Transvaal to instigate a revolt of British residents in the Boer republic. The uprising did not take place, and the 'Jameson Gang' was captured.

[31] The Krugersdorp Commando, 800 strong, had arrived at the front in September 1899. General Jan Smuts believed that the unit 'distinguished itself more than any other commando in the Natal campaign'; see Van Aardt, JMH, Die aandeel van die Krugersdorpse kommando aan die Tweede Vryheidsoorlog (1899–1902). MA thesis. Potchefstroomse Universiteit vir CHO, 1950, pp 20–22; Hancock, WK and Van der Poel, J (eds), *Selections from the Smuts Papers*. Vol I. Cambridge: Cambridge University Press, 1966, p 566.

[32] JL van Wyk was only a field-cornet, not a commandant.

[33] The Hungarian homeland army in Austria-Hungary, established in 1867.

[34] The Hungarian Revolution of 1848–1849 was crushed by the Austrian and Russian armies.

[35] Cavalry captain Gyula Illés, also known as Julius von Illich (1856–?), had participated in the occupation of Bosnia and Herzegovina. In March 1900, he organised an Austro-Hungarian corps; see Pap, L, 'Magyarország és a második angol–búr háború', PhD thesis, University of Debrecen, 2015, pp 238–239; Schmidl, EA, 'Österreicher im Burenkrieg, 1899–1902', PhD thesis, Universität Wien, 1980, pp 174–175.

[36] Baron Felix Luzsénszky (1856–1921), a retired Hungarian officer; see Pap, 'Magyarország', pp 219–220.

[37] Franz Rumpf (1872–?), a mining engineer from Voitsberg, and his brother Karl had come to South Africa as volunteers in January 1900. Karl Rumpf (1875–1900) was killed during the Battle of the Tugela Heights. Franz joined a foreign volunteer unit under Baron Anton von Goldegg. He was perhaps the only Austrian to receive the *Dekoratie voor Trouwe Dienst*

(Decoration for Devoted Service), the South African award for Boer veterans of that war; see Schmidl, 'Österreicher', pp228–229.

[38] Lieutenant Anton Buzukov (1869–?), a graduate of the Military School in Sofia. He had taken part in anti-Ottoman expeditions led by Bulgarian military officers into Turkish-ruled Macedonia to provoke the struggle for independence on the part of its Slavic population: see Gerdzhikov, M, *Spomeni, dokumenti, materiali*. Sofia: Nauka i Izkustvo, 1984, p 396; Peltekov, AG, *Revolyutsionni deytsi ot Makedoniya i Odrinsko*. Sofia: Orbel, 2014, p 56; Tanev, S, *Otvoreni pisma. Spomeni i ispovedi na glavniya redactor na v.'Utro' pisani v Tsentralniya zatvor*. Sofia: Universitetsko Izdatelstvo 'Sv. Kliment Okhridski', 1994, p 27.

[39] This was probably Waldemar Wagner, who had served in the 5th Royal Bavarian Field Artillery 'King Alfons XIII of Spain' Regiment. It had a horse artillery detachment; see Van Niekerk, 'Adolf Schiel', p 204.

[40] A title given by Miguel de Cervantes to his fictional creation, Don Quixote.

[41] Rocinante was Don Quixote's horse.

[42] German mercenaries of the 15th and 16th centuries.

[43] Ludwig II (1845–1886), King of Bavaria.

CHAPTER 5

Life on commando

It was a period of calm, even though the British felt obliged to send us a dozen shells or so every day. Yet that did not worry us much. We had become thoroughly accustomed to the shelling and stopped fearing it, even though their range increased by the day. The fearless Nikitin decided to educate the Boers a bit, and folded the sides of a shell casing into a hearth on which he grilled and roasted sizzling, succulent pieces of steak.

Let me say a couple of words about Nikitin. He arrived in the Transvaal as soon as he'd become an officer, right after the completion of his training at the Odessa military school, where he received first prize, a gold watch.

We often had a bit of a laugh at him, partly because of his prize watch, whose inscription he tried to explain to curious Boers, partly because even while lying in the trenches, he would open up his tactical handbooks and all the manuals and instructions he had brought with him from his regiment, in order to check the course of the battle.

'The British are idiots!' he would grumble as he sat in his trench returning the enemy fire. 'They're marching their reserves in columns, while it says clear as day in the *Military Manual* that when you're in the line of fire you need an open, deployed formation. Ah well, all the worse for them!' And he'd snap the bolt of his rifle with a click.

All the fellows grew sincerely fond of him for his down-to-earth, outgoing nature. With his courage, which was the calm, sober courage of a true soldier, without bravado or boastfulness, he managed to earn such respect from the Boers that they later called him '*dappere Nikita*' [brave Nikita], unlike another Nikitin, a lieutenant from one of the Caucasian Grenadier regiments who joined us later.

We had meat in abundance: every day an ox or several fat sheep were slaughtered for the commando. The squad commandant handed out delicious white rusks, rice, salt, tinned pork and Ceylon tea or coffee. When the fancy took me, I cooked a borsch[1] with meat and the hyacinth bulbs that grew wild on the slopes of the mountain. The borsch was quite filling, although it had a peculiar taste.

Sugar was sometimes in short supply, but we replaced it with jam or fruit marmalade in round tin boxes. We also contrived to make Russian hotcakes, doughnuts and flatbreads from flour and baking powder.

A springbok or partridge, shot on occasion, and a peach *kompot*[2] gave some variety to our dinners, and the Boers, whose table was less exciting because the blacks did their cooking, glanced with envy at our rich soup with onions, huge beefsteaks with rice and browned griddlecakes with jam. Sometimes we generously treated them to our culinary works of art, especially because they never got us involved in the dirty work of cutting up carcasses and always gave the best parts – the fillet or tongue – to our team.

The Boers often received delicacies from home – rich pies or fruit baskets – via military post and they always remembered to share with us. Generally, they treated us, the Russians, with more consideration and kindness than other foreigners.

To tell the truth, we also behaved more modestly than the other volunteers. We did not make a display of our officer's rank and obeyed the corporals put in charge of us without protest, whereas the Hungarians, Germans and other volunteers frequently showed contempt for the Boers, tried to impose their expert advice and often got into vehement squabbles with them.

Of course, the Boers did not always treat the volunteers properly either. It was utterly beyond the simple psychology of an unsophisticated Boer to resolve this seemingly incomprehensible phenomenon: how was it that these foreigners, these complete strangers, who did not know his language, his faith or his customs, had sailed to him from across the distant seas and were prepared to fight and suffer and die with him, and yet demanded no payment or reward?

I would often be sitting in the tent of some esteemed Boer, and, as

I drank my coffee, he would strike up a conversation like this: 'Do you also have cows in Russia?'

'Yes, we do.'

'And sheep?'

'And sheep.'

'And railways?' he kept on asking.

'And railways!'

Then the Boer would puff on his pipe as he digested this information, until he suddenly asked: 'Now when will the Russian Tsar stand up for our people?'

People would read with rapt attention the fanciful news that often appeared in the Johannesburg newspaper, *The Standard and Diggers' News*, concerning military preparations by Russia, the mobilisation of troops in the Caucasus and Turkestan military districts, of Russian troop movements towards Herat, etc.[3]

Every time such an article appeared, it caused lively discussions among the Boers. To be honest, we too, deprived as we were of any news from our distant fatherland, were sometimes perturbed by the possibility of complications in the East. What if Russia suddenly declared war on England and we, abandoned by fate on the other end of the earth, had to fight here with lower ranks for what was in fact a completely alien cause, without any benefit to our service record?[4]

If a British bullet were to cut any of us down, we would not even land up on the pages of *The Invalid*,[5] and our powerless wives and orphans would lose their widow's pension. We thought hard about this at times.

But at least we were somewhat comforted by Lieutenant Nikitin's sensible arguments that in the event of a war between Russia and Great Britain, we would be doing Britain no less harm here than if we commanded half a company in the Pamirs.

'As for me,' declared the free-thinking Diatroptov frankly, 'although I am just a *praporshchik* in the reserve, I will do everything in my power not to take part in a war caused by diplomatic misunderstandings or by aspirations to seize foreign territory. Here I can defend the sacred *droits de l'homme*, freedom, equality, fraternity and the like with a rifle in my hands.'

The affable young Pavel R looked at things even more simply:

'Ours is not to reason why: ours is just to have a drink and carry on fighting!'

At the time, none of us doubted that the outcome of the campaign would be successful. We were sure that we would rout those despicable seafarers, who had once invented boxing and now lyddite bombs and dum-dum bullets, and that we would enter Durban as victors with our hats dashingly cocked. Diatroptov had even made up a song for that occasion to the tune of 'Resound the glory trumpet':[6]

> *At Tugela's distant stream,*
> *We had fought old Buller's team.*
> *And the glory of our names*
> *Echoed through the Transvaal hills.*

In fact, we had no time to dream of the past or ask anxious questions about the future; the concerns and needs of everyday camp life fully absorbed what little time we had left between sorties and guard duty. We took turns to prepare lunch and make tea; the others would bathe or wash clothes under the arches of a ruined bridge, beyond the reach of flying shrapnel. In the evenings we had to drive our horses from the pasture. We tied them for the night to hitching posts made of railway sleepers and wire, and diligently cleaned and brushed the animals as taught by the experienced Austrian cavalry officers.

By now, pointlessly sitting in trenches on the mountain and observing British batteries and armoured trains from Chieveley through binoculars had lost its former interest. The enemy's shells sometimes exploded very successfully, but the sight of the dead and wounded no longer disturbed us, as we had somehow grown inured to other people's suffering. In short, our life amid the ranks of Boer warriors was by no means a constant picnic.

All the charms of unfettered camp life paled in comparison with the torments we suffered as a result of the unbearable heat and the insufferable stench of cattle innards and leftover food lying all about. We were horribly plagued by swarms of bothersome flies, against which neither tobacco smoke nor the shade of a tent or a bath in the river offered any salvation. Swimming in the warm, muddy water was not particularly pleasant either. Every now and then the current would carry past the bloated, crab-eaten body of a horse or a soldier.

It is small wonder, then, if in the end we were overcome by some kind of apathy. Our thoughts would become sluggish, and we would lie as if drowsy for days on end in the tent, only coming to life when it was our turn for guard duty.

◆

The black mountain tips sleep in silence; the only sound is the dull roar of the fast-flowing Tugela. In the distance, on the far side of the river, the lights of the British camp cast a shimmering glow in the dark sky.

I am alone at my guard post; all around me is quiet. It is at such times that memories of the distant homeland I abandoned for some phantom of an idea awaken in me with an unstoppable force.

It is winter there now. Crisp snow has covered everything. The wind drones and howls through the boundless fields and dense woods. My eyes wander longingly over heaven's vault, but there is no sign of the North Star, the Bear or even a single familiar little luminary. The Southern Cross shines indifferently from its unreachable height, but it is a stranger to me. What ill wind brought me here?

Now, with a carbine in my hand, I am just a Boer sentry, nothing more: a corporal posted me here and a corporal will relieve me; but once, not long ago, my name was listed among the field and non-commissioned officers. Now I must stare with watchful eyes at the enemy's positions, although I am so sleepy that I cannot keep my tired eyes open. One by one, in an endless chain, I see scenes of military life: keeping watch on the Tugela, patrolling, guarding the bivouac in compliance with the new manual of field service …

Did I not theorise about it at the tactics drill of the officers' assembly not so long ago? With a sinking heart, I stick pins into the woods and marshes on a map of the great and glorious town of Alexandrovsk[7] and environs, all under the formidable gaze of my commander. The enemy is expected from the northwest. With some help from Levitsky, the problem is solved.

The grave-looking instructor is listening to my explanations. 'Now why are you only telling me about pickets and advance parties? And at the bivouac, sir, have you put down a place for doing laundry?'

The empty walls of the sombre guardhouse.

A paraffin lamp is smoking on the table. Boredom, wistfulness. For the hundredth time you read the instructions regarding access to the money box, written in the elaborate copperplate of some commander's aide-de camp. On the other end are quaint arabesques and rhymed nonsense, the fruit of the imagination of those esteemed gentlemen, the idle officers of the guard.

I remember the sunlit streets of Krakowskie Przedmieście: shining shop windows, gilded restaurant signs, carriages rumbling along the roadway paved with wooden blocks; happy, dressed-up crowds swarming over the pavements: men in top hats and beaver collars, and ladies ... ladies like the pictures from some fashion magazine. And I, in a brand-new coat made by a tailor on credit, join the crowd; soldiers salute and the other people I know bow to me. And there she is! How her dark eyes sparkled under that fur hat ...

'Pasop! Pasop! Daar kom die Kakies!' [Watch out! Watch out! There come the khakis!] a Boer – he must have stolen up on me – whispered, pointing at the opposite shore. I roused myself, rubbed my eyes and, clenching my loaded rifle, pressed myself to the ground next to the Boer, whose sensitive ear had detected a rustle and movement in the bushes across the river.

I was all ears and eyes, but all I could hear was the flow of the river and the quiet rustle of the thick bush. We spent several minutes in breathless anticipation. Then I saw it clearly: the dull clatter of hooves, silhouettes taking shape over the dark surface of the river – they were swimming towards us. The British! A rifle shot crackled right next to my ear. Another one. Then yet another one. More shots rang out somewhere in the distance. A groan of pain rang out over the sleeping river and died away.

'Skiet not, porca madonna! Skiet not, maledetto!' [Don't shoot, damn it! Don't shoot, bastard!] the voices of the men swimming towards us boomed out in a wild chorus.

'Ons mense! Italiaanse korps!' [Our men! The Italian corps!] my comrade sighed with relief, uncocked his rifle and ran to them.

The other members of our watch, who had been lying behind us under cover, also came running. They gathered in bewilderment around the riders, who by now had reached the shore. We saw that there were about 15 men. Two of them were dragging a third one, apparently wounded. His hands hung helplessly and his head was shaking slightly. He looked around at the people surrounding him as if trying to guess who his unintentional murderer was.

The gloomy Boers kept quiet and did not react to the frenzied swearing of the Italians.

Captain Camillo Ricchiardi's Italian corps.

Their leader, of whom I had heard stories, Captain Ricchiardi,[8] a tall man with an aquiline nose and a jet-black beard, pounced on our corporal, brandishing his revolver. '*Porca madonna!*' [God damn it!] he shouted in a voice breaking with anger. 'You, eyeless giraffe! You killed-a my man! You wounded-a my two horses! I am going to smash your skull!'

It turned out that his commando was returning from patrol after a skirmish with a British picket, from whom they had captured two horses. And now, heading for the ford, they could not have expected to run into our watch or imagine that the Boers would mistake them for the British in the dark and open fire. The brave captain was particularly infuriated that one of the horses they had captured from the British, loaded with trophies, had been wounded by a stray bullet and carried off by the swift current.

Soon the sun began to rise. The Italians were still swearing as they set off to their camp, taking the dying man with them. A few days later the sad episode was forgotten.

On another occasion our watch managed to capture a fugitive from Ladysmith. He was taken to the field-cornet for questioning. He said that he had slipped past the siege lines unnoticed, hidden in gorges during the day and made his way to the Tugela during the night. His pale, exhausted face, feverishly burning eyes, bloody legs and clothes which hung in tatters on his thin body spoke volumes about the deprivations he had suffered on his journey.

The Englishman, a private from the Gordon Highlanders regiment, ravenously attacked the meat and rusks offered him. When asked how long the garrison in Ladysmith was still going to hold out, he gave an answer worthy of a true soldier: 'For as long as we have ammunition and shells!'

'And how long will that be?' the Boers asked ironically.

'Until Buller has chased you, sons of bitches, back for Majuba!' It was a response for the textbooks. The good-natured Boers were not offended, however, and continued plying the Englishman with food and drink.

They already knew full well from line-crossers and African spies that the situation in Ladysmith was critical, with dysentery and fever rampant among the garrison and inhabitants, as the underground shelters in which the populace hid from bombardment had been flooded with water. A whole third of the garrison was unable to fight, provisions were coming to an end, rations were cut further every day and the people ate almost only horsemeat.

They were starting to experience a shortage of ammunition as well, mainly of shells for the large-calibre naval guns from the battleship *Powerful*.[9] But the thought of surrender did not even occur to White, and Ladysmith's tenacious defence should serve as vivid testimony of the endurance and resilience of the British soldier, and will take its place of honour in the history of the British Army, together with the defence of Gibraltar in 1704 and Lucknow in 1857.[10]

◆

Only a few days had passed since the disastrous failure at Spion Kop,[11] but already by the beginning of February, Buller considered it possible to launch a new attempt at breaking through the Boers' army of observation. This resolve on the part of the British serves, to some extent, as proof of their soldiers' high spirits and the confidence they placed in their leaders. And yet it should be clear that the entirely passive nature of the Boers' defensive tactics, especially their continued inability to take advantage of the situation, as well as a whole sequence of failures, such as the repelled attacks at Colenso on 15 December and at Spion Kop on 24 January, were in any case unlikely to have dampened either the troops' morale or Buller's resolve.

Those chief traits of the British national character – their perseverance and stubbornness – are clearly visible when evaluating the subsequent actions of the British commander. Buller's operations from 5 to 7 February were aimed at capturing Vaalkrans, a hill that lay near the Tugela's northern bank.[12] ...

We only heard the distant echoes of artillery fire in the Krugersdorp Commando. Thus far we had not been disturbed. Several days before Buller's march on Vaalkrans, our prudent commandant, Van Wyk, had already requisitioned two wagonloads of entrenching tools from the main camp behind Grobler's Kloof, where all the ammunition, food and so on was stored. In anticipation of a possible British attack on Colenso he proposed that the men start deepening and widening the trenches.

We also had to arm ourselves with shovels and pickaxes and get to work. This was not the same as shouting the command, 'Dig towards your toes!', lighting a cigarette, and with the entrenchment instructions tucked in your pocket, strolling behind your company as it dug around in the loose sands of the Bielany base.[13]

It would have been silly even to consider showing off our knowledge of fortifications to the Boers. They selected the line of fire unerringly, as though guided by some deeper instinct; the outlines of the parapets blended in so well with the adjacent terrain that even at a distance of a few steps it was impossible to guess the location of the rifle trench, so well concealed was it behind the bends and twists of the soil and the scattered rocks and boulder fragments.

The trenches usually reached to your waist or a bit deeper. The outer wall of the ditch was dug in the shape of an arch, so when you were in a sitting position it made up to some extent for the absence of a dugout. Rocks were used as steps to stand on when shooting, and for exiting the trench.

The trenches did not stretch in an uninterrupted line, but were built for groups of six to ten men at a time. In places where it was impossible to create a two- or three-tiered defence by arranging the trenches on different levels, they were connected with shallow passages. There was a noticeable trend to place the trenches in such a way that they exited into some gorge or gully, so as not to attract the enemy's attention when entering or leaving the trench.

Every Boer placed bags of rusks, tins of corned beef manufactured in Chicago and flasks or canvas bags of water in the trenches, without waiting for 'orders from above'. Ammunition was handed out in unlimited quantities, and not in packs but in entire crates or bags.

Incidentally, on occasion I saw crates with a British stamp, 'Rifle Cartridges', followed by some numbers and letters; they also kept dum-dum cartridges, not with sawn-off tips but with four lengthwise incisions. Many Boers were armed with Lee-Metford rifles taken from dead Englishmen, and they used English dum-dum bullets without any qualms.

The trench tools, large-size shovels and pickaxes, had been confiscated by the government of the republic from the warehouses and stores of the Beckett Company, which specialised in equipment for gold prospecting.[14]

We were not used to this kind of work, and initially it seemed downright unbearable; each blow of the pickaxe against the rocky ground sent sparks flying in all directions. Our hands became covered in bloody calluses and we were drenched in sweat, but it was essential work, otherwise one could get hit by a piece of lyddite shell before you knew it.

Settling into someone else's trench was viewed by the esteemed

Boers as tantamount to theft, and we pooled all our efforts to dig our own trench. Poor young Pavel R soon lost any desire to continue his practical studies in the field of fortification and earthworks, and after he broke his shovel, he magnanimously gave us the pit he had only dug a quarter-deep, declaring that this would have to do: 'If we get bombarded, I'll build myself a wall with dead bodies.'

Our participation in the events of 5–7 February[15] was limited to a request received by the Krugersdorp Commando for a hundred men to lift a Long Tom[16] to the top of Doornkloof with the aid of cables, levers and pulleys. The massive cannon (manufactured at the Creusot factory) was unlike anything in the British artillery and was transported by 60 oxen from End Hill, near Ladysmith. It now required the combined effort of 200 men to drag it up the mountain.

The day before, 200 Boers had been working on the construction of a road, a platform of oak planks, and a parapet made of sandbags. Fifty men carried the shells up. To hide the construction of the battery from the English and distract the enemy, the crafty Boers occasionally resorted to the following trick: on one of the adjacent heights not occupied by them they laid out rocks in rectangular heaps and smeared them from the outside with lime. To make the illusion complete, they left some unrideable horses there.

The British gunners seized the opportunity and opened heavy fire on the make-believe battery, pounding it for the entire day and only noticing their mistake much later, by which time the Long Tom's formidable muzzle already poked out from the embrasure of the completed battery. The dashing young artillerymen, some of them still dressed in their French-style, black-cord-embroidered uniforms,[17] bustled around the cannon, gauged the distance by sight, set the required angle of elevation and loaded a giant projectile.

At the signal of General Botha, who was standing immediately next to the battery, the gunner jauntily pulled the cord, and a shot went off with such force that the hill shook. I thought I had burst an eardrum. Dark rings flashed in front of my eyes and I inadvertently leaned against the parapet.

The gunners were brimming with the sacred fire that always takes hold of inveterate artillerymen during battle: the steel monster, as if imbued with the will and thoughts of his cannoneer, obediently opens his gaping jaws to receive the next shell, and belches it out again and again with a deafening groan, sending death and destruction to the bewildered ranks of the enemy.

Despite the onset of dusk, the British artillery answered our fire. Shells started falling left and right. Shrapnel bounced off the stones with a crack or thumped dully into the parapet bags, covering us in fine sand and earth. The familiar suffocating smell of lyddite gas filled the air. Lieutenant Nikitin, who was standing on the platform, expressed his heartfelt admiration for the British artillery's accurate aim at the top of his voice. 'They took aim without a bracket, the devils! That first shell fell right on target!'

But other shells came whizzing and squealing in after the first one, and I was gripped with terror at this precision, for they all exploded right next to the battery. I could not help but feel admiration for the young artillerymen as they kept their cool perfectly under the continuous hail of shrapnel, and cheerfully, even dashingly, without any fuss or panic, carried one shell after the other to the cannon, loaded and took aim as if they were on the training ground.

There were some casualties, however, and the blood-drenched platform became slippery to walk on; Red Cross wagons gleamed at the foot of the hill.

'Hip hip hurrah!' the Boers shouted when the dry grass and bushes between the hill and the Tugela suddenly began to smoke and burst into bright flames from their shells. Now the shooting could continue all through the night.

It was a majestic sight, that fire: its rolling waves grew wider and wider and enveloped the dense bush; we could see the long tongues of flame shoot up and flicker above the dark river, revealing the location of the enemy troops crowded in disarray. Every minute that went by, their return fire grew weaker.

The Boers, triumphant in their imminent victory, began to sing a song to some music-hall tune in their jarring voices. Locking hands, they started dancing in a circle around the cannon:

> *En Buller vlug terug*
> *Long Tom skiet en ruk!*
> *Pasop vir die Vaalpense!*[18]

[Buller runs away / The Long Tom shoots and
shakes! / Watch out for the Transvalers!]

The chorus boomed and thundered:

Pasop! Pasop! Pasop vir die Vaalpense!
Pasop! Pasop! Pasop vir die Vaalpense!

The first voices began again with a high tenor ...

Kom burgers bymekaar ...
[Burghers, come together ...]
Aandag! Skiet voorwaarts!
[Attention! Shoot forwards!]

The menacing shout of the lieutenant, the chief gunner, put an
end to this unbridled merriment, which for some reason reminded
me of some dance by cannibals around an idol bespattered with the
blood of human sacrifice.

The song ceased and the shooting continued throughout the night
and until sunrise, when the last British columns had fled behind the
Tugela.

◆

At that time, a new volunteer joined our commando. He was Lieutenant Guchkov, an officer of the Kuban army who was doing his
stint of reduced pay.[19] He brought his own tent with him, as well as a
good many other things: real Moscow tea and sugar, pea sausage and
papirosas, which we had not seen for a long time. For the brave young
Pavel R he brought a letter from Pretoria. Such was the bliss and delight on the beardless face of young Pavel that even the gaunt coun-
tenance of the Royal Bavarian lieutenant, whose beard had grown
quite bristly and unkempt, displayed something like a smile when he
stood by at the reading of the letter: '*O, ich habe auch geliebt*' [Oh,
I also knew love] ...

Guchkov brought a valet with him from Moscow, old Ivan
Petrovich, who looked after his baggage and tent.[20] He caused us so

many moments of merriment that I will devote a couple of lines to remembering him here.

Fyodor Guchkov (1913).

He was dressed in boots with pleats at the top, which provoked the astonishment and envy of the Boers, and a red calico shirt, on top of which, despite the heat, he always wore a warm waistcoat and a watch and chain. On top of his bald head was a peaked cap, which made him look like some petty clerk at a roadside inn who had been whisked off, God knows how, across half the world and the seven seas, to a Boer commando. But Ivan Petrovich was the embodiment of the virtues of the immortal Sancho Panza and Gogol's Petrushka,[21] and quickly got used to his unfamiliar surroundings. Deft, eager to please and good-natured to the highest degree, he willingly took on the duties of head waiter and started managing our kitchen: 'You lads go and do your fighting, and I'll make you some steaks or meatballs in the best fashion. Thank the Lord, I learnt to cook in the service of the noblemen!'

He converted two little African boys, whom the field-cornet had magnanimously placed at our disposal, to the Christian faith and gave each a Russian name.

'You, little Vanyusha, bring water to me, you understand? And you, little Petrusha, bring wood, you understand? That thing to make fire, you get it?'

The little black boy just stood there, blinking uncomprehendingly.

'*Hamba lapha*, boy!' [Get out of here!] I shouted at him in Zulu, to help Ivan out.

'Don't bother us, master. I'll explain everything properly myself. He'll understand!' Ivan Petrovich grumbled.

He had a low opinion of the Boers and openly sympathised with the English.

'They rebelled for nothing! They don't even have anyone in charge. Them English, now there's a different story. We have some English merchants in Moscow, and they're quite a clever bunch.'

We laughed till we cried when he heard shells screaming ominously above his head for the first time. With a single leap he landed beneath a nearby ox-wagon, and only crawled out from under it at nightfall.

But he soon grew accustomed to this music and eventually would only close the pots more carefully to prevent any clods of earth or rubble from the explosion of a projectile from ending up in the borsch or roast.

'Such unchristian behaviour, my word! They could at least call a truce when good people are at their cooking!'

Our peaceful camp life was not fated to continue for long. Menacing thunderclouds were gathering above us, and soon the catastrophe took place that led to the total rout of the Boer army.

On 15 February, the enemy began to show increased vigilance. Closely packed columns of troops, batteries and baggage trains stretched past our position. Buller was clearly planning to attack our left flank, which lay along a series of steep hills on the other side of the Tugela. Although these movements happened out of cannon shot, the Long Tom was moved to the top of Grobler's Kloof, the hill lying closest to us, and now both British and our shells criss-crossed the sky above our heads. The cannonade aimed at the Krugersdorpers' hill also grew more intense.

We no longer slept in tents but spent all our time in the trenches, in anxious apprehension of a British offensive from the direction of Colenso.

Notes

[1] A Russian beetroot soup.

[2] A Russian sweet beverage made from cooked fruit.

[3] In early 1900, Russia increased its troops on the Afghan border, but British diplomats prevented further escalation. *Anglo-burskaya voyna 1899–1902 godov …*, vol 3 (2012), p 165.

[4] On 8 March 1900, it was rumoured in Pretoria that the Russian military agent with the Boer troops had been recalled and that Russia had declared war on England. *Anglo-burskaya voyna 1899–1902 godov …*, v 6 (2012), p 28.

[5] The *Russky Invalid* daily was the organ of the Ministry of War of the Russian Empire.

[6] A Cossack song recounting events of the Russo-Turkish War of 1877–1878.

[7] The name of several small Russian towns. Possibly, the present Žemaičių Naumiestis in western Lithuania.

[8] Captain Camillo Ricchiardi (1865–1940), commander of the Italian corps of about a hundred men. He had fought in the Philippine-American War (1899). In South Africa, Ricchiardi joined the Krugersdorp Commando before forming his corps; see Uys, *South African Military Who's Who 1452–1992*, p 198.

[9] HMS *Powerful* was an armoured cruiser.

[10] A reference to the capture of Gibraltar by Anglo-Dutch forces in 1704, during the War of the Spanish Succession (1701–1714), and to the British relief of the siege of Lucknow during the Indian Rebellion of 1857.

[11] The Battle of Spion Kop (24 January 1900), one of the bloodiest clashes of the war. An attempt by Lieutenant General Sir Charles Warren's troops to establish themselves on Spion Kop hill to cover General Sir Redvers Buller's advance across the Tugela River to lift the siege of Ladysmith was foiled by the burghers under the command of General Louis Botha. Over 240 British soldiers were killed, many of whom were buried in their trenches. Sixty-eight Boers fell in the battle, two from the Krugersdorp Commando.

[12] A ridge of hills near Spion Kop.

[13] Bielany is a district in northwestern Warsaw. A fort was built there as part of the city's fortifications in the second half of the 19th century.

[14] Thomas William Beckett (1851–1924) was a prominent general trader and mining entrepreneur.

[15] The Battle of Vaalkrans.

[16] A 155 mm French field gun, one of the four that the Boers had purchased before the war.

[17] Incorrect. The uniforms of the Transvaal State Artillery were in the Prussian style.

[18] One of the few army songs that the Boers sang (note by Avgustus).

[19] The Kuban Cossack army. Cossack officers were required to go on reduced pay for three to four years.

[20] Pavel Kumaniyev, aged 40, a peasant from the Tula province. The servant returned to Russia with Guchkov; see Voropaeva et al (comp and eds), *Anglo-burskaya voyna 1899–1902 gg*, p 237.

[21] Sancho Panza is Don Quixote's squire. Petrushka is a servant of the main character, Pavel Chichikov, in Nikolai Gogol's novel *Dead Souls* (1842).

CHAPTER 6

The Battle of the Tugela Heights

By the end of the war's first phase, the Boers had been victorious everywhere. All Buller's efforts had been shattered on the Tugela. In the Cape Colony, General Gatacre[1] wanted to put an end to the Boers with a night attack, but he was ambushed himself and suffered a painful defeat at Stormberg. Things did not go better for General French, the dashing sportsman, who was dealt one defeat after the other at Colesberg by De Wet, one of the best Boer leaders.[2]

Methuen, who spoke with undisguised contempt about the Boers, those farmers with their unkempt beards, wanted to crush his un-yielding opponent with a full-frontal attack, according to the rules of boxing, but witnessed, instead, the ruin of his Guards Brigade and Scots Guards, the cream of the British Army, in the battles of 27 November and 11 December.[3]

The English press tried to justify some of these shameful defeats by claiming that the terrible British losses as a result of the Boers' destructive firepower had left the attacking troops in utter disarray.

But one only has to look at the statistics, and you will realise that the true reason for these defeats was not the high percentage of British soldiers put out of action but the lack of combat training and a true shortage of morale.

Russian losses in the campaign of 1877–1878[4] sometimes reached 40–90 per cent (at Plevna, Gorni Dubnik and Nova Zagora); the German regiments at Gravelotte, Saint-Privat[5] and Weert suffered 15–45 per cent casualties. And the British? On the bloodiest days at Spion Kop, Magersfontein and Colenso, the British lost no more than four to nine per cent of their men on average.

These eloquent numbers speak for themselves, and it is depressing to think that a false assessment of the British might had hung for so long like a nightmare above Europe and had driven Russia to the Congress of Berlin.[6]

A small, hitherto almost unknown nation had boldly accepted the challenge of the formidable 'Mistress of the Seas' – the same country to whom France yielded a couple of years ago in the Fashoda Incident[7] – and had inflicted several shameful defeats on them.

The Boers failed to take full advantage of their position, however. There is almost not a single occasion where the Boers went on the offensive and crushed the British army as it was retreating from a repulsed attack. Nor has there been an instance where the Boers, who, with their mounted troops and light artillery drawn by hardy mules, are perfectly adapted for continuous movement, performed any significant partisan raids on the extended, initially almost defenceless communication lines of Methuen or Buller, even though they had both knowledge of the country and the sympathy of the local Afrikaners on their side.

The main reason for the Boers' subsequent failures should be sought in their innate inclination towards passive resistance, their unwillingness to submit to strict discipline, which does not require independent reasoning, as essential a military virtue as that may be, and the absence of a popular leader who would be able to embody in his person and his will all the forces at work in society and the will of the people.

But they lacked such a leader, such a man, whose one word or mere appearance on a scene would inspire and carry with him this mass of brave men, dashing riders and sharpshooters, ready to fight for their freedom and independence to the last drop of blood.

It was no secret to anyone that the elderly Kruger was waiting day after day for help from outside, that the phlegmatic Piet Joubert and the crafty Cronjé, who would subsequently perform the role of a latter-day Marshal Bazaine,[8] were members of the party that wanted reconciliation with the British and were even willing to make concessions. Botha, De Wet and President Steyn did not enjoy any fame at that stage, and could therefore not play a decisive role in influencing the character or means by which the war was being waged.

Thanks to the inaction of the Boers, all of these factors resulted in the British gaining the necessary time, fixing their mistakes and taking advantage of the disproportionate size of their forces, to crush their enemy in an uneven struggle.

In England, the news of their continuous losses had a startling effect. The British had to acknowledge that at no time since the Crimean campaign of 1855 and the Sepoy rebellion of 1857[9] had their nation experienced such a critical moment. A few more victories and the Cape Afrikaners, who were just waiting for an opportunity to shake off the hated British rule, would rise up en masse and that would mean the end of British dominion in southern Africa, and perhaps eventually even the collapse of their clay-footed colossus's global monarchy.

But at this point the tenacity and energy of the British made itself known. Instead of accusing their generals of treason or cursing the army for not living up to their hopes, the government and society made every possible effort to emerge from their plight with honour...

◆

The treason of Cronjé, together with his entire army, was a heavy blow for the two republics. In a single day the Boers lost every advantage they had gained during their hard-fought war in the other theatres of war in Natal and the Cape Colony. Their success at the beginning of the campaign had come too easily, and their leaders had been filled with an unwavering belief that the English would remain true to their reckless tactics of frontal attacks while using the railways as lines of operation. Both the British at the beginning of the war, and now also the Boers, paid dearly for the same mistake, which was to treat the enemy with disdain and contempt – a common occurrence among victors after their first successes.

Roberts's actions illustrated how to take advantage of the war's lessons and proved that well-considered preparation is the primary key to successfully executing a planned operation.[10]

Although the mere capture of a small Boer militia by a regular force of 35 000 troops cannot be considered a remarkable feat, the British army demonstrated such strength and endurance of hardships during their intensive marches through the sandy and waterless desert that Cronjé's capitulation will endure forever as a glorious page in the annals of British soldiery.

◆

Meanwhile, everything stayed the same at our camp on the Tugela. Our horses still grazed on the vast meadow between the river and the railway. Patrols were still being sent out at night. From our trenches we could see that the enemy was not going to trouble us and that their columns were going past Colenso towards the mountains on our left flank. The fact that the British began shelling our mountain more intensely than usual did not worry us much. The news of Roberts's movements or the relief of Kimberley[11] had yet to reach the Krugersdorp Commando.

But on 18 February, at lunchtime, General Lucas Meyer arrived, riding at full speed, and gathered the commandant and the field-cornets. Soon thereafter shouts of 'Mount! Mount!' filled the air.

There was a great commotion. The Boers had been peacefully snoring a minute before, but now they were hastily rushing from their tents and dugouts, putting on their rifles and bandoliers and driving their horses together. The field-cornets rushed about the camp like mad, calling their men and hurrying them on. The blacks drove the horses from the pasture, and the earth trembled under the hooves.

Those who finished saddling did not wait for the others but, with drawn-out cries to their horses, took to the road and disappeared in clouds of red dust. The commotion that suddenly spread over the camp did not escape the attention of the British, and they opened rapid fire on our mountain.

The sinister whistling of shrapnel, the wild screeches of the blacks, the thud of the crazed horses, the hoarse screams of the Boers, out of whom we could get no sense, had a stupefying effect on us.

We managed to catch and saddle our horses, but I ran to the commandant's tent to find out what was the matter. He was no longer there. In the tent, our acquaintance, the Kovno Jew, was busy packing up. In a voice trembling with agitation, he told us that the Free State Boers had abandoned their positions on the left flank hills, the

British had appeared on the Tugela and Botha was calling on the Krugersdorpers to come and help, and intended to take the offensive and repel the British.[12]

'An offensive at last!' Nikitin rejoiced. 'Let us go, gentlemen!'

We agreed to stick together, whenever possible, and rode off after the Boers. The camp was now empty.

I shall never forget that furious race over mountains and gorges. There was no way we would be able to stay together. The riders tore along at full gallop and scattered all over the place. The wind whistled in our ears, shrapnel screeched and hissed and rained down behind us. I could see nothing in front of me. I was aware of nothing. And, suddenly, for some reason, I had a vivid recollection of a one-armed beggar with medals from the Turkish campaign[13] whom I had often seen on the porch of the cathedral in my childhood. 'Mustn't get crippled!' the thought crossed my mind. Then something flashed in front of my eyes, and I was thrown out of my saddle with a terrible force. 'Of course. I'm dead,' I thought. I do not remember how long I lay senseless, but when I regained consciousness, the first thing I instinctively did was to touch my nose. My pince-nez was missing; it had come off and landed at a distance. I got up, only slightly bruised by the sudden fall.

A few paces away, my horse was thrashing, his ribs heaving in pain, bloody foam caking his mouth. A piece of shrapnel had disembowelled him, causing all his intestines to fall out. With a shot through his ear I put an end to the suffering of my Bucephalus, found my pince-nez, swinging about on a grass stalk, and thought about my situation. Where could I go without a horse? The shooting still rang out in the distance, but the big shells were no longer directed at my location. Riders darted past here and there, but they soon disappeared from sight without hearing my shouts, and now I was alone as the silent mountains shone around me in the glare of the midday sun.

A black man on a bay horse appeared. I recognised him: he was from our commando and always carried saddlebags with provisions and a kettle behind his master.

'I'll take his horse. He can carry his sacks without it!' I thought quickly.

But the man apparently guessed my intention, and his bare heels began working hard, urging the horse into a full gallop. I tore off my rifle and aimed, but did not have the heart to do away with him.

'To hell with him. I'll walk!'

But at that moment, none other than Herr Wagner rode up to me at a relaxed trot, leading another horse by the reins.

He was evidently in good spirits and light-heartedly humming a song. Wagner listened to my story and shook his head. 'So, so! I always said that it is helpful to have a spare horse in cases like this. So I chose another horse for myself after everybody had left the camp. I'm sure he'll grow into an excellent trotter.'

'Please, let me have him now!' I begged.

'And what if they kill the horse I'm riding?' Wagner responded imperturbably.

'And if they kill you instead, what good will two horses be to you?'

'That is also possible! I suppose you are right,' Wagner said thoughtfully. 'I can let you have my spare horse, but I want a written proof of receipt, including an undertaking that he will be returned to me at the first opportunity. Here, write it!'

With a gracious smile, he handed me a soiled *Taschenkalender für Königlich Bayerische* ... [Pocket Calendar for Royal Bavarian ...], which he used as a notebook.

I had no choice. 'Why didn't I kill that black man?' I sighed. I scribbled the receipt for him, but then Wagner started thinking again, 'I do not really know which horse to give you: mine is good, but maybe the other one is better?'

He duly got off his horse and spent a long time in contemplation of the poor fleabag, which the Boers had obviously discarded as useless.

'Very well, you can have it,' he said magnanimously in the end. 'If you were a *Rittmeister* or someone else, I would never have agreed; it is only for you, remember! But you wrote the receipt incorrectly: you should indicate all the distinctive marks of the horse and put your full rank next to your signature.'

I did as he asked, but after saddling and mounting the horse, I turned the air blue with such a volley of warrant-officer swearing that even the fleabag of a horse twitched his ears out of decency.

'What did you say?' Herr Wagner asked with a pleasant smile after we set off. He understood about as much Russian as my horse.

'Oh, nothing!' I assured him. 'But remember, if the British ever capture you and I have the chance to free you, I'll require a written receipt from you as well.'

We spurred our horses on until we caught up with an unfamiliar group of Boers. They were from the Ermelo Commando. Botha had also sent for their help, and they were making haste to rejoin their unit near the pontoon bridge. From there, they were evidently supposed to attack the Boschrand, which had already been occupied by the British. Now we knew the situation: Buller had bitten off more than he could chew, and perhaps a new Spion Kop awaited the British. I only hoped I could find my commando and companions.

The Boers had built a wide pontoon bridge where the Tugela turns sharply east, in an area where the high mountains rise up to the very shore.[14] Something incomprehensible was taking place there. The gentle, easy slope and the bridge were crowded with so many people, riders and wagons that at first it was hard to understand who was heading where.

The air was filled with the continuous rumbling and groaning of bellowing oxen, and the shouts and screams of a thousand-strong crowd, whom I identified as Free State Boers by the yellow bands on their hats. '*Die kêrels vlug terug, godverdom!*' [The fellows are fleeing, damn it!] the Ermelo Boers muttered and began to make their way to the bridge. We dismounted and followed them, leading our horses by the reins. There was a terrible crush and congestion on the bridge. Its covering of railway sleepers was shaking, and water was seeping over under the weight of the wagons, guns and ammunition boxes. Horses slipped and reared. The harnessed oxen bellowed mournfully, frightened by the swift, seething current and the cries of the agitated crowd.

Somehow, I managed to cross the bridge, up to my knees in water. My sides were bruised, and I held only the reins in my hand – my horse had remained on the bridge. But even now it was impossible to move forwards: a thousand people crowded on the opposite bank. Our Krugersdorpers were also here; the slender figure of General Botha on a large white horse stood out among the crowd: he was telling them something and waving his wide-brimmed hat, but his voice was drowned out amid the unceasing bellowing of animals and the cries and clamour of confused people. From afar came the mute roar of a waterfall, and from behind the mountains came the muffled thunder of cannons. These sounds all merged into an overwhelming, dispiriting chaos.

General Louis Botha.

The armed crowd was panic-stricken; indeed, we were witnessing the staggering scene of a wild, disorderly stampede. But this abandonment of so many impregnable positions was caused not by the appearance of the British or their victory, but by the fatal news that an immense force led by Roberts had invaded the Free State and that General Cronjé, the 'Lion of the Transvaal', that mainstay and stalwart of the Boers, was plotting treason.

This rumour, started by someone unknown, had spread among the Free Staters with lightning speed; they abandoned their trenches, took the transport and cannons, and resolved to return home to protect their farms and families.

Botha's attempt to persuade them otherwise came to nothing. They did not obey him. His speech was interrupted by angry exclamations: 'It is all very well for you to say, General! Your family is safe while our women and children are left there!'

'Cronjé, Joubert and the rest of you are traitors!' an old Boer bellowed, shaking his sinewed fist. 'You've sold us out to the English!'

'We fought at Boschrand for three days, without water, without rusks! You didn't support us! It's too late now, General!' another Boer, his head tied with a bloodstained cloth, cried out. Anger and desperation could be seen on every face.

The shots from the mountain grew more frequent, and we clearly heard the familiar volleys of the British infantry.

'*Daar kom die Kakies! Die Kakies!*' [There come the khakis! The khakis!]

This crazy scream, uttered by some vile creature, startled and terrified the people – the same people who till recently had repelled attack after attack of an enemy ten times its strength. Everybody rushed to the bridge in wild disarray, carrying along those who had already crossed over to the other side of the river. Wagons were toppled over, oxen rushed about, and the horsemen crushed the horseless. I was also knocked off my feet by the rush of the mad crowd; I barely managed to fight my way to the shore, bruised and bloody. But I avenged myself by grabbing the nearest riderless horse, mounted it and joined my comrades. The horse was a spirited half-blood, and I felt no regret at the thought that Wagner's skinny nag had stayed behind on the bridge.

New groups of retreating Orange Boers were descending from the mountains. But then the commanding voice of Botha thundered again, and the Transvalers gathered around him. There were our Krugersdorpers and members of many other commandos: Ermelo, Winburg, Carolina, Boksburg, and so on; even some Orange Boers joined them. The commotion subsided slightly. Botha spoke, and his impassioned, self-confident speech rang out again, his face radiating courage.

'Lead us, General!' hundreds of voices boomed in reply.

At that moment, I, a stranger among that people, also experienced and understood the burst of fervour that drives a soldier to death at the wave of a leader's hand.

Someone put his hand on my shoulder. I turned around and saw my comrades; they had the same light in their eyes. We silently shook each other's hands.

'*Kom aan! Kom aan, Krugersdorpers!*' [Come on! Come on, Krugersdorpers!] shouted our commander, old Van Wyk, swinging his colourful umbrella, from which he was never parted, whether on the march or in battle. We were told that we would go around the mountains already occupied by the British. It was getting dark, and a breath of cool air came wafting from the river.

We had to travel along the riverbank, walking on a barely visible ledge of steep rocks. We walked one by one, in single file, leading our horses by the reins. A majestic waterfall, as wide as the river, seethed and roared below, but we had no time to admire the magnificent view. One wrong step and we would plummet down, horse and rider, into the yawning chasm where the wild waves boiled and foamed.

After traversing that dangerous trail, we stopped near a wide gorge where we were ordered to dismount and leave our horses behind. The commandant, who had always ridden at the front, stepped aside and started to count the burghers passing by him along a trail in single file. He counted 420 Krugersdorpers. This was the first time I saw the men being tallied. Then, without commands, shouts or talking, we learnt that we had to occupy the top of the mountain, where we expected to meet a British picket.[15]

With amazing deftness, avoiding the faintest rustle, the Boers quickly started climbing up the mountain's steep slopes, strewn with sharp spurs and rocky edges. It was very quiet at the summit: the British clearly did not expect to be attacked at night. But then somebody kicked loose a stone and immediately shots began crackling. A swarm of bullets flew over our heads. A Boer crawling next to me waved his arms, dropped his rifle and rolled down with a long mournful bellow.

But I had no time for him! The flat summit was near, and I saw shadows darting over it. In the dark, pinpoints of light flickered as rifle shots rang out. I stumbled over bodies.

The small British picket quickly vacated the mountain, and the Krugersdorp Commando took their place; the same night, we started building barricades, digging up rocks with our bare hands and placing them in heaps. Thus, we worked through the night until first light. Nails and skin peeled off our fingers. When the day came, the Boers were already lying behind formidable barriers of skilfully laid rocks and chuckled at our shelters made from cobbles. Meanwhile, the sound of the British artillery was already booming in the distant mountains. The shells did not reach us, falling way ahead, but the ominous hissing of rifle bullets could be heard ever more often. We reluctantly decided to continue our work; as much as we felt like cursing Buller and Chamberlain and Cronjé and Kruger at that moment, it was far more important to have reliable cover against the coming bombardment. Pooling our strength, we heaved out some huge boulders and rolled them to the breastwork. Meanwhile, Diatroptov, who had once attended university lectures, could not help saying a few words about Permian and Triassic formations, etc.[16] Only the amiable young Pavel R shirked his work as usual, pleading faintness at the sight of the disfigured corpses of British soldiers lying behind us. Instead, he readily volunteered to fetch water from the Tugela in our flasks, which was really a feat because the slope that led to the river was being enfiladed by the British from the nearby mountain.

We endured terrible thirst and heat; the rocks became so hot under the rays of the scorching sun that it hurt to touch them. Boxes of cartridges were delivered to us, but they forgot bread, so in addition to thirst we now also experienced hunger; only Fyodor Ivanovich's crammed cigarette case helped to stiffen our fading resolve to some degree.[17]

Meanwhile, the British rolled out battery after battery. Their shells were destroying our barriers. The measured banging of the machine guns enfilading us echoed over the mountains. The British infantry always kept a respectful distance, refraining from advancing in the hope of driving us out with artillery fire. The shelling was so efficient that we could hear the rattle of the dying and groans of the wounded ever more often. My heart sank at the thought that we might meet the same fate, and that the rays of the setting sun were smiling their last farewell to us.

Despite the tragedy of our situation, I could not help but laugh when I saw how Nikitin, crouching behind the barrier, enthusiastically disassembled and assembled the Lee-Metford rifle he had captured from an Englishman the day before, and how he argued with Buzukov whether the rifle's firing range should be measured in yards or metres, and all of this while shrapnel was exploding above our heads.

A day or two passed in this fashion, and by evening we learnt that it had been decided to retreat. On a dark night, in a terrible thunderstorm with heavy showers, we abandoned the mountain, unnoticed by the British, went down to our horses and took the same route back to the river.

It was a terrible night. The tropical thunderstorm was so intense that the enormous rocks shook and groaned under the constant peals of thunder. Every now and then blinding zigzags of lightning cut through the impenetrable darkness of the night, briefly lighting up the raging river cascades and vague silhouettes of a thousand riders clambering down the steep cliffs.

Once the troops had crossed the river, the bridge was dynamited.

The disorderly Boer hordes had by now seemingly lost all communication with each other; horsemen rushed about in small groups or alone and disappeared into the night.

The wounded lay helplessly on the sides of the road. Torrents of rainwater gushed over them and their screams were drowned out by the raging howl of the foul weather.

I shouted myself hoarse until, through some miracle, I found my comrades. They were all there. Exhausted, hungry, sullen and soaked to the skin, we had no time to talk. We set off in silence, not knowing where to go.

Then, at last, the thunderstorm died down, the rain stopped and in the east the sky grew scarlet. Fyodor Ivanovich shared his last cigarettes with us, and we started to discuss our situation.

'We need to find the Krugersdorpers: the Boers will probably take up new positions in these mountains,' Nikitin was saying.

What new positions? We need to eat and sleep first!

Then we came across a camp that had obviously been abandoned by the Boers not long before: fires still smouldered here and there among the toppled, broken wagons and discarded tents; crushed boxes, broken pots and torn sacks of maize and rusks, mixed with mud and manure, lay all about. We made an enormous fire, fell on the rusks and slept like logs. Fyodor Ivanovich, the most sensible among us, said that we should post a sentry and volunteered to be the first. We answered him with loud snoring.

Only Wagner could not sleep a wink; he was still sitting by the fire, reading my receipt again and again, obviously puzzled by the fact that his tailless, bay-coloured fleabag had turned into the stately black horse I had captured during the river crossing.

But we were not able to sleep long. Buzukov's strident voice rang out above my ear: 'The English! Get up! The English!' The erstwhile Macedonian campaigner, who during his adventurous days as a robber had acquired the commendable habit of resting with his bandolier and rifle on, had heard suspicious sounds in his sleep, jumped to his feet and realised to his horror that British engineers were building a bridge over the Tugela close by the place where we lay. It took us a minute to gather the horses and be on our way. In an hour, we were safely in the company of our Krugersdorpers, who had already considered us irretrievably fallen.

Old Ivan Petrovich, whom we had left behind on the day of our march-off, ran up to his master with cries of joy. For three days he had languished in uncertainty over the fate of Fyodor Ivanovich Guchkov.

'I only bumped into our fellows just now. I recognised their boss by his umbrella, but we couldn't understand each other, so I couldn't figure out where they'd left you. But now we're all together! Praise the Lord! I'll straightaway make you some tea!' Ivan Petrovich fussed around the cheerfully crackling fire; he had tea, sugar, rusks and even three or so jars of jam; the mugs and kettle he got from the brave Hungarians. We were immensely surprised to find them all in good health, well-fed, red-cheeked and all spruced up. While we were savouring our hot tea, the *Rittmeister* twirled his moustache as he confided his heroic exploits to us. As it turned out, he and his compatriots had remained in the camp and withstood a fierce battle while defending the drift at Colenso: 'The bullets were whistling past like bumblebees. Can you imagine it? A couple of times the English regiments went on the attack with their banners unfurled ...'

'Actually, the British don't have banners; they keep them in the Tower of London,' I ventured to interrupt the worthy descendant of Kossuth.[18]

'So you do not believe the word of an officer?' a lieutenant of the Austrian infantry with a rooster's feather on his Tyrolean hat exclaimed and jumped up.

'*Baszom teremtette!*[19] a third one proclaimed with a challenging look.

'As soon as we've finished our tea,' Nikitin grumbled. His muscles commanded a measure of respect among the Hungarians, and they chose to leave with a look of insulted dignity, whistling the 'Rákóczi March'.[20]

Buller's army crossed the Tugela, and the white tents of the British now stood in the same place where those of the Krugersdorp Commando had been a few days before.[21] But the Boers were preparing for a vigorous defence; the commandos that had been depleted after the panic of 19–20 February were reinforced with men called back from leave; many of those who had fled after the first setbacks and were ashamed of their cowardice also returned. The famous Long Tom gun was transferred from its position near Ladysmith and set up at Grobler's Kloof, which remained in Boer hands; wagons with entrenching tools were brought in, and on all the mountains work was in full swing: the Boers were building batteries and entrenchments.

Our unit was positioned on Pieter's Hill, a group of heights connected by upfolds and intersected by deep gorges. Meanwhile, as one shift of men was working on the hill and setting up watch points, the other was resting two versts[22] behind the hill in a large valley through which flowed a winding little river hidden in a dense thicket of acacias. Here there was a large farm only recently deserted by its owner, one Pieters, who was reputed to be one of the richest men in the whole of Natal. He was the owner of vast pastures between the Tugela and Klip rivers, where great flocks of sheep and cattle grazed. After Buller's success, this Pieters, himself of Boer descent, took his family and part of his belongings and fled to Pretoria, realising that he would face severe punishment for aiding the Transvalers. The British were not soft on Natal and Cape farmers of Boer descent.

The farm, which was surrounded by the velvety green of thick-leaved orange trees, was now a sad sight. The hedges of enormous cacti and sumptuous oleanders in full bloom were crushed or cut down; horses and oxen grazed in the garden; everywhere lay the remains of the owner's property: smashed chests, broken threshers, a horse's harness, wagon wheels. A Red Cross infirmary had taken up position inside the house. An overwhelming smell of carbolic acid emanated from the building. Blood was spattered over the white walls of the rooms, the furniture and the straw-covered floors on which the wounded lay. They did not groan or whine, but silently placed themselves at the mercy of the doctors, who gave them first aid and sent them on their way. They were a depressing sight, these wretched men, of whom increasing numbers had been crippled by artillery shrapnel.

There was one whose whole head and face were wrapped in bandages that had turned black from all the blood, struggling to rise, but then falling back helplessly. '*O, my vrou! Katrina!*' [Oh, my wife! Katrina!] the wounded man wheezed. He writhed and a stream of scarlet blood gushed from his mouth.

'The poor man is delirious,' I thought. But at that moment a tall, slender woman in an enormous, snow-white bonnet emerged from the adjacent room with a teapot in her hands. Her luscious hair spilled out in golden curls from under the bonnet. Her wonderful face expressed such profound, boundless grief that I immediately guessed her to be the suffering man's wife; she had abandoned her house and family and hurried here to ease his suffering, to comfort the man who was dearer to her than anyone in the world with her caresses. She placed the teapot on the floor, quietly bent over the wounded man and began changing his bandage. More wounded men were carried in. 'What are you hanging around here for?' a Boer orderly with a sweaty face, covered in blood, lashed out coarsely at me. 'Oh, these Uitlanders! It's all their fault; they caught the whiff of gold, started the war, and now they're fighting for us too!'

I stepped out obediently and headed for the garden. Here, in the shade of a flowering oleander, the Boers had just buried one of these

Uitlanders, the quiet, humble Rauch, one of two Styrian brothers who had been everyone's darling.[23] They carried his lifeless body, with a gaping wound on the forehead, down from Pieter's Hill, and on the mound of his grave his brother had placed a wooden cross. It bore the inscription: 'Born in Styria 1 May 1875. Killed on Pieter's Hill 21 February 1899.'[24]

As before in the camp near Colenso, so now at Pieter's Farm, the Boers would gather in the evenings without their fatigues when the field-cornet called for prayer. With their bare heads reverently bowed, they listened to the words of the field-cornet as he read a chapter from an old leather-bound Bible with brass clasps. Then someone would begin saying the prayer in a hoarse, insecure, drawn-out voice; the crowd would join in and the sounds of the old hymn would rise and flow until they filled the valley. When the last echo of the prayer had died away, there would emerge from the crowd of closely huddled men some impromptu preacher, inspired by grace from above. Throwing back his head in devotional rapture, as if contemplating the constellation of the Cross – that symbol of suffering and victory – burning in the dark vault of heaven, he would be silent for a minute or two, and then his passionate, booming speech would begin, interspersed with sighs and exclamations of '*Geliefde broeders!*' [Beloved brothers!] And he would say that God almighty, all-powerful, was angry at his chosen people, but once the hour of tribulation had passed, the forces of heaven would take up arms in defence of the believers.

And then the stern faces of these warriors would come alive, and hope would shine in their hearts anew for aid from the Almighty, and the next day they would return to battle – for their fatherland, for freedom, fearing neither death nor suffering. I loved being present at these evening prayers. I was touched by their childlike, innocent faith. But every time the thought occurred to me that the English were also pious Christians, that they were calling upon the same God, singing the same hymns, listening with adoration to sermons just like these. Why is it that none of the Christian nations is guided by the inspiration of Christian conscience? Why do these nations even go so far as to seek God's blessing for the ringing and rattling of arms as they exterminate each other in bloodthirsty ecstasy?

But it was not for me to ask, or answer, such questions. I had more

A Boer position at the top of Hart's Hill.

substantial and important duties: to chase the horses into their wire-fenced kraal for the night, to clean my rifle and to prepare myself something for supper. Many fowl – turkeys and chickens – had been left behind on the farm, while herds of goats, rams and pigs roamed about the surrounding countryside, and large turtles and crabs lived in the stream. But there was no time to try my hand at the culinary arts. We were under constant bombardment by British artillery and spent days and nights in the trenches repelling the enemy onslaught. Buller did not spare his people to dislodge us finally from the last positions that stood between his army and Ladysmith.

I remember the fighting on 24 February[25] when line after line of infantrymen, agitated and swaying, advanced in a wide semicircle over the slope of the mountain held by the Krugersdorp Commando. The accurate fire of our machine guns tore out whole rows of British soldiers. But their lines closed up again and thickened as new masses pressed in from behind. It seemed as if the formidable avalanche would wipe out everything in its way and crush the handful of brave men in their hastily dug trenches, but those men, stained with blood and mud, waited fearlessly for the British to approach.

And when the masses of the advancing enemy were at point-blank range, the Boers met them with such a hail of bullets that the entire mountain became strewn with dead bodies. And still the crazed

The British attack on Hart's Hill.

enemy burst forth with manic persistence: fresh battalions started ascending the mountain, and some bold spirits ran up to us so fast that we could see their sweating red faces and their bayonets glaring in the sun. However, this time it did not come to hand-to-hand combat: all the efforts of the Irish Brigade were thwarted by the fortitude of the Boers. For example, the Royal Inniskilling Regiment that attacked our trenches lost over 300 men, and Buller was compelled to request a ceasefire to remove the dead and wounded. The sight of the battlefield was more terrible than at Spion Kop.[26]

After the ceasefire the British attacks were renewed with the same fury but also with the same success; they dug in within 300 paces ahead of us and battered us from there with their Maxim machine guns. The British gunners quickly got the hang of it: their bullets began whizzing above our ears the moment we lifted our heads above the breastwork.

Without food and sleep, we held out for another four days. In the end, I grew so fatigued that I would fall asleep right there, under heavy fire, in the trench heaped with hideously swollen blue corpses. There was nobody to bury them, nor was there any need: flocks of kites flew over us, and at night we heard a monotonous howling of jackals that made our blood run cold. Only sometimes, in the rare periods of lull, did we throw the corpses over the breastwork.

No more than 80 or 90 of the 420 burghers Commandant Van Wyk had counted at the Tugela were left. Many had been lost at Pieter's Hill,[27] but the majority had probably dispersed, believing that the cause was lost. The dashing Hungarians had also disappeared; I was told later that they had found a pretext for a quarrel with the field-cornet, took a wagon, mules and three blacks and departed for the Free State, to reap new laurels.

It was also at this time that young Pavel R, everyone's favourite, died a hero. A lyddite bomb fell right into his trench and maimed him beyond recognition; his blood and brains splattered on his comrades lying nearby. He was never to see the end of the war and live as a farmer with his beloved, as he used to dream sitting with us around the bivouac fire on dark nights.

The Royal Bavarian lieutenant had to pay dearly for the undisguised contempt in which he, a professional artilleryman, held his small-bore rifle: he had never cleaned or disassembled his Mauser and neglected it so much that on one of those days, when we had to fire off shots by the hundreds, the barrel and bolt blew up in smithereens. He was in a dead faint, his face covered in blood, when they dragged him to the dressing station. But Pieter's Farm was overflowing with wounded, and they no longer had either dressing or medical personnel. So Fyodor Ivanovich, with the help of his valet, sent Wagner to Glencoe, along with Diatroptov, who had been injured the same day. It was said that there was a Russian Red Cross hospital there.[28]

I was lucky. I got off with just three days of moaning and convulsively holding my side. This is what happened. A British bullet pierced my bandolier, flattened the bullets in the clip and bounced off without even touching my skin, although the blow was so hard that the wind was knocked out of me and I staggered over. In all probability it was a ricocheted bullet that hit me, otherwise I would have been done for, and, like Captain Kopeikin,[29] I would have shed my blood, in a manner of speaking, and forever been deprived of the right and the pleasure of commanding a half-company for the rest of my life.

Of all the volunteers, only Nikitin, Buzukov and I remained. Impelled by some silly quixotic impulse, we gave each other our word that we would hold out until the end.

On 27 February, the last battle broke out. The mountains shook and groaned under the thunder of bombardment.[30] We were lying face down under the crumbled bank of our entrenchments, suffocating from the pungent lyddite gases and covered in sand and shards of rocks and shells that furrowed the ground in every direction. We lay that way until the evening when we caught sight of the round helmets of the British on the mountains to our left, which had previously been occupied by the Boksburg Commando. We were outflanked on both sides.

The Boers had been lying still in the trenches, but now they began to stir. Shots rang out helter-skelter. The Boers' screams were mixed with the menacing shouts of the enraged British, 'Amajuba! Son of a bitch!'[31]

A clean-shaven Englishman in a wide-brimmed helmet, apparently an officer, ran straight at us. 'Hands up, bloody fools! Buggers!' he croaked, shaking his revolver. Here and there the Boers were fighting hand to hand, defending themselves with the butts of their rifles and their fists. Then some white cloths were waved. It lasted no more than ten minutes, during which I was in a kind of stupor. I do not remember how I slipped out of the throng of enemies, giddy with their victory; only the barrel of my rifle was left in my hand. Of the last 80 Boers, only 17 returned, including Nikitin and Buzukov, who were saved by some miracle.

Those who still had horses followed the main Boer force, which had retreated in the morning. My horse and Nikitin's had both been killed the day before, and we began to walk in some insensible kind of daze. Jagged rocks cut our feet and thorny branches hit us in the face, but on and on we kept walking, northwards, to where the sullen peaks of Lombardskop rose in the moonlight. The gusty wind drove scraps of cloud over the sky, and those clouds were rushing north as well, as if guiding us along our way. An oppressive silence reigned all around us; only rarely would a rush of the wind carry to us the dull thudding of hooves or the creaking of wheels ...

Notes

[1] Lieutenant General Sir William Forbes Gatacre (1843–1906), who commanded the British 3rd Division and suffered a defeat at the Battle of

Stormberg (10 December 1899).

2   Avgustus refers to Christiaan Rudolf de Wet (1854–1922), a Boer general.
    However, it was General Koos de la Rey who was responsible for the British
    defeats around Colesberg. CR de Wet's brother, General Piet de Wet, was
    also active on the Colesberg (southern) front, which may explain the confu-
    sion, but he was not the senior of De la Rey.

3   A reference to the Battle of Modder River (28 November 1899) and the
    Battle of Magersfontein (11 December 1899).

4   The Russo-Turkish War of 1877–1878.

5   The Battle of Gravelotte (18 August 1870), the largest engagement of the
    Franco-Prussian War.

6   A meeting of the representatives of the leading European powers, the Otto-
    man Empire and Balkan states to determine the territories of the countries
    in the Balkan Peninsula after the Russo-Turkish War of 1877–1878.

7   A diplomatic conflict (1898) over territories in East Africa that resulted in
    France's acknowledging British control over Egypt and the Sudan.

8   François Achille Bazaine (1811–1888), a Marshal of France, who surrendered
    the last organised French army to the enemy in the Franco-Prussian War
    (1870) and was convicted of treason. General Piet Cronjé and his 4 000 men
    surrendered after the Battle of Paardeberg on 27 February 1900.

9   A reference to the Crimean War and the unsuccessful anti-British Indian
    Rebellion of 1857.

10 Field Marshal Frederick Sleigh Roberts (1832–1914) had been appointed
    commander-in-chief of British troops in South Africa.

11 The Boers had laid siege to Kimberley in October 1899. The British only
    managed to lift the siege on 15 February 1900

12 On 17 February 1900, the British attacked Cingolo and Monte Cristo hills.
    General Louis Botha, concerned that the Boers would not be able to hold
    the Tugela line, requested reinforcements.

13 The Russo-Turkish War of 1877–1878.

14 After the British forced the defenders of Monte Cristo and Green Hill to
    withdraw, the Boers crossed the Tugela River by a bridge they had constructed
    of wooden railway sleepers; see Gillings, K, *The Battle of the Thukela Heights*:
    12–28 February 1900. Randburg: Ravan Press, 1999, p 11.

15 Botha realised that the high ground extending from Colenso downstream
    represented a natural defence line. He deployed the 3 000 Boers remaining
    at his disposal along the distance of more than ten kilometres.

16 A reference to the Permian and Triassic geologic periods.

17 Avgustus refers to Fyodor Guchkov.

18 Lajos Kossuth (1802–1894), Governor-President of the Kingdom of Hungary
    during the revolution of 1848–1849, also known as 'Father of Hungarian
    Democracy'.

19 A Hungarian obscenity.

20 The unofficial state anthem of Hungary.

21 The British crossed the Tugela on 22 February.

22 Roughly two kilometres. A verst is a Russian unit of length equal to 1.0668
    km.

23 It was Karl Rumpf; see Schmidl, 'Österreicher', pp 228–229.

24 Mistake by Avgustus. The battle took place in 1900, not in 1899.

25 The Battle of Hart's Hill started on 23 February, as part of the series that

has come to be known as the Battle of the Tugela Heights. The 5th (Irish) Brigade, comprising the 1st Royal Inniskilling Fusiliers, the 1st Connaught Rangers and the 2nd Royal Dublin Fusiliers led an offensive against the positions of the Krugersdorp Commando on the hill. Five thousand British soldiers participated in the attack; see Gillings, *The Battle of the Thukela Heights*, p 25.

26 On 25 February, Botha and Meyer granted Buller a partial armistice to attend to the wounded. The total British casualties on the hill on the previous day had been about 450 men. The Boers had lost over 50, including at least 11 Krugersdorpers; see Pretorius, F, *Historical Dictionary of the Anglo-Boer War*. Lanham: The Scarecrow Press, 2009, p 326; Van Aardt, 'Die aandeel van die Krugersdorpse kommando', p 77.

27 Evidently, Avgustus refers to the elevation now known as Hart's Hill, where the battle took place, not to Pieter's Hill.

28 At Glencoe, the Russian Red Cross ambulance had set up an admission room for ambulatory cases.

29 In Nikolai Gogol's novel *Dead Souls*, Captain Kopeikin is crippled during the French invasion of Russia (1812) and becomes a brigand.

30 The Battle of Pieter's Hill. The final assault of British troops on the Tugela Heights was covered by the largest number of guns used in a single battle in the war so far. The British gunners were instructed to fire ahead of the advancing troops, despite the risk of shelling their own men.

31 It was an anniversary of the Battle of Majuba Hill, the final defeat of the British in the Anglo-Boer War of 1880–1881.

CHAPTER 7

Falling back

We walked all night, stumbling at every turn, clinging to rocks and clambering across sheer cliffs overhung with prickly acacia branches that tore at our clothes and lashed our faces.

The sharp stones ruined our shoes, and I could only barely keep up with Nikitin, whose dark outline would disappear one moment, only to appear again the next.

His silhouette took on a monstrous shape in the utter darkness that enveloped the chaotically scattered rocks and cliffs, and an unaccountable fear took hold of me that the figure walking before me would suddenly coalesce with the gloomy shadows of the quietly rustling trees and disappear, leaving me on my own, abandoned and forgotten by all until the Lancers caught up with me.

I collapsed in total exhaustion on a stone ledge and called out to Nikitin in a faltering voice.

At once his powerful figure rose in front of me, and his voice, as sharp as usual, but now with a tinge of unfeigned concern, asked me: 'Are you worn out? Very well, let's rest a bit. There's no point in pushing on right now; if we go on like this we'll lose our way.' He lit up his pipe and sat down beside me. 'The Boers are bastards. They rode off just in time and forgot about us. I hope they end up at the bottom of the sea! The English are a fine bunch too: they outflanked us on both sides and killed our horses; worst of all is that I left a pair of new shoes and some canned peas in my saddlebag. As for Buller ... Buller! No pursuit of his defeated enemy!'[1]

I couldn't help but smile as I listened to his thoughts zigzagging unpredictably from one topic to the next.

But I was not in a condition to talk; terrifying images of the day's events floated up before my mind's eye, flared and faded out. My arms and legs refused to obey me, as if they had been weighed down by a leaden weight. I wanted to embrace the damp ground, sleep the sleep of the dead and forget that we were far behind our own people, that perhaps we had lost our way and would be overtaken by the menacing Lancers.

'Well, well! He's nodding off! We've had our rest. Time to be on our way again! Dawn's breaking already!'

The sun would be rising before long. Above the sharp peaks of the mountains the edges of the clouds were beginning to glow crimson; a white veil of mist quivered over the gorges and ravines, from where we could hear the cooing of turtledoves. When dawn broke, we could see by the light of day that we had wandered far off to the left, and, instead of going along the path left by the Boers, had been moving along the steep slope of a mountain strewn with rubble and boulders.

We rejoined the road. The deep tracks of the heavy wagons, broken carts and abandoned bags and boxes all indicated that the Boer convoy had recently passed this way.

On the advice of my companion, I tore up one of the bags, wrapped my feet in the rags and tied them up with string. Now I felt able to walk at least a slow three-step parade march.

At last we caught sight of our wagons piled up at the bank of a stream; this was only the tail of the convoy: ahead of us we saw endless lines of wagons extending far into the distance; some of them were still slowly ascending the slope, while others had halted on both sides of the small river, apparently to rest.

The oxen and mules, exhausted by the night march, had scattered over the valley and were nibbling on the tall, succulent grass.

Fires smoked here and there among the wagons, and around them sat Boers boiling water and roasting their customary biltong on rifle ramrods. No one paid much attention to us.

'*Waar is Krugersdorpsche menschen?*' [Where are Krugersdorp men?] we asked them in broken Dutch. But we could hardly get any sense out of anyone; the Boers sat like stuffed dummies, gloomily kept silence or pointed somewhere in the direction of the already departed wagons.

Suddenly, somebody called out to me in a weak voice. I turned around and saw the familiar face of our corporal leaning out from underneath the roof of a wagon. How thin and pale he had become! A cloth, black from his blood, was wound around his forehead. His eyes burned with a feverish fire and it seemed that every word required a terrible effort. We learnt that he had been wounded on 26 February, not in the Pieter's Hill trench but while he, as commissioner in the rear, was arranging meat and rusks for the front line.

'I thought I'd never see you again, my friends! But the Lord has saved you!' he said with difficulty, and a weak smile lit up his haggard face. 'Well, the republic is gone for now, and you should return to your country.'

'And he calls himself a corporal!' Nikitin grumbled. Pointing to the blue mountains in the distance, he tried to comfort the wounded man, *'Daar, lekker posisie! Alle burgers bymekaar!'* [There, good position! All burghers together!]

But the corporal shook his head.

'No, everything is lost now if Europe does not intervene,' he insisted.

Of course, such talk could not give us much comfort or cheer, but we also learnt from the corporal that the Krugersdorpers were far ahead, the blockade of Ladysmith had been lifted the day before[2] and the Boers had managed to retreat with all their guns.

It was still unknown what course of action Joubert and Botha would take; in all likelihood the Boers would retreat all the way to the Drakensberg and only venture to repulse the British at the passes of Majuba.[3]

The corporal could not tell us anything else but, noticing that I only had a stock and barrel left instead of a rifle, asked me to accept his Mauser carbine as a keepsake. On the small of the butt, the corporal's name and the dates of the battles in which he had taken part were skilfully carved:

Christoph Vlies, Doornkop, Glencoe 20 Oct.,
Dundee 22 Oct., Colenso 15 Dec. 1899

'The commandant will give you horses,' the corporal concluded, much wearied by this long conversation, wished us a safe journey and shook our hands firmly.

We moved on and soon caught up with the Krugersdorpers. Already from a great distance we spotted the familiar sight of the field-cornet's umbrella. The wagons moved slowly, halting almost every two hours to allow the exhausted oxen some rest. At every halt the Boers unsaddled their horses, built fires of dry manure or acacia twigs, rested for an hour or two, then harnessed the oxen again and continued their retreat. One could only wonder at the recklessness of the Boers, who moved without any cover, but the behaviour of the British seemed even more incomprehensible: after defeating the Boers at all their positions and freeing Ladysmith, which Dundonald's cavalry entered on the evening of 28 February, Buller gave no thought to any pursuit, as if reckoning that the Boer army had already ceased to exist.

Nikitin was particularly outraged at the clear disregard for the principles of tactics by both the Boers and the British: 'No rearguard, no rearguard patrols,' he said, looking with some anger at the respectable burghers riding at a gentle trot beside their large wagons. If only a cavalry unit or two to three squadrons would jump out from behind that mountain and charge into attack, lances and sabres at the ready! Now that ... now that ...,' and choking with delight he painted me a brilliant picture of a dashing cavalry attack on a wagon train blithely on the move without any cover.

'But what about the two of us?' I said, trying to bring him back to reality. 'We don't have any horses, so we'll be the first to fall under the sabre blows.'

'Us?' he protested vehemently. 'We'll form a wagon fort and fire in bursts at the cavalry!'

As can be seen, the retreat definitely benefited us in terms of refreshing and broadening our tactical knowledge. On the other hand, it was not without its discomforts. We had to deal with such mere trifles as scabs and scratches covering our feet, seeing that we could not find ourselves new horses; also, we had to live hand to mouth, on mouldy rusks and biltong, pieces of meat poorly dried in the sun that swarmed with wriggling, fat white maggots. The Boers had no other provisions. Moreover, it rained, and our clothes were wet throughout. We had no opportunity to dry them: fires were not allowed at night, and during the short night halts we shivered in the piercing wind and shrank, teeth chattering, into some corner of a wagon filled with Boers, who were not particularly sympathetically disposed towards our invading their family arks. Wrapped in warm blankets and waterproofs, they calmly smoked their pipes, but we only had the clothes we had worn in the trenches of Pieter's Hill; our blankets and waterproofs remained strapped to the saddles of our dead horses. None of our hosts, however, even thought of sharing a spare blanket with us. But we did not really protest against such treatment, fully aware that they had other concerns. Many of them had lost a son, a brother or a father in the bloody battles, and the war would require countless other sacrifices. We were just accidental newcomers who had forgotten the wise saying, 'Jerome, Jerome, why stayed you not home?' So we tried not to lose heart, but to endure with courage the adversities, even if they ended up giving us a chronic cold or typhoid fever. In for a penny, in for a pound.

◆

Our peregrinations ended the following day when we reached Elandslaagte station. I could not help feeling sad when I remembered how we had arrived at that station only a month before on our way to the Tugela, filled with hope and expectation. Now defeated, hungry and ragged, we took shelter in a small house, where we managed to make fire. Buzukov had joined us along the way, and the three of us sat in silence around the red-hot iron stove, trying to dry our clothes.

Large drops of rain pattered on the zinc roof, and the hum of a hundred voices, the bellowing of draught oxen and the shrill whistles of steam engines burst through the broken window glass.

At the station, into which a thousand agitated people, vehicles, ammunition wagons and guns had been crammed, a scene reminiscent of Zola's *Débâcle*⁴ was taking place. On the platform where the train stood read to depart, Boers thronged, screamed and rushed about in search of free room in the carriages. Where did the usual phlegm and composure of those people go? Shoving and cursing each other with utter profanities, they climbed on top of the carriage roofs and tender platforms, lost their balance and fell off.

Elsewhere there were bitter fights for the gangways used to load wagons and caissons onto the platforms; the logs of the gangways cracked and broke under the weight of the clumsy wagons; horses and oxen, frightened by the whistling and rumbling of locomotives, rushed about, stumbling against the rails and falling under the vans. Trains were constantly leaving, yet the crowd at the station was growing; new groups of Boers on horseback were arriving in the hope of using the railway to depart promptly for Majuba. And the rain was teeming down. The stifling smoke and soot from the locomotives, whose constant whistling dominated the discordant rumble of screaming and bellowing, hung over the station like heavy clouds.

The Boer commandants and generals shouted themselves hoarse trying to restore some kind of order, but all their efforts led to nothing. People did not listen to them, knocked them off their feet, seized vans and locomotives without permission and loaded their horses and vehicles, ignoring the numerous wagons of the Red Cross with the wounded. The doctors and orderlies who had been awaiting their turn since the morning, preoccupied with the plight of their patients, walked confused among that horde of armed, crazed people, who cared only about saving their bacon and had completely forgotten about the common cause.

Blacks were removing sacks, boxes and barrels from the buildings on both sides of the railway bed, where enormous quantities of provisions had been stored during the siege of Ladysmith. Only a part of it could be loaded into railway vans; the rest was thrown in a heap, helter-skelter. The Boers broke the boxes and barrels open with the butts of their rifles, filled their sacks with sugar and coffee, and grabbed clothes, boots and underwear. Nikitin and I also availed ourselves of that mess: we got new clothes and some provisions, including a few boxes of tinned food, butter and sweet rusks. But then a smell of burning came from somewhere; the Boers swarming in the empty stores disappeared in dense puffs of suffocating smoke, and tongues of flame that hissed and writhed, fighting with the drenching rain, enveloped the station from all sides.

The Boers decided to burn everything that they could not take away by railway to prevent it from falling into the British hands.

Deafening peals of thunder rolled every now and then. The Boers were blowing up the railway buildings, water-pump station, turntables, pipes and bridges.

In the environs, wreathed in a grey veil of constantly pouring rain, smoke clouds swirled and pillars of fire rose up into the sky: these were coal mines and abandoned farms burning. Heaven gazed down sullenly at this scene of total devastation, the ominous fires and utter panic that had gripped a thousand people. This mass of people seemed to be possessed by a dark demon of hatred and destruction. Retreating in frenzied fear of a dangerous enemy, whose columns could appear in the distant mountains any minute, the Boers unleashed their instincts of spoliation and decided to raze everything to the ground in the land they were abandoning.

Night fell and the endless lines of cumbersome wagons slowly began moving northwards again. Their wheels got stuck in the watery mud on the roads; the wagons creaked and rocked on the steep slopes and rises; the black drivers, bespattered with mud, cracked their long whips now and then and shouted some strange, guttural words to goad on the exhausted oxen. And the Boers in the wagons puffed on their short pipes with perfect calm and pensively gazed at the distant sky where the glow of the burning station and the coal mines was flickering and blazing up.

◆

The Boers' retreat only came to a halt when they reached Glencoe.

When the President learnt by telegraph of the misfortunes that had befallen the Boers on the Tugela, he immediately took an emergency train from Pretoria to Glencoe, and here, in the open air, he addressed the crowds standing tightly packed around him.

The dignified old man's words were not in vain. The retreating Boers regained the fighting spirit that had been crushed by the latest defeats, and the *Krijgsraad*'s decision to delay any further attack by the British on Biggarsberg was met with total understanding by the entire nation.

Unfortunately, I had to miss Kruger's visit to Glencoe. The shoes I had grabbed at the Elandslaagte station, and wore without socks, chafed at my blistered and bruised feet even harder; it is therefore not strange that I lagged far behind the Boer wagons, even though they were trudging at a snail's pace.

The overcast, rainy days came to an end. The sky cleared, and the mountains and verdant plain of the Sundays River were bathed in the bright rays of a basking sun. On and on I hobbled, using my carbine as a walking stick, until Glencoe, drowning in a sea of green, finally appeared beyond the last peak of the Biggarsberg mountains. Here I hoped to rest and find my companions. But I was too exhausted to make it to town before nightfall. My feet burned as if they were on fire, my throat was parched, and in a state of utter exhaustion I collapsed on the ground, determined to spend my last night in the shelter of a prickly cactus.

Not far from me, a little stream murmured as it rushed glitteringly from a crevice in the rocks. I quenched my thirst with the ice-cold water and caught a large crab. No matter how it struggled with its pincers, I clutched it tightly in one hand while I used the other to gather some dry twigs and branches and lit them with a match. The crab, impaled on my ramrod, quivered over the fire, and I was getting ready to gobble it up with the delight of a cannibal, when I heard a voice.

'*No goed, baas*' [No good, master].

I looked around and saw an old black man with a wrinkled face, in a tattered coat and trousers but with a starched shirtfront. His appearance was so unexpected that I grabbed my rifle. But the old man, noticing my movement, shook his head reproachfully.

'*No goed, baas*,' he repeated. Then he sat down by the fire and offered me some large cobs of golden-hued corn from his pocket. '*Lekker mielies*' [Fine corn], he said. Then he buried the cobs in the hot ash and two minutes later offered me the corn with a toothless grin. I ate the sweet kernels of corn with immense pleasure and magnanimously gave the old man a shilling out of gratitude for the treat. He seemed pleased with the gift, nodded his curly head, waved his hands and ended up inviting me to follow him.

In a clearing by the side of the road, huddled between the wire fence of the railway on one end and a cornfield on the other, there stood a group of round huts woven from reeds and leaves and enclosed behind a similarly constructed lattice hedge. I had previously seen native villages like these, which in this part of Natal had maintained their characteristic lifestyle and culture, but only at a distance, and now I gladly accepted the old man's invitation and followed him into a clean-swept enclosure. Here we were met by a whole bunch of naked children; two dogs of a peculiarly South African breed, not unlike greyhounds, rushed at my legs with angry snarls, but at the sound of their master's voice obediently retreated to the back corner of the enclosure, where a woman wrapped in a colourful blanket was milking a goat with growths on its forehead.

I was admiring the cone-shaped hut, which resembled a huge, overturned basket, artfully woven from thin cane stalks, when the old man, still grinning good-naturedly, pointed at a small opening in the wall and crawled in first. I took off my rifle and crawled on all fours behind him. I was still growing accustomed to the darkness when a woman came in, and showing off her dazzling white teeth, placed in front of me some earthen bowls with milk, pumpkins cut in half and flat cakes of maize flour baked in ash. The woman said something in her sonorous African language. The melodious sounds and rich vowels resembled Italian: '*Manu ela, baas, figa lana.*'

The scent of her bronze body, naked to the waist, wafted over me; her saggy breasts dangled right in front of my nose.

First I drank the milk, which had a peculiar sour taste, then I devoured the flat cakes and poked around in the pumpkin. All the while she continued to babble and laugh, poured me more milk, unwound the dirty rags from my feet, made me a soft sitting place out of mats and deftly threw off my bandolier.

'Two shillings, two shillings, baas!' the old man said, raising two fingers of his left hand, and his wrinkled face broke into a broad smile. My charming hostess burst into high-pitched laughter and moved even closer to me. At last, I realised what was happening. No wonder the railway and the telegraph passed so close by the hut: civilisation had done its job, and when I had trustingly entered the hospitable dwelling of this Uncle Tom, I actually found myself in the charming company of a black pimp and his charming lady, abundantly garnished with a foul-smelling oil.

Quite frankly, the thought of playing the role of pious Joseph[5] had never crossed my mind, but on this occasion, I was saved by an event that even the most extreme representatives of naturalism never mention in their novels or dramas. In short, the sour milk I had drunk had its trademark effect on my stomach, and I had to rush headlong out of the hut. No wonder the French have a saying: 'L'estomac est l'ennemi de l'amour' [The stomach is the enemy of love].

I spent the night in the most chaste conceivable manner, far from the embraces of my chocolate-coloured Circe, in the yard on a pile of dry maize cobs.[6]

The next morning the old black man treated me to hot flat cakes and milk again, as if nothing had happened; the milk was fresh this time, but I decided to avoid any temptations and set out for the road immediately. In a couple of hours I was in Glencoe.

President Kruger had already departed from the town. His efforts to bolster the burghers' fallen morale and convince them of the necessity of taking a defensive posture at the Biggarsberg mountains, which represented the last obstacle to Buller's march on Majuba, seemed to have enjoyed some success. A commandant was appointed at the station, normal rail communication between Pretoria and Glencoe was restored, the commandants and field-cornets were actively gathering the people from their districts, warehouses were set up at the station with supplies of clothing, undergarments and boots, and the field bakery worked day and night. At the bakery they gave me a freshly baked loaf of bread without any questions, but when I poked my head into the boarded barrack where undergarments and shoes were being issued, the commissioner, a Hollander, gave me a suspicious look and announced that he only issued supplies and clothing upon receipt of a note from a field-cornet.

In vain did I show him my bloody feet and torn jacket, which I wore directly on my naked body.

'All the clothes we received from Pretoria have already been distributed among the commandos. Find your commando and they'll give you everything you need.'

I spat in annoyance and headed for the station. I did not encounter a single Krugersdorper among the numerous Boers who had pitched their tents along the railway line; no one could even tell me where the commando was at that moment.

I did run into my old acquaintances, the brave Hungarians. As it turned out, they were now the owners of a squat little tent and a wagon with all sorts of goods – canned food, saddles, blankets and the like. The bold *Rittmeister* Illich, surrounded by his hangers-on, was hotly arguing about something. They seemed to be debating what to cook for lunch, a slaughtered lamb or some chickens that were being plucked by a black man. Baron Luzsénszky gave me a nod. He was wrapped in a blanket and began complaining to me about his rheumatism.

'There's a new Russian volunteer who recently arrived, Prince Ganetsky, and he's been looking for you,' the Baron informed me. 'You know, we're planning to form our own Hungarian scouts legion and acting independently – *auf eigene Faust* [off our own bat]. These Boers are in any case useless!' I could not help but recall the valiant behaviour of these worthy descendants of Rákóczi and Görgei[7] during the battles on the Tugela.

The moustachioed *Rittmeister*, a living advertisement for the miracle of Hungarian pomade, began painting me a glowing picture of their future partisan activities and invited me to join them. I thanked him for the honour but gave a bow and went my way.

I had to find shelter for the night. Storm clouds covered the entire sky. In the distance, a fiery ribbon of lightning lit up the darkling horizon. There was going to be a downpour any minute now. Every building was already occupied by Boers I did not know. The warehouses and barns were locked for the night. I only had one choice – to return to the Hungarians or hide in some empty carriage. In the end I was lucky enough to find myself an empty spot in a dilapidated building near the station. I lit a match and saw a broken threshing machine, some tin maize chutes and a couple of blithely snoring figures. The floor was littered with bags, hides and an assortment of rags, and after all the many nights spent on sharp stones, I stretched out blissfully on the soft floor. The wind creaked and howled in the rafters, the tin plates of the roof booming and ringing. My neighbours snored loudly but would sometimes shout something incomprehensible in their sleep. Suddenly, something heavy and alive stirred on my chest. I grew cold with horror. A chill ran over my skin and I straightened up, throwing the bags and skins away from me.

'Rats! Damn the bloody creatures!' I cried out.

A dark figure stirred nearby and moved towards me: 'Are you Russian? How did you get here?'

By the light of the lit match, I could make out the clean-shaven, smiling face of an unfamiliar young man.

We struck up a conversation. My chance companion turned out to be a former pupil of the Libau Gymnasium,[8] the son of a well-to-do merchant. Some years earlier, having read too much Mayne Reid and Cooper,[9] he abandoned his family and his school, and fled to America as a stowaway in the hold of an American steamer. For three years he served as a cabin boy on the high seas, until he tired of the harsh world of a seaman. In Cape Town, he deserted his ship and, without a penny in his pocket, made his way to Johannesburg, where he gained employment as a clerk on the gold mines. He managed to earn a tidy sum, and as soon as war was declared he was one of the first men to report to Schiel when he was setting up his German corps.[10] Now he was a member of Krantz's unit, which after the relief of Ladysmith stood camped near the station.

Grünstein – that was the name of the Libau student – lit a candle stub and took a packet of cigarettes and a chocolate from his bag. He had obtained all these items from the shops in Dundee, where the German volunteers went 'foraging' daily, or, to put it more plainly, where they ransacked the houses and shops abandoned by their owners. The candle was almost spent, and the rats were starting to race about the floor again, but Grünstein continued telling me about his adventures and plans.

'As soon as the war is over, I'll start working at the Simmering mines[11] again and playing the stock exchange. As soon as I've made a million, I'll return to Libau and join the Dragoon regiment as a volunteer.'

I did not get to sleep anytime soon.

◆

The next day I went to the station and wandered around aimlessly on the platform, hoping to meet one of my companions.

A man with a red band around his arm and a two-headed eagle on his straw hat approached me. 'Good Lord, just take a look at you!

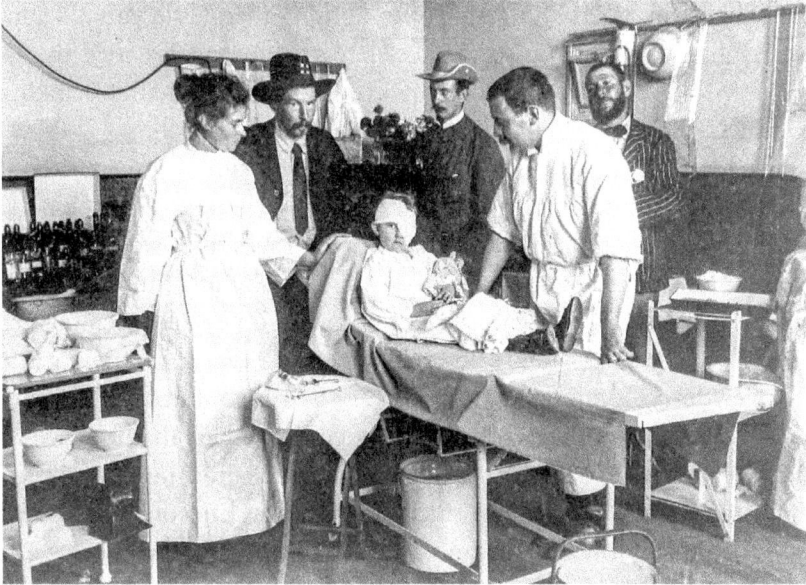

After an operation at the Russo-Dutch Ambulance, Kroonstad (1900).

I hardly recognised you. Come live with us for a bit, get some rest and you'll get on your feet again.'

I was somewhat embarrassed by the kind invitation of the doctor, who, as it turned out, was the head of the Russian Red Cross ambulance here in Glencoe.[12] I knew that our dear countrymen, the members of the Russian ambulance, regarded the Russian volunteers with ill-concealed mistrust, considering them all to be vagrants and adventure-seekers, but so great was my desire to see and speak with my own people at that moment that I only mumbled a few words and followed the doctor immediately.

In a well-arranged infirmary over which the Russian flag was fluttering, I was warmly greeted by Captain Potapov of the General Staff,[13] who was attached to the unit, my comrade Diatroptov, who had already recovered, as well as our military orderlies. I was unspeakably happy to see the familiar high-cheekboned faces of our plucky soldiers from the Guards regiment.

I was given tea, rusks and jams. The orderlies crowded around me as if they were on official business, and with a feeling of superiority over me, a fellow who had been 'struck from the regiment and squadron rolls' benignly asked: 'So you've been fighting there? Did you kill a lot of Englishmen? Do you receive any pay or allowance?' I tried to satisfy the soldiers' curiosity to the best of my ability, and after drinking countless glasses of tea bade my hospitable hosts farewell.

I had still not given up on the thought of finding my unit and decided to apply for the necessary letters of reference to General Joubert or General Botha, both of whom, I was told, were in Glencoe. In Botha's tent, I found a Mr Sandberg, who introduced himself as the general's aide-de-camp, chief of staff and personal secretary.[14]

He conveyed the following news to me in excellent French: the Krugersdorp Commando had not yet assembled, but Field-Cornet Oosthuizen[15] had been appointed its commandant in the place of Van Wyk, who had succumbed to his wounds, and I needed to contact Oosthuizen in order to receive everything I needed. So I went to Oosthuizen, but he informed me that he had neither horses nor clothing; he would only be receiving these in a few days, and for the interim he magnanimously issued me an 'order' to receive bread and meat from the warehouses at the station.

To my question where the men of the Krugersdorp Commando were, he merely shrugged. I had to return empty-handed to my hut, where I met my new acquaintance of the previous day and Second Captain Shulzhenko; we were joined by Buzukov, who brought with him another Bulgarian, the young, friendly Kolarov. We began to discuss our situation. Grünstein recommended that we all join Krantz's German corps, but Shulzhenko, who had served for three months with the Germans, would have none of it: 'Even Ricchiardi and the Italians are a better choice, or some Boer commando.'

The Bulgarians, and especially Kolarov, vehemently opposed the latter option: 'Even the armed bands in Macedonia obey their superiors and observe at least some level of military discipline; the Boers do not even have a trace of that. Now that they've been crushed you won't get any horses or clothing from them.' He related a great number of facts that painted the Boers' attitude to foreign volunteers in a very unattractive light:

'They took away my horse during the retreat; a corporal took my Lee-Metford rifle and gave me some eight-line Winchester in return. I'm going to Pretoria. I'm going to complain to Reitz. Just think of it. For the sake of these Boers, I left my country and my job, and I've been fighting for them for almost three months!'

Chance also brought me into contact with the Prince that Luzsénszky had told me about. Ganetsky[16] made the most pleasant impression on me, and when all one saw before one were dirty, shaggy-looking Boers, how could one not admire this tall, dashing figure with his carefully trimmed beard and his elegant, spick-and-span suit that one would not be ashamed to wear on a bicycle ride along the shady alleys of the Bois de Boulogne. Ganetsky, the son of a famous battle-hardened general, had served for several years in one of Saint Petersburg's dashing Guards regiments before retiring, but soon after war was declared his name appeared in the Petersburg newspapers as one of the first Russian volunteers to join the Boers. A short tour of Europe had somewhat delayed his departure for the Transvaal, and he only arrived in Pretoria at the end of February in the company of three French officers with *Dreyfusard* features.[17] …

Notes

[1] Buller wanted to encircle the retreating Boers, but the latter effectively covered their men with fire. The British were forced to stop pursuing the Boers at night; see Cloete GP, *The Anglo-Boer War: A Chronology*. Pretoria: JP van der Walt, 2000, p 112.

[2] Ladysmith was relieved on 28 February. The siege lasted 118 days.

[3] The Boers continued to retreat in the direction of the Biggarsberg.

[4] *La Débâcle* (1892) is a novel by Émile Zola, set during the Franco-Prussian War of 1870–1871.

[5] Saint Joseph, the legal father of Jesus Christ, who, according to the Gospels, did not consummate his marriage with Mary.

[6] In Ancient Greek mythology, Circe was the daughter of Helios who kept Odysseus with her for a year. In the figurative sense, Circe is a cunning seductress.

[7] Francis Rákóczi (1676–1735) led a major Hungarian uprising against Austria. Artúr Görgei (1818–1916) was a prominent general in the Hungarian Revolutionary Army.

[8] A city on the Baltic Sea, currently known as Liepāja in Latvia.

[9] James Fenimore Cooper (1789–1851), a writer of historical romantic novels of the American frontier.

[10] Adolf Friedrich Schiel (1858–1903), a German-born Boer officer who organised the German Commando at an early stage of the war.

[11] The Simmer & Jack Gold Mining Company, a South African business founded in 1887.

[12] Apparently, it was Vasily Davydov (1863–?), a Saint Petersburg surgeon in charge of the Russian Red Cross detachment in Glencoe.

[13] Second Captain Alexey Potapov (1872–?), a member of the Russian Red Cross ambulance and unofficial agent of the Russian Ministry of War.

[14] Adjutant Christoph Georg Sigismund Sandberg (1866–1954), military secretary to General Louis Botha.

[15] Sarel Oosthuizen (1862–1900), nicknamed 'Rooibul' (Red Bull), a future general.

[16] Second Captain (*stabs-rotmistr*) Alexey Ganetsky (1868–1908?), formerly a dragoon officer in a Guards regiment and assistant to the Russian Minister of War. *Anglo-burskaya voina 1899–1902 godov* ... Vol 8 (2012), pp 15–16, 281.

[17] A reference to the swirling moustache worn by Captain Alfred Dreyfus. His supporters were known as 'Dreyfusards'.

CHAPTER 8

A Russian corps is born

Almost all the Russians who had managed to return from the Tugela gathered in Ganetsky's large, comfortably furnished quarters. Diatroptov was here, in a red calico shirt and greased boots he had bought from one of the soldiers working as a Red Cross orderly. Battle-worn Nikitin and Second Captain Shulzhenko were also present, as was Guchkov, who brought with him some new volunteers, recently arrived in the Transvaal from Russia. One of them, Mr Nikolaev, a self-employed man, looked like the director of a provincial theatrical company or the owner of a grocery store. It was said of him that he had arrived in Pretoria with a team of Montenegrins in tow and had offered his services to the government as the leader of an independent commando. The two others were students from Saint Petersburg who had just graduated from the Institute of Technology.[1]

We briskly made our acquaintances and a lively conversation ensued. The congeniality of our hospitable host, the sounds of our mother tongue and the awareness that we were at last among our own kind, and that all of us had been drawn here, to the sultry skies of a foreign land, by the same thought, the same idea – all this had an exhilarating effect on the group. There was a clinking of glasses and enamel cups, which we used as goblets, and the fumes of wine and cognac fogged our heads until our eyes lit up and our voices rang with the fervour of youth and hope; we all longed for heroic deeds and glory on the battlefield.

'Gentlemen!' Ganetsky announced. 'I trust I am not mistaken that all of you who got lost or scattered among the different Boer commandos and among Boers who are unfriendly, sometimes even distrustful of foreigners, have more than once had the idea, the desire, to rally together and form your own, independent commando. We are not many, but it seems to me that if all those of us present were to join together and select a worthy leader, our commando, filled with Russian men and Russian in spirit, would outshine the Germans, the French and the Irish alike. The glorious deeds of our valiant partisans, the immortal Seslavin, Davydov and Figner,[2] can serve as an example to us as well.'

Second Captain Alexey Ganetsky.

'Stuart's raids in the North American war[3] could also serve as a model of guerrilla warfare to us!' Nikitin interjected. 'I brought his book with me to the Transvaal, but in the meantime, you can uncork another bottle of brandy for us!'

'Of course, of course!' our host responded and bustled about.

'Gentlemen, be my guests, Here are the hors d'oeuvres, canned food, sweet rusks, and here are the cigarettes!'

'Gentlemen,' Ganetsky proclaimed, becoming more and more animated. 'Just think what vast fields of action lie open to us here, in an actual war: incursions, raids on the enemy's communication lines, sabotaging railways, blowing up bridges, night attacks, capturing of convoys … Some of you, and I bow down to you in respect, have been shelled and covered in gunpowder, and this while you acted under the Boer commandos, incapable of active operations where it is possible to demonstrate daring, courage and fearlessness. The whole time you were just sitting in trenches and shooting back, instead of participating in dashing cavalry raids and attacks on batteries. The bullets will whistle as we cut down the gunners! We all have that spirit of daring, that thirst for risk and danger. That proves that we've shaken off the burden of peaceful garrison service and exchanged our safe quiet for the tribulations and horrors of war!'

> *A battleground is filled with bliss,*
> *As is the lightless edge of the abyss*
> *And all the raging ocean's brine*
> *Amid the storms and darkling waves.*
> *Thus, all that holds a seed of death*
> *Is for the mortal's heart a breath*
> *Of indescribable delight—'*

… the young technologist declaimed.[4] I noticed that he was holding the unopened bottle of brandy ready.

'Well, I'm not so sure,' the incorrigible Nikitin grumbled. 'What bliss is there in battle? The main thing is to make sure your sight is straight …'

'Exactly!' Ganetsky echoed. 'Composure, endurance and discipline under fire are more important than anything in modern warfare, and we must organise our commando's operations in the most sensible, rigorously considered way. Only then, with a combination of courage and deliberation, will we achieve the best results. We will strike fear into the British. Our thunder will be heard far beyond the borders of the Transvaal. They will write about us in foreign newspapers. All manner of spoils of war will come our way. Now, however, gentlemen, you are deprived of even essential clothing.'

'It was not for honour, money or glory that we came to fight for the Boers,' Diatroptov interrupted the eloquent speaker. 'We knew what to expect from the war; we are not afraid of deprivations now, nor of any hardships in the future. If the idea of forming our own commando arouses our deepest sympathy, then it is not because we are attracted to the opportunity to raid, pillage and loot with impunity.'

At this Ganetsky checked himself. 'Gentlemen, that is not what I meant. You misunderstood me. Surely you must agree that the guerrilla activities that form the purpose of our commando are impossible without capturing prisoners, convoys and even sums of money.'

'Correct. Even army regulations make provision for that,' Nikitin interjected again. 'Correspondence, the telegraph and sums of money may be seized.'

Ganetsky brightened up at this unexpected support. 'Well, there you have it,' he said. 'Of course, we won't follow the example of the Italians, who take advantage of the fact that everything in war is permitted and plunder English and Boer farms alike. We will set ourselves broader, purely tactical goals. The first thing we need to do is get everybody re-equipped, obtain horses, arms, dynamite, and so forth. I will arrange everything. I have extensive connections in Pretoria.'

Our conversation continued late into the night. From the station came the hissing sound of a steam locomotive. Its lanterns burned like the fiery eyes of a monster, casting a scarlet glow on the tracks. Excited by the talk and the wine, we wandered along the railway track for a long time. Breaking up into separate groups, we worked out the formation of a Russian partisan unit in the finest detail. There was universal support for the idea of electing Ganetsky as our leader.

We had endured, suffered and felt a lot while we were sitting in the trenches on the muddy Tugela. We had learnt that neither republican valour nor the selfless bravery and courage of individuals can make up for a lack of military organisation and military discipline. Now we had the opportunity of setting the Boers an example of correct organisation. Perhaps our Russian corps, weak in numbers but strong in spirit, would in future serve as a core around which the uncoordinated Boer militia could be consolidated. We fell asleep, lulled by rosy dreams of the future, in which our unit grew by leaps and bounds, and hundreds of dashing cavalrymen and quick-firing batteries fought in formation. Our long-range raids would cause panic among the British. We would even capture Kitchener[5] himself, and with the dignity of a well-bred gentleman he would hand us his sword and his Order of the Garter.

◆

The formation of an independent Russian corps was essentially already decided in Ganetsky's tent, during our first meeting. These dreams, which had been born under the influence of wine fumes and the ardent speeches of our host, did not dissipate without a trace like smoke but took on a tangible form; we moved from words to deeds.

One thing bothered us, however: the small size of our future legion. Four of us had returned from the Tugela. We were joined by Grünstein, the erstwhile schoolboy from Libau, and two students from Saint Petersburg; we could not count on Guchkov, who had left for Pretoria – his weakened health required a more or less pro-longed period of rest. Mr Nikolaev, at the head of his Montenegrin lads, prudently stood aside, not wishing to give up his prestigious role as the leader of a separate unit. This cost him dearly, however: the Montenegrins each received ten shillings per day from their 'boss man'; naturally, they had no intention of leaving such a generous leader and joining us. How Nikolaev had contrived to recruit the 12 Montenegrins, armed with daggers, revolvers and rifles, how he had brought them to the Transvaal and what sources of money he was using to pay for their keep – five roubles each per day – these questions were all wrapped in a mystery, and Nikolaev himself cut a very romantic figure.

He would lie for days on end in his tent, drinking countless cups of tea as he related the history of the Montenegrin people to the at-tentively listening Boers. Plump, with gentle blue eyes, he produced a comical effect among the athletically tall, moustachioed Monte-negrins standing submissively in front of him with their hats off. Who could then have imagined that this money-squandering idealist fighter had in fact been some business clerk in Kiev, who had got so carried away by the Boers that he secretly fled to the Transvaal with somebody else's passport, taking with him, as befits a brave and light-fingered cashier, a tidy sum of money. Nikolaev subsequently returned to Russia and his case has recently been dealt with by the Kiev District Court.

At the time we suspected nothing of the kind and were quite upset when we learnt from Ganetsky that Nikolaev refused to join us.

We were even more surprised by Nikitin, who had regarded the idea with scepticism from day one, and in the end frankly declared: 'Nothing good will come of this. You will make bad subordinates, and in my opinion Ganetsky is an unsuitable leader: he's just too much of a smooth talker. I, for my part, decline the honour of serving in your unit.'

It was an unexpected and unpleasant surprise for us to lose Nikitin, that fearless soldier and good companion, with whom we had shared two months of fighting life on the Tugela. When all my entreaties and argumentations with him failed, Ganetsky himself tried to persuade him.

'You're not acting like a fellow soldier,' he said, seizing Nikitin by the only button of his tattered jacket. 'You are sowing discord in our enterprise. You're wrong to doubt my abilities as a commander. Did you know I was one of the top students at officer school? I also have more years of service than all of you; I'm well acquainted with combat situations and whistling bullets; in the Caucasus I took part in raids against the infamous bandit Kerim Pasha!'[6]

But the stubborn Nikitin just repeated the same thing: 'No, thank you. You are on your own and I am on my own. In Natal I studied mountain war, and now I'm going to the Free State to familiarise myself with war in the steppes. To tell you the truth, I didn't come to the Transvaal to form squads and test Duron's findings. I will not join your corps, my dear sir!'

There was no question of trying to persuade Nikitin. He left Glencoe without changing his stance, and I have lost sight of him ever since. Only recently, after I returned from British captivity and re-entered the service, did I come across Nikitin's name while looking in *The Russian Invalid* [*Russky Invalid*] through the list of wounded and killed in China. How fate mocks us indeed! He had survived a hail of British bullets and grenades only to be crippled for life by some slanty-eyed cutthroat.

After Nikolaev's refusal and Nikitin's departure, we all became somewhat despondent and lost faith in our ability to realise our goal. Only Ganetsky did not lose heart and continued to act with the same tireless energy. All day he was on his feet, bustling about, running around the station to meet new volunteers arriving from Pretoria; he sent me to recruit a squad of Lithuanian emigrants who were part of the eight men on guard duty at one of the guard posts along the Pretoria–Glencoe railway line. I gladly volunteered to carry out the assignment. Before reaching Hattingspruit station, eight versts from Glencoe, I came across a guard post where the man in charge was the brave Lithuanian Savitsky, a former bombardier of the First Guards Artillery Brigade. I explained the purpose of my visit to him, and employing every bit of eloquence at my disposal, attempted to persuade him to join Ganetsky's corps.

'Well, that sounds like a good plan,' Savitsky said sedately. 'If your leader is the son of the General Ganetsky who commanded us at Plevna, I think that will be a good thing.[7] The Germans, the French and the Irish are all working together. If you, our esteemed gentlemen officers, can get together, we'll do the same. It's a good plan. There's another six of us at another bridge around here. Tomorrow we'll get together to discuss it and let you know. In the meantime, enjoy a bite with me, Your Honour. It's not much, though. Wartime stuff!'

I asked how they had ended up in the Transvaal and how they enjoyed life here. They were all from Kovno. They had arrived two or three years ago in South Africa and had settled down rather nicely in Johannesburg. They had even sent for their wives and relatives from faraway Russia. Some worked on the gold mines; others had their own workshops, butcher shops and bakeries. The war, which had led to a general stagnation in business, had forced many of them to enlist with the Boers. There were several reserve soldiers among my new acquaintances; all of them, including the bombardier, responded enthusiastically to my offer. Only one thing worried him: 'How will I leave my post? They'll have to send a replacement.' I dispelled his doubts with the assurance that Ganetsky would arrange things with Joubert. He had clearly not forgotten his soldier's training.

The Lithuanians were unsure what food and drink to serve me. They were citizens of an independent republic, thousands of versts from Russia, and yet they were embarrassed to shake my hand and addressed me very formally. A bottle of whisky appeared on the table: 'Your Honour, please don't refuse to have a glass with us – we are going to be fighting together!'

Naturally, I did not refuse and ate some perfectly roasted wild partridge with the drink. After supper, I drew their attention to a piano standing in the corner of the barracks.

'Where did you get this?'

They smiled: 'There are abandoned and looted farms all around us here. While we're posted here, we decided to make the place a bit more homely. The piano, crockery, books … we got everything from the farms. It'll all go to waste anyway. Getz, who's stationed at another post two versts down the track, even found an abandoned child. He took him and sent him by rail to his family in Johannesburg. It's all so sad! When Ladysmith was liberated, the Boer farmers fled and forgot a child in the rush. That's the way things are!'

'Does any one of you play?'

'Of course! Jagello can play all sorts of polkas and things!'

Jagello, a handsome boy of about 17, smiled and sat down at the piano. His fingers ran quickly over the keys. The broken strings rang and rattled. The polka was followed by a krakowiak, then a mazurka, and then he suddenly played a couple of chords and begin to sing in a resonant tenor:

> We take our leave forever,
> Another land awaits …

Here in Glencoe, the sounds of this song from home, the song of a Russian soldier and factory worker!

> … But nothing will divide us,
> Except the soggy earth …

How tiresome the song had become back home! It's forever being played on shrill street organs, bawled out by drunk craftsmen, but here a shiver ran down my body and I got a lump in my throat.

The chorus boomed exuberantly:

... It's not the wind that whistles.
The roar of war resounds
No one suffers as much
As a beloved at war.

The sharp whistle of a steam locomotive rang out. The train rushed over the bridge with a deafening rumble. When its red lights had disappeared in the impenetrable darkness of the night, I suddenly remembered that I had to return home, to the camp, to report back to Ganetsky about the outcome of my trip. I took leave of my kind hosts and made them promise that they would visit us the next day, and started the horse at a trot along the familiar road.

◆

The next day a large crowd of people gathered in front of Ganetsky's tent.

Savitsky had brought six Lithuanians; well dressed and armed with rifles and bandoliers, they posed a striking contrast to the tattered Portuguese, who looked like meat for the gallows. Ganetsky had dug them up somewhere and generously accepted them into the unit, believing in their passionate avowals that they wished to fight against their traditional friends and patrons, the British. Second Captain Shulzhenko, beaming as though he had met some old acquaintances, was chatting in some incomprehensible guttural language with a group of men with hawkish noses and dishevelled black hair. They were Greeks who had previously served with the American troops and had deserted from Cuba. The language he spoke to them was Turkish![8]

Standing to one side, waiting to sign up for the squad, was a group of animated dark-complexioned Italians; Cornetti, a former non-commissioned officer of the Bersaglieri who had fought in Ricciotti Garibaldi's unit against the Turks at Larissa during the Greco-Turkish War of 1897, had brought them to Ganetsky.[9]

The tall, slender figure of Ganetsky, the '*capitano russo*', towered above them all. Grünstein, the former student from Libau, who acted as his personal secretary and interpreter, sat next to him with pencil and paper.

Jean du Breuil de Saint-Germain.

Putting the finishing touches to this motley assortment of lan-guages and nations were the Prussian Lieutenant Döseler, in a foppish yellow jacket and with a well-groomed moustache; the tall Marquis du Breuil;[10] Baron von Busch, a Baltic German wearing golden spectacles;[11] and an archetypal Jew of about 30, who had in-troduced himself to us as a reservist corporal from the 8th Smolensk Dragoon Regiment.

Strange business indeed! People from all over the world had con-gregated here like ravenous jackals at a bloody feast. Most of them had a shadowy past, and quite a few of them were probably wanted men at home; many had simply been drawn to the Transvaal by a concealed lust for looting and plundering. Throughout the war, the governments of the two republics had undertaken no recruitment drives, and the volunteers who had come here at their own risk and peril received no pay; the Boers themselves treated these latter-day crusaders with distrust, at times even gruffly. Meanwhile, the volunteers poured into the Transvaal in their hundreds and thousands, and, having spent their last money on the voyage, arrived in Pretoria without a penny to their names. However, few of these 'knights without fear, but hardly without reproach' remained in the towns, even though these presented a relatively safe hunting ground, given the present impotence of the authorities and the reigning state of anarchy. Instead, the majority of them rushed eagerly to the front and into battle. What drove them into that carnage? What gave them the patience and resignation to endure thirst and hunger, heat and cold, and expose themselves to English bullets? After all, they were paid no money, nor did they expect any rewards, medals or glory. This can only mean that even among these people, of whom Botha had once said that 'all European volunteers are either idiots or rogues',[12] there were men with convictions and honest, idealistic aspirations, in whose veins there flickered a flame of courage and bravado, a chivalrous impulse to aid and deliver the weak and oppressed.

Many of them fell in bloody battles, their bones now fading in the plains and mountains of the sultry Transvaal or lying under silt at the bottom of the turbid Tugela River; many of them are languishing sick and crippled in British captivity. These nameless heroes sealed their willingness for self-sacrifice with their own blood!

◆

Once Ganetsky had registered the volunteers with all their nationalities and professions, he assigned them to different squads: the Italians and the Greeks formed their own unit headed by Cornetti; Shulzhenko was appointed their squad leader; I was placed in command of the Russian unit. Du Breuil and Döseler were left without anything to do. Döseler was at first on the verge of taking offence but calmed down when promised command of the Germans and Dutch if their numbers increased. For now, only Baron von Busch was under his command.

Diatroptov agreed to take charge of the commissary unit, but that was also only a prospect, as the unit lacked all necessities – horses, tents, provisions and the like.

It fell to me, as Ganetsky's most zealous collaborator, to perform the rather delicate task of writing the 'service regulations' for our unit. In the opening paragraphs I sought to clarify the purpose and nature of the corps and outlined the need to observe a degree of discipline. Each article had to be written with extreme circumspection; the concept of discipline could only be loosely applied to these outlaws, and everything had to be adapted to the instincts and ideas of a group of people who had not yet become united into a whole, distrusted one another and only respected brute physical strength. In their original form the service regulations, which could easily have been adopted by Churkin's gang,[13] declared the following, for instance:

> Superiors can only be appointed and removed by a majority vote in an election.
>
> The authority of the superior is relative at camp and on the march, but absolute when under fire.
>
> A superior shall have the right to kill a subordinate for failure to comply with an important order when in view of the enemy.
>
> The purpose behind a planned operation and the means of carrying it out shall be discussed by all ranks in the corps.
>
> All spoils of war shall be the common property of the corps.
>
> Any individual found guilty by his comrades of failing to comply with the provisions of these regulations shall be expelled from the corps and his horse and rifle confiscated.

And so on, and so forth.

These service regulations, translated into French, Dutch and Italian, were read by all and adopted by general consent. The Italians, Portuguese and the rest of the rabble were very pleased finally to have found a place to settle in and be united by a common cause. In the hands of a competent leader, capable of using the force of his authority to instil a feeling of duty, camaraderie and mutual support in this motley crowd, this gang of outlaws could well have been transformed into a formidable force.

◆

We still had to receive permission from Commandant-General Joubert for the corps to actually exist.

A delegation consisting of Ganetsky, Grünstein, Shulzhenko and myself set off to see Joubert, whose quarters were located in Glencoe, about two versts from our camp.

The four-coloured flag still fluttered above the commander-in-chief's green tent; newspapers, a map of Natal and letterheads with the pencil-written reports of field-cornets still lay spread out over his table. But his face had become sunken, there were more grey hairs in his beard and his eyes had grown dull, without their former shine and sparkle.

General Piet Joubert with his men in Newcastle, Natal (1900).

How many cruel blows had fate dealt this old man? How many moral torments had he had to endure? He had flown like an eagle over the Drakensberg and inflicted a whole series of bloody defeats on the English, and his name had thundered across the world – but now luck had betrayed him. One failure followed upon the next, and now, in his twilight years, all his dreams of seeing his nation triumph and achieve freedom and full independence for their republics had collapsed.

Joubert listened indifferently to Ganetsky's ardent speech about the creation of a *sotnia*[14] of Russian Cossacks, leisurely reached for his pen and wrote his signature in large, uneven handwriting on the requisition form that we would be required to present to the Chief Commissariat in Pretoria.

'*Alles van die beste!*' [All the best!] Joubert said in a muffled, decrepit voice. That was my last meeting with him.

◆

The hardest task now lay ahead: supplying all 36 men of the commando with the necessary clothing, horses, weapons and the rest.

The head of the commando, Ganetsky, volunteered to go to Pretoria; Diatroptov, Grünstein and I were appointed to help him obtain the weapons and equipment. Our dragoons, the Prussian Lieutenant Döseler and Leiba Kaplan,[15] were taken as experts to take ownership of the horses.

Just before the train departed, one of the Italians came flying into our carriage and asked us to make sure none of us had accidentally taken his Lee-Metford rifle, which had disappeared without a trace from his tent that very morning. The search led to nothing, of course – we all had our own rifles with us – and we shoved the poor Italian out of the carriage with a laugh. The train started, and for a long time we could still see him, surrounded by his comrades, gesticulating with his hands. It was good to sit on a soft seat and watch the tents of the different encampments, the herds of grazing horses and oxen, the ruined farms, green valleys and distant mountain masses rush past the windows of our carriage in an endless line.

Somehow the feeling of total safety, the certainty that all the horrors of death and the afflictions of camp life had remained behind us in the distance, beyond the blue horizon, and the rhythmic clacking of the wheels soothed my strained, exhausted nerves. My eyes began to close involuntarily. I stretched out on the soft seat and was about to indulge in some sweet dreams, when Döseler burst through the door of my compartment with widely gaping eyes and a pale, distorted face. He was shoved in from behind by none other than Leiba Kaplan, who for some reason was holding a rifle in his hands.

I jumped up in bewilderment. 'What's the matter?'

The lieutenant did not respond. His face twitched nervously, and his eyes darted restlessly from Kaplan to the rifle, and from the rifle to me.

'What's the matter now?'

The reservist lance corporal was apparently enjoying the lieutenant's embarrassment in the same way that an artist admires a striking painting.

'This', Kaplan finally said, hammering out each word, 'is the rifle of our Italian. It was neatly wrapped in newspaper, tied up with string, and I found it behind the seat of this officer. This is bad! One mustn't steal from a comrade. We need to report this to the captain. I just wanted to get your advice what to do.'

The lieutenant had managed to regain some self-control and began to explain to me, in a disjointed, incoherent voice, that this was a complete misunderstanding, that someone must have planted the rifle there, that the Jewboy had no right to rummage through his things and that he had probably wanted to steal something himself. Who was more trustworthy, he continued, an officer of the German Army or some vagabond yid?

At this, Kaplan flew into a temper and started rebuking the hapless lieutenant in his best German-Jewish lingo: 'So what if I'm a yid? Yes, I'm a simple, shady Jew. God himself commanded me to rob and cheat the Goyim. But I'm a soldier, I served in the regiment for five years and I know there is no greater sin than stealing something from your fellow soldier you sleep and eat with; especially when you are at war! You were caught red-handed, and that's all. You should be ashamed, doubly ashamed, as an officer! What will Ganetsky and his comrades think when they hear that the rifle was found in your possession? What will the Boers think of you? At the very next station I'm informing the commandant and taking you to jail. It won't matter a thing that you call yourself a German officer. There's no place for you among us. You'd be better off joining the

English so you don't land up in jail!'

'Don't hand me over! I...I...did it by accident. I won't do it again,' the wretched fellow mumbled. He was a sorry sight.

The train slowed down. Red lanterns flashed through the windows. Someone knocked on the door. I shut the latch fast and turned to Kaplan. This whole scene had upset me tremendously. 'Can't we settle the matter somehow? Come on, it will be better that way. Come on, Kaplan! Can't we keep it quiet? Let's return the rifle to its owner, and Mr Döseler can either leave the corps for ever or give us his word to make up for his guilt in the very next battle with his death. And you, lieutenant, if you ever actually wore an officer's uniform ... You have no choice but to wash this shame off with your blood. Remember Count Zeppelin's heroic death at Elandslaagte![16] I promise you that everything will remain between us. Everything depends on you now, Kaplan. Remember, we're all only mortal!'

The charmless, pockmarked face of this son of Israel suddenly lit up with a kind smile, and he held out his calloused, grubby hand to me in agreement.

'I'll keep quiet, Your Honour, if you want me to. I'll keep quiet, because it's war now, and the Boers need every man they can get. I'll give the rifle back to its owner myself. I'll think of an excuse. I'll say I took it out of absentmindedness. I'll talk myself out of it. And you, Mr Döseler, had better not come back to us. There's better work for you in Pretoria or at the Johannesburg mines!'

Notes

[1] Vladimir Roubanov (1874–1910?) and Vladimir Semyonov (1874–1960), graduates of the Saint Petersburg Institute of Civil Engineers. Semyonov, who was wounded in the South African War, became the chief government architect of Moscow in the 1930s. *Anglo-burskaya voyna 1899–1902 godov*...Vol 8 (2012), pp 277–282.

[2] Commanders of Russian guerrilla units during the French invasion (1812).

[3] A reference to the Confederate cavalry raids organised and carried out by Major General JEB Stuart during the American Civil War.

[4] A quotation from Alexander Pushkin's play *A Feast in Time of Plague* (1830).

[5] Major General Horatio Herbert Kitchener, 1st Earl Kitchener (1850–1916), Field Marshal Lord Roberts's chief of staff at the time.

[6] Abdul Kerim Pasha, better known as Abdülkerim Nadir Pasha (1807–1883), was not a Caucasus bandit but an Ottoman military commander. During the Russo-Turkish War of 1877–1878, he commanded a division of the

Danube forces. Although Ganetsky did not take part in that war, he served in a dragoon regiment in the Caucasus in 1891. *Anglo-burskaya voina 1899–1902 godov* ... Vol 8 (2012), pp 15–16.

[7] Alexey Ganetsky was a son of General Nikolay Ganetsky (1815–1904). However, a prominent Russian military leader in the Russo-Turkish War of 1877–1878 was Alexey's uncle, General Ivan Ganetsky (1810–1887).

[8] Shulzhenko was born and brought up in the Baku Governate (present-day Azerbaijan), and was therefore fluent in Azeri, a Turkic language.

[9] Camillo Cornetti, a former Bersaglieri warrant officer, who had fought under the son of Giuseppe Garibaldi with the Greek Army against Turkey in 1897.

[10] Retired French dragoon officer Jean du Breuil de Saint-Germain (1873–1915).

[11] Victor von Busch, a 28-year-old volunteer from the Russian Empire.

[12] It was General Philip Rudolph Botha (1851–1901), the elder brother of General Louis Botha; see Pottinger, B, *The Foreign Volunteers: They Fought for the Boers (1899–1901)*. Johannesburg: Scripta Africana, 1986, p 240.

[13] Vasily Mikhalkin, nicknamed Vaska Churkin, was a famous robber and extortionist operating on the outskirts of Moscow in the 19th century. In the 1880s, serialised novels about his adventures appeared in the popular newspaper *Moskovsky Listok*.

[14] A Russian military unit comprising 120–135 men.

[15] Apparently, it was Niklaas David Kaplan. When the war entered the guerrilla stage, he fought with General Ben Viljoen's commando. At the end of the war, Kaplan was said to have been promoted to Commandant; see Saks, D, 'Jewish Bittereinders of the Anglo-Boer War', *Jewish Affairs*, 2019, Rosh Hashanah, pp 6–7.

[16] Count Heinrich Eugen 'Harra' von Zeppelin (1870–1899), a nephew of the inventor of the Zeppelin airship, was a member of Adolf Schiel's German Commando. He was killed at the Battle of Elandslaagte on 21 October 1899.

CHAPTER 9

In Pretoria after Cronjé's surrender

Although our journey was short, we could see from our wagon that the Boers had not lost faith in the success of their resistance effort. As we passed through the Drakensberg, we caught sight of thousands of blacks swarming over the peak of Majuba, which commanded the Laing's Nek Pass. They had been herded there by the Boers to build trenches and batteries for the Long Toms.

Endless trains of ox-wagons carrying the Natal Boers' families and their household goods stretched out along the country roads. The hapless farmers expected nothing good to come from an invasion by Buller's victorious army and were rushing to take their families to Pretoria. Posters had been pasted up at all the stations in Wakkerstroom, Standerton and Elandsfontein to announce to the people that Kruger had decided at a meeting with Steyn to abandon all peace talks with England and to continue fighting to the last man and the last cartridge.

Nothing had changed in Pretoria. At the station, enterprising Jews, hotel clerks and orange pedlars scurried about in expectation of the train from Lourenço Marques. The streets were a hive of peaceful activity: children romped about in the gardens; piano music rang from the open windows of the houses; trade was brisk in the crowded coffee shops and boarding houses. Total silence only reigned in the buildings over which the Red Cross flag fluttered. There, in rooms with drawn curtains, lay the wounded, the sick and the dying. Crowds of men, women and children stood at the hospital gates, expressions of grief and anxious expectation on their faces. They had clearly been searching for their relatives in the hospital, had not found them and now, upon seeing us, besieged our group with questions: were we from the Ermelo commando, did we know Piet Vorster, and so on. A tall woman dressed in mourning, with the classical face of a Roman matron that still retained traces of its former beauty, kept asking me if I knew a Samuel Potgieter. 'He's my last son. Two were buried at Spion Kop, one is with Cronjé in captivity, the fourth is lying at home with only one leg, and I haven't heard a thing about the last one, the youngest ...'

I sensed a mute reproach in the way all these mothers, wives and children were staring at us – we who had returned healthy and un-harmed from the war and from the battlefields that had robbed them of so many dear lives. 'Why have you come back from the front?' many of the people asked us. 'The *oorlog* [war] isn't over yet, is it? Or are the khakis so close already?'

We were surprised to see that the people in Pretoria had only the vaguest idea of the course of military operations, and especially of the recent fateful events. Many of the people we spoke to regarded the news of Cronjé's surrender and the relief of Ladysmith as false, or at least as exaggerated rumours. Telegrams from 20 to 24 February hung on the walls of the station and government buildings; the government had for the time being wisely refrained from publishing the latest news.

This time we did not stay with our Berdichev countryman, but went at Ganetsky's invitation to the European, one of Pretoria's best hotels.[1]

The owner of the hotel, one of those fat cosmopolitan Jews, greeted our commander with a low bow.

'I'll have the same suite prepared for you as previously, *mon prince!*' he said with a pleasant smile and personally led Ganetsky up the carpeted staircase. He paid no attention to us, dirty, ragged, with our sunburnt, begrimed faces. A servant gave Diatroptov and me a small dark room with windows overlooking the backyard. Even this seemed luxurious to us after the nights we had spent sleeping on bare rocks: the washbasin with its whole bar of fragrant soap, an electric bell, the bed with its clean linen and down pillow.

'Ah, a samovar and some sweet bread rolls would be just the thing now!' Diatroptov said dreamily. 'I'd feel as if I were back home in Zubtsov!'[2]

We had lunch at the hotel from the table d'hôte. So unaccustomed were we to the atmosphere of a large, brightly lit hall, the clinking of dishes and the chatter and laughter of the well-dressed public that we sat there light-headed, as if in a daze. We were joined by some fine-looking gentlemen. They offered us whisky and beer and enquired where we were from and why we had come to Pretoria. Suddenly, a lieutenant – the one with whom we had had that most unpleasant incident along the journey[3] – elbowed his way through to me. He had shaved and was dressed to the nines, so that I hardly recognised him. With a patronising look he took me by the arm and said: '*Herr Kamerad.* My old friend, Herr Mach, the editor of the *Kölnische Zeitung*, would like to meet you.[4] Come with me.'

Mach, or Bach (I can't remember any more), an imposing grey-bearded old man with golden spectacles, had occupied a separate table in the middle of the hall. It was laden with vases of fruit and bottles of chilled champagne. He stood up from his table, walked courteously up to me and a lively conversation ensued between us.

'I read about you in the *Volksstem*. You fought on the Tugela the whole time. How did you manage to get back here? How are things there now?'

I tried my best to satisfy his curiosity, although I could not resist taking a few jabs at the war correspondents.

Mach smiled good-naturedly.

'You were also able to scribble some reports for the Russian newspapers from here. I mean, did you not send some letters to the *Novoye Vremya* along the way?[5] But you have a *nue âme de tambour* [naked soul of a drum].[6] You couldn't sit still while you were here and traded your pencil for a carbine. I know the feeling. In my young days, I was also a reporter in 1870–1871 and 1877–1878.[7] I smelled enough gunpowder in my life!'

Mach switched to Russian, a language in which he was fairly fluent. He had participated in the 1877–1878 campaign as a newspaper correspondent, and had known Skobelev, Radetsky, Totleben and other prominent participants in that war personally.[8] He interspersed his lively characterisation of these individuals with various little-known episodes and facts …

◆

'Did you know that here in Pretoria, in the same hotel as us, there's a Colonel Maximov, of the Gendarmerie, who arrived recently from Russia? They say he's a secret agent of our government, that he's been given extraordinary authority, and he's also under instructions to write a detailed report about the actions and behaviour of the Russian volunteers in the Transvaal.[9] It's a highly unpleasant story!'

'What rubbish is that? How could you believe such gossip?'

This conversation took place in our hotel room. It was already after two when Diatroptov and I returned from the common room.

I had undressed and was already stretching out voluptuously on the soft feather bed, but my brave rival was pacing nervously from one corner to the other, all the while voicing his fears about the mysterious colonel.

'While you were prattling on in German with some fellow in glasses, I went to the smoking room to smoke a pipe. Suddenly, I hear someone speaking Russian. Who do I see? Ganetsky sitting at one of the tables arguing with someone. The next thing a short little gentleman walks up to me, introduces himself and says he heard that I'm a 'Red'. I didn't know how to answer him!'

'Calm down, Alexey Nikolaevich!' I mumbled in my sleep. 'This is all a bunch of nonsense. We'll talk tomorrow! Go to bed!'

But Diatroptov did not give me any rest.

'You're not behaving like a brother-in-arms. Of course, you don't care. If you go back to Russia, you'll enlist in your regiment again. But I often had a lot to say about freedom, I expressed my views openly, and he's probably aware of all of that. You're not the only one I told about my grandfather, God rest his soul, who went blind and deaf in the dungeons of the Peter and Paul Fortress.[10] If I make it back to Russia, they can put me away where the sun doesn't shine.

'So, I'm asking you, my dear fellow, to do me a favour. If you see Colonel Maximov tomorrow, explain to him that I've realised for myself that a monarchy is superior to a republic as a form of government. Here, in this republic, I've become the most ardent conservative. And now it's my sincere, unwavering conviction that only the tough, fatherly authority of governors and city administrators can protect the state from downfall. Parliaments, freedom of speech and all that kind of thing only lead to doom in the end.

Listen to me!' he cried and unceremoniously shook me from my sleep. 'You need to tell all of this to Maximov tomorrow. He'll believe you as an officer.'

'Will you leave me in peace at last?' I roared, my patience now at an end. 'What kind of power do gendarmes and the Russian police have over you now? What do they care about your political beliefs? Just leave me in peace or as God is my witness, I'll put a rifle bullet through you, and tomorrow I'll report to your secret agent that I felt duty-bound to do you in as a malicious nihilist!'

◆

The next day we all headed for parliament, with Ganetsky in the lead. The commissariat officials treated us with more kindness and consideration this time. The mere mention of the Russian count's illustrious name was enough to ensure that all the formalities surrounding the issuing of the necessary forms and authorisations were sorted out in a few hours.

The Russian Jews who had swimmingly taken up the role of suppliers to the government welcomed us just as kindly. Tents, kitchen utensils, trench-digging equipment, clothes, linen, boots, saddles and saddlebags – we obtained everything exclusively from these agile agents, who had received the contract for the supply of clothing and equipment from the Boer government. At the beginning of the campaign, the treasury paid them in banknotes or hard currency, and when the supply of money was exhausted, they prudently refused to accept South African bank bonds or shares in the Dutch railway line from Pretoria to Lourenço Marques instead of money, and payment was made in gold bullion. Thanks to the generosity of the government, the Jews' sympathies were entirely – and up to the last moment, of course – on the side of the Boers, although the venerable Mr Abramovich, from whom Ganetsky had ordered a Russian national flag and similar tricoloured cockades for our hats, was already quietly stitching together a British Union Jack in anticipation of Pretoria's occupation by British troops in the near future.

The Jews, most of them immigrants from Russia, generally fared quite well in the Transvaal. For some reason President Kruger was well-disposed to them. He granted one a monopoly to build the country's only distillery – Eerste Fabrieken, near Pretoria – while another was given the monopoly to manufacture matches in Johannesburg.[11] The former made millions in only a few years and wanted to erect a monument to Kruger in the square in front of the parliament building in Pretoria. The pedestal of polished granite, surrounded by scaffolding, already graced the square, but the war prevented further work on it. The statue, commissioned from a famous Italian sculptor, remained in Europe. The scaffolding collapsed, and the empty pedestal probably still rises gloomily above the square, unless the English got the bright idea to crown it with a bust of Chamberlain or Roberts.[12]

The following story did the rounds about the Johannesburg Jews: after they had built a magnificent synagogue for a sum of several million, they sent an invitation to the president to honour the consecration ceremony with his presence. Old Kruger put on his top hat and tailcoat with a wheeze and went to the synagogue. After the rabbi had performed the consecration ritual, he asked the president to mark the occasion with a few words. The president went to the front, folded his hands devoutly and without any hesitation, said distinctly to the whole synagogue: 'I declare this synagogue open in the name of the Father and the Son and the Holy Ghost!'

It was a terrible scandal and the Jews, cursing the day they had decided to invite the president, decided to abandon the synagogue and immediately began building a new one.[13]

◆

By the evening, two enormous wagons filled with bales of clothing, sheets, boxes of rifle and revolver cartridges, dynamite and cooking pots were already standing in the hotel courtyard. Black bearers carried bags full of sugar, coffee, rice and canned meat to us. Just like Skobelev before the Akhal-Teke expedition,[14] Ganetsky was excitedly helping with the packing of the goods and shouting threats at the blacks, of whom ten were to become our full property as 'boys', ie official servants.[15]

That same evening, I saw and spoke to Colonel Maximov, by

General Willem Johannes Kolbe and Lieutenant Colonel Yevgeny Maximov, Orange Free State, April 1900.

whose graces our *libre penseur* [free-thinker] Diatroptov had spent a sleepless night.

The saying 'Never judge a book by its cover' can easily be applied to Maximov. Small in stature, lean, wiry, with sharp features, in a shabby Austrian-cut jacket and tall boots, he could not be said to make a charming impression at first sight. But an hour or two of talking to him – of hearing his sharp, passionate voice and observing the darting muscles playing in his face – was enough to catch that slightly mocking, penetrating look of a man who on more than one occasion had to stare the terrible spectre of death in the face. His entire appearance exuded something elemental, the impression of an impetuous man, a man of powerful passions and indestructible strength. Such men are incapable of living in the narrow confines of peaceful, everyday life. They crave open spaces and freedom. Men of his kind either leave their mark as fearless explorers of new and unknown pages in the book of history, like seafarers, like warriors, like national leaders in times of great upheavals or disasters, names like Dezhnev, Przhevalsky and Razin,[16] or they become the victims of human stupidity and indifference, and live out their lives with clipped wings, suffocating in the middle of nowhere with the rank of retired captain…

Maximov was evidently in his forties, but his eyes blazed with a youthful sparkle, his nostrils flared and quivered when he spoke about his past or about the plans he hoped to carry out in the Transvaal. His past had indeed been quite stormy: he was one of the Chernyayev lionhearts who, already as a young officer, had fought in the fields of Đunis and Aleksinac, participated in the war of 1877–1878, then gone to Geok Tepe, followed by travels across Asia and Abyssinia.[17] If he was now in the Transvaal, it was not only to experience, like us sinners, the acute pleasure of risking one's life, but also because he hoped to serve the greater cause of defending the weak and oppressed – and not only as a run-of-the-mill soldier. He had greater designs.

◆

As can be seen in the preceding chapters, the corps of Russian volunteers, organised and authorised by the commander-in-chief back in Glencoe, could only be considered a reality and ready to go on commando once its men had been supplied with horses, weapons and general combat supplies.

After two days of running around the offices of the War Ministry, where our old friend De Souza was still operating, and around the warehouses and stores of the quartermaster and his suppliers, everything was at last organised. Thirty-four horses of all ages and colours, all selected by expert horse masters, were still in the stables of the Pretoria Mounted Police. These horses would horrify any commander of a wagon train battalion or even the owner of a posthorse exchange: some of them were wild, unbroken three-year-old Basotho ponies, but the majority were pitiful, weak-legged, broken-winded Rocinantes with stooped backs.

The government could not give us better horses; the best ones had already, before our arrival, been confiscated for military needs from the city tram service, private owners and even cabbies.

But our pride was two wagons filled to the brim, sporting a full new harness and six pairs of mules. The wagons held boxes of rifles and rifle and revolver cartridges and explosives – dynamite, detonators and Bickford fuses. The tents, water supplies, pots, drinking cups and even a couple of meat grinders were neatly packed in the wagons. There was coffee, rice, sugar, wheat rusks, canned meat and jars of jam in abundance. Nor had they forgotten to give us a bag of tobacco and a set of pipes. An enormous box with linen, clothes, hats and shoes took up almost half a wagon.

With baggage like this, our commando could easily head for the most remote, unexplored wilds of Africa – not to carry out guerrilla raids, of course, but to engage in barter trade with the savages.

The blacks assigned to our commando at Ganetsky's request were huddled underneath the wheels of our wagons, from where they peeked out at their new masters. Of note among them was a strapping grey-bearded Zulu who could still remember King Cetshwayo and a Basotho who turned out to be literate and was all the time reading an English Bible gifted to him by a missionary. The others, wrapped in pitiful rags of flannel blankets, belonged to the Mashona tribe. I had taken some interest in these representatives of the Transvaal's indigenous population and had made up my mind to engage in some scientific research in the field of anthropology and ethnology.

With pipes clenched between our teeth and attired in our brand-new motley suits, we made our final rounds of the wagons to check if everything was tightly fastened and stowed away. We decided to postpone our departure to the station and the loading of the goods to the next day. To be honest, we were sad to part with our soft hotel beds; the mere recollection of the nights we had spent in trenches and in the hills among the savage cliffs and thorny acacias filled us with dread. The fervour and fascination I had once felt when rushing into battle was a thing of the past. I did not want to believe that it had really been me somewhere out there, at war, amid the smoke and flames of the Natal mountains, that I had sat among the writhing, moaning wounded and dying, untouched by any lyddite bombs … it all now seems some half-forgotten nightmare. Was it worth going back, worth living again through all the horrors and privations of war? How good, how unspeakably good it was to be here, surrounded by peace and quiet.

The warm breeze barely stirred the dark leaves of the tall palm trees and the magnolias. The silver light of the full moon lay scattered in fantastical patterns about the footpaths of the garden. The caressing air of this southern night was drenched in the intoxicating scent of tropical flowers, moths circled above the white crowns of the flowers, and the fiery sparks of fireflies rushed on high above my head. In the distance I could hear the soft chords of a piano; the sounds grew, shimmered and faded. I heard laughter and the ringing voice of a woman. My heart ached with a feeling of boundless loneliness and longing, an unstoppable desire for peace, for bliss; surely happiness is not to be sought in suffering, or in the eternal alternation of new and vivid sensations? What am I here for? Oh, to go home again, to my country, my uniform, caution money,[18] the peal of wedding bells!

What shame, what ignominy to get so carried away! Everyone knows how Hannibal's extended stay in Capua ended,[19] and I am perhaps no Hannibal, but here I was, trying to aid my digestion by taking a walk in Pretoria's botanical gardens. I had grown completely soft. Tomorrow I set off for commando!

◆

Back at the hotel, I managed to shake off all sorts of melancholy feelings and began listening attentively to the conversations of the guests who had not yet retired to their rooms and were chatting animatedly in the halls and corridors. A Dutch official arrived with the news that Kruger and Steyn's peace talks had failed to bring the desired results: in a harshly phrased note, Roberts, the commander-in-chief of the English army, had demanded both republics' utter and unconditional submission to England. Kruger followed up with a proclamation urging the people to continue fighting; it said, among other things, that the Almighty Lord was heeding the prayers of his grieving people, that the forces of heaven would rally to the cause of His chosen people, and that a second Majuba would dawn for the English. The proclamation also hinted that one could sooner or later expect the intervention of foreign powers, to whom it had been decided to dispatch a special embassy.

This news roused a multitude of utterly conflicting opinions among those present. The majority were sceptical about the prospects of continued fighting, regarding it as futile. Some bitter interjections were directed at the president. 'Old fool!' muttered some of the 'gentlemen' gathered around the hotel owner, who did not hesitate to express his fears that he was unlikely to get his money from the government if the war continued with the same measure of success. All these esteemed Uitlanders, many of them apparently Jewish, had grown fat and wealthy in the Transvaal, and had been Oom Paul's most ardent admirers at the start of the war; now they were already starting to weigh up the killing they could make by providing supplies to the quartermaster of the victorious English army.

But no sooner would some Boer appear in the doorway with his bearded sunburnt face, a bandolier slung over his shoulder and a pipe in his mouth, than the conversation took an entirely different turn: then they would praise the courage of the Boer nation and curse the despicable *rooinekke* [rednecks] for all they were worth. 'Just let the English show up at the walls of Pretoria! We'll show them!' exclaimed the distinguished gentlemen. Some of them were members of the 'Spesiaal Polisie', recruited from among the civilian population of Pretoria to maintain public order, and they were not a little proud of the revolvers hanging from their belts.

The adjacent room housed a bar with hard liquor, and here a company of government officials had gathered to toast Field-Cornet Spruyt following his escape from English captivity.[20] The sale of spirits had been officially prohibited throughout the country, and the bars, even in a first-class establishment such as the European Hotel, had been boarded up, but on such an occasion and for such influential guests, the owner had deemed it permissible to break the law.

On the table stood arrayed a dazzling assortment of bottles with the seductive labels of 'Scotch Whisky' and other products of the English liquor industry. They drank, as is their habit, without any hors d'oeuvres, mixing whisky with Seltzer water. They were all quite inebriated already and listened with flushed faces and bleary eyes as Spruyt regaled them for the tenth time with his account of the encirclement and surrender of Cronjé, his own daring jump from a station platform onto a speeding train, and the many adventures that had brought him through the entire British army until, at last, he found himself in Pretoria. Shaking his hairy fists and straightening up to his considerable height, Field-Cornet Spruyt roared hoarsely: 'Cronjé sold out his people like Judas the traitor for 30 pieces of silver! I told him: "Run, Piet Cronjé! The khakis are all around us like field locusts … Run, while there's still time!" Give me another bottle, *my jong*! My heart is burning! "Mind your own business, Field-Cornet," he answered me. "I'm a Commandant-General!" And he just went on greasing the wheels of his trolley. And now the *rooinekke* are already there, in Bloemfontein. The Free Staters have raised white flags and our people are running. Give me more wine! Why leave it all for the English! Your health! Oh, woe to us!'

A blond burgher, some parliamentary official, began to sing, his whole body rocking back and forth:

Cronjé is gevang
Met al syne man
Pasop vir die rooinekke …

[Cronjé is captured / With all his men / Watch out for the English …]

I recalled the singing and dancing of the gunners at the Long Tom battery, back in the glory days of the battle of Vaalkrans. The tune was the same, but the words had changed.

'*Pasop, pasop, pasop vir die rooinekke!*' His fellow revellers took up the song with wild, unsteady voices; they drummed the beat on the table with their fists; bottles and glasses jumped up, tumbled over, and the sound of breaking glass cut through the air.

Die burgers vlug terug
Met Mausers op die rug
Pasop vir die rooinekke

[The burghers flee / With Mausers on their
backs/ Watch out for the English …]

The drunken voices thundered in chorus. The field-cornet's powerful bass drowned out the other voices. But suddenly his voice broke;
he buried his face in his hands and collapsed at the table.

Muffled sobs broke out: 'My wife … My children …'

'I'm switching off the gas!' declared a German waiter with a pimply face. 'Time to finish up! To your rooms!'

The coolness of dawn wafted through the open window. The same
wordless silence hung in the streets outside. The field-cornet half
rose, cast a dull gaze over the empty room, crashed down onto the
floor and immediately began snoring. He had fallen asleep with the
same deep slumber that used to overcome him in the crevices of the
kopjes after wearying watch duties and marches.

◆

In the meantime, two members of the Russian volunteer community
were engaged in a momentous conversation in my room. It would be
of great importance for our newly organised commando; to a certain
extent this conversation would determine the commando's fate.

I caught Ganetsky and Colonel Maximov just as the argument was
coming to an end. They were both highly agitated and their voices
sounded heated and impatient. Diatroptov was also sitting in the
room: the conversation had clearly become not only tiresome but
also highly unpleasant for him, and he wanted to get some sleep.

'So you are breaking your word of honour that you gave me on
the ship? I ask you for the last time, in front of these witnesses!' the
Colonel demanded from Ganetsky.

Ganetsky could barely contain his anger and turned to us as if
expecting support. He replied: 'We formed the commando together, but the idea was entirely mine. I made you no promise. You are
wrong, Colonel. And what is more, the commander is elected by

a majority of votes, and the comrades' choice settled on me! I have no intention of renouncing the honour of commanding the Russian corps in your favour!'

'Is that your last word on the matter?'

The Dutch corps under Yevgeny Maximov, Orange Free State, April 1900.

'Yes, it is my last word!' Ganetsky declared with a defiant look. 'It will be even better if you ask for the opinion of our companions. You are presumably already aware of the views of Lieutenant Alexei Nikolaevich Dreyer[21] and Second Captain Shulzhenko. Yevgeny Fyodorovich Avgustus will probably also speak out in my favour. As for the rest who stayed behind in Glencoe ... I doubt that they will refuse me.'

'So that is it,' Maximov said sharply, every word dropping like a newly minted coin. 'I will lay my cards on the table. Now is not the time to discuss who was responsible for spreading rumours among the Russian volunteers that I'm a gendarme and a secret agent; that we will discuss another time!'

It became clear from Maximov's subsequent words that during their journey on the steamer, Ganetsky had told him of his wish to form a corps of Russian volunteers and had not concealed his hope of commanding it himself, but with the proviso that he was willing to give up the role of commander if another, worthier person was found, on which he had given his word of honour to Maximov.

But now, when the creation of the corps and the selection of Ganetsky as its commander was already a fait accompli, Maximov's pretensions were unexpectedly rebuffed not only by Ganetsky but also by Diatroptov and Lieutenant Dreyer, a new Russian volunteer but recently arrived in Pretoria. Some kind of misunderstanding had arisen between Dreyer and Maximov, and it had almost degenerated into a quarrel.

Thus Ganetsky's ambition and his unwillingness to submit to Maximov, together with those mysterious rumours that had made poor Diatroptov view him as a political spy, had deprived Maximov of any hope of occupying the position that he fully deserved thanks to his combat reputation and personal qualities. Ganetsky's political game was a complete success.

The fate of our commando was decided.

Notes

[1] It was located in Scheiding Street, close to the Hollandia Hotel. It belonged to Herman Hamburg; see *Longland's Pretoria Directory for 1899*, p 192.

[2] A town in the Tver Governorate of Russia.

[3] A reference to Lieutenant Döseler.

[4] Richard von Mach, a special war correspondent of the *Kölnische Zeitung*; see Bender, S, *Der Burenkrieg und die deutschsprachige Presse: Wahrnehmung und Deutung zwischen Bureneuphorie und Anglophobie, 1899–1902*. Paderborn: Ferdinand Schöningh, 2009, pp 42–43.

[5] Avgustus's letters from his voyage to South Africa appeared in the *Novoye Vremya*, a popular Saint Petersburg daily.

[6] Perhaps meaning that Avgustus was a born soldier.

[7] The Franco-Prussian War of 1870–1871 and the Russo-Turkish War of 1877–1878.

[8] Mikhail Skobelev (1843–1882), Fyodor Radetsky (1820–1890) and Eduard Totleben (1818–1884), Russian generals who took part in the Russo-Turkish War of 1877–1878.

[9] Yevgeny Maximov (1849–1904) was made lieutenant colonel while serving in the Special Corps of Gendarmes, the uniformed security police of the Imperial Russian Army. This and his close relations with Boer leaders suggested that he was on a mission from the Russian government: members of the Russian corps believed that Maximov spied on his compatriots. Their

assumption was incorrect because he had resigned from security police long before; see Voropaeva et al (comp and eds), *Anglo-burskaya voyna 1899–1902 gg*, p 514.

[10] A citadel in Saint Petersburg that served as a prison for political criminals.

[11] De Eerste Fabrieken in de Zuid-Afrikaansche Republiek was co-owned by the Russian Jews Samuel (Sammy) Marks and Isaac Lewis.

[12] The statue was commissioned by Sammy Marks. It was designed by Anton van Wouw, a South-African-based Dutch sculptor, who completed the project in Italy. The Kruger statue, cast in Europe, was stored in Lourenço Marques during the war. It was only in 1954 that it was installed in Church Square on a new pedestal.

[13] Kruger did not say the words attributed to him by Avgustus and many others. Instead, the president declared, 'I call those my people who obey the laws of the land.' The Jews are God's ancient people. I respect the Jewish and other faiths without distinction'; see Fisher, J, *Paul Kruger: His Life and Times*. London: Secker & Warburg, 1974, p 150.

[14] A reference to the Russian campaign to conquer the Teke Turkomans in 1880–1881, which was led by General Mikhail Skobelev.

[15] Black *agterryers* (auxiliaries) were commandeered by the republican governments and provided to burghers on commando; see Nasson, 'The war for South Africa', p 218.

[16] Semyon Dezhnyov (c. 1605–1673), a Russian explorer of Siberia, who was also the first European to sail through the Bering Strait. Nikolay Przhevalsky (1839–1888), a Russian explorer of Central and East Asia. Stepan Razin (1630–1671), the leader of a major uprising in Russia in 1670–1671.

[17] Mikhail Chernyayev, a Russian major general, was commander-in-chief of the Serbian forces in 1876. Russian volunteers such as Maximov served under him in the Balkans. Maximov, a veteran of the Herzegovina uprising, the Serbian-Turkish and Russo-Turkish wars, and the Russian conquest of Turkestan, had broad experience in guerrilla warfare and commanding volunteer units. *Anglo-burskaya voina 1899–1902 godov … Vol 6 (2012),* pp 64–72, 80.

[18] Financial contributions made by army officers in Imperial Russia to provide for their future family life after marriage.

[19] During the Second Punic War (218–204 BC), Hannibal, based in the city of Capua in southern Italy, lost the initiative, abandoned his plans to conquer Rome and returned to Carthage.

[20] Apparently, this was Cornelis Johannes Spruyt (1857–1901), Field-Cornet of Heidelberg. While advancing to Paardeberg to relieve General Cronjé, he was captured by the British on 20 February 1900 but managed to escape and continued to fight on the republican side. Promoted to Assistant Commandant-General, he was mortally wounded near Val in the Eastern Transvaal; see Preller, GS and Engelenburg, FV, *Onze krijgs-officieren: album van portretten met levens-schetsen der Transvaalse generaals en kommandanten*. Pretoria: 'Volksstem' Kantore, 1904.

[21] Lieutenant (*poruchik*) Sergey Dreyer (1874–?), formerly of an infantry regiment in Russia. He fought on the republican side for four months, sustained a head injury and was captured during the fighting for Pretoria. *Anglo-burskaya voyna 1899–1902 godov … Vol 8 (2012), pp 277–282.*

CHAPTER 10

To the front again

◆

Editor's note: This part of the account begins with Avgustus's deviating from the main course of his narrative and commenting on the conduct of the Russian corps, on Boer morale after the capture of Cronjé and on the efficiency of guerrilla units and methods in a war against a regular army. It was written with hindsight, long after the author had left South Africa.

◆

It is a daunting, ungrateful task, to say the least, for me now to narrate the ensuing military operations and exploits of the Russian corps. My memories of these experiences are still too fresh, and they are sad and gloomy rather than pleasant memories.

Here is what I had to read in the *Novoye Vremya* upon my return home:

Highlights from the provincial press

A certain Mr Gringof, a technical mechanician,[1] has returned to Saratov from the Transvaal, and was interviewed as a 'qualified expert' by a reporter of the *Saratov Daily*, to whom he spun the following tale.

'How did the Russian volunteers in the Transvaal behave?'

'Oh,' Mr Gringof said with a smile, 'badly, very badly! For starters, upon their arrival in the Transvaal they received horses and rifles from the Boers, but the very next day they exchanged the horses for alcohol.

The same thing would probably have happened with the rifles, but the taverns did not accept them as payment! After they lost their horses, they got new ones in the following ingenious way: by cutting the cabbies' horses from their harnesses, and then writing out receipts to the cabbies that they claimed would allow them to obtain compensation from the Boers! There was no order or discipline among our volunteers. And that is easy to understand – they had no cruel superiors of the kind to which Russians are accustomed, and the Boers understood discipline somewhat differently: when there's no fighting, they have no distinction between ranks, everyone is friends, and they don't need whips to keep them in tow, a friendly word is all that's needed.'

'Did the Russians participate in any battles?'

'Yes, a couple, but in the end their debauchery caused the Boers to stop taking any Russians with them, and the leader of the corps, Captain Ganetsky, ran away from the volunteers back to Moscow.'

Those Russians who had been in the Transvaal will doubtlessly not hesitate to respond to this frivolous and indecent blather by someone who is 'pretty well a yid'.[2]

I thought it unnecessary to rebut in print the accusations of Mr Gringof, an individual completely unknown to me, although I ought to have exposed the total absurdity of his fabrications, not on behalf of those who safely returned to their fatherland decorated with the tawdry laurels of Transvaal heroes, and through their participation either regained their reputations or became known as knights without fear or reproach, but on behalf of those who laid down their bones on the battlefield, and thus redeemed all their sins – willingly or not – by dying a soldier's death.

The esteemed contributor of the *Saratov Daily* first of all enquired from the 'knowledgeable expert', with all the severity of a form master, how the Russian volunteers had behaved in the Transvaal, and only after recollecting himself posed the question: 'Did the volunteers take part in any battles?'

As it turns out, these Russian volunteers, who had bartered their horses and rifles for drink at the taverns, still managed to take part in several battles.

Thank you at least for that, Mr Gringof.

Following this article, a letter by Maximov appeared in the columns of the same newspaper. Although it contains some inaccuracies, for instance regarding Philip Botha's attitude to the Russian corps, I quote it here in full due to its importance in outlining the types of Russian volunteers.

Russian volunteers in South Africa

A letter to the editor
The Saratov Daily recently published several slanderous statements about the Russian volunteers in South Africa, based on the assertions of one Mr Gringof.

I had close relations with government officials of the Transvaal and the Orange Free State, was personally acquainted with almost all the Boer generals and commandants, and also had numerous friends among the Boers, but never heard as much as a hint of those abominations of which Mr Gringof accuses us, Russians, nor did I ever observe anything of the kind. Not all the Russian volunteers were up to our great task of fighting for the noble cause of truth and justice, but there were few such who wisely settled in warm spots far away from the battlefield; they, however, behaved with modesty and decency, and did not go chasing after glory and higher ideals. (There were two exceptions, whom I will name when the need arises.) The majority, however, did not bring shame to Russia's name in distant Africa. I will name a couple of them: Lieutenant Guchkov, Lieutenant Strolman (killed),[3] Second Lieutenant Nikitin, Count Komarovsky,[4] Second Lieutenant Nikitin[5] Lieutenant Avgustus, Praporshchik Diatroptov and others. Let Mr Gringof name the persons about whom he has fabricated these defamatory claims, and I, who know all the volunteers who were in the Transvaal, can say with confidence that I will disprove his slanderous lies against these Russian men.

There may have been some complaints about the Russian corps of Lieutenant Ganetsky, but they were not about the Russians, who only made up a fifth of the unit (there were about 30 people in Ganetsky's unit), but about that multinational rabble that formed a portion of the unit. Naturally, there were some individuals of very low moral quality in that mob. The Boers knew this, and therefore never confused the Russians with them. If General Philip Botha

was dissatisfied with the Russian corps, one must blame the com-
mander of the corps, who was unable to discipline the rabble in his
unit, not the Russians who made up a minority.

Let me repeat that it is difficult for me to write about our fur-
ther adventures related to the combat activities of the Russian corps;
I need to pull myself together, which is why I will for now move from
personal recollections to another, strictly academic theme: the next
section will be dedicated to an outline of the military operations of
March 1900, which are not devoid of some interest when examining
Roberts's campaign that followed on the heels of Cronjé's capture of
27 February.

◆

Lord Roberts's successful operation against Cronjé's army at Modder
River had as its direct consequence not only the lifting of the siege
of Ladysmith; it also diminished the size of the Boer commandos
earmarked for the invasion of the Cape Colony. Cronjé's subsequent
surrender caused the Boers to panic. Both the Free State Boers on
the Tugela and the Boers in Stormberg, Dordrecht and Rensburg left
their positions without permission, fearing that they would thus be
deprived of a way of retreat. The elected commanders had no means
of combating the cowardice gripping the burghers. This clearly
illustrates a shortcoming inherent to all militia troops: the personal
interests of every burgher, who feared for the safety of his farm and
the fate of his family, caused him to forget the war's most important
objectives. The narrow-minded outlook of the Boers, each of whom
considered the defence of his home district to be the main purpose of
the war against the British, was incapable of grasping the importance
of team play in the different theatres of military operations, where
every man had to forget his own plans and considerations completely
in favour of one common, overarching idea.

The Boer militias of that phase of the war had not yet developed an
awareness of the importance of discipline. The almost total absence
of such discipline explains the panic that gripped the Boer commandos, which had hitherto been operating so successfully in the north
of the Cape Colony. Men started withdrawing from the occupied

areas not just one by one but as entire detachments. On 1 March, General Clements entered Rensburg without a fight, followed by Colesberg, which had been abandoned by General Schoeman and his commando.[6] The retreating Boers still held out for a couple of days at Norval's Pont, but in the end they blew up the railway bridge over the Orange River and relocated to its northern bank.

Clements's troops followed in the footsteps of the retreating Boers, crossed the river almost unhindered and on 15 March began building a pontoon bridge and restoring the destroyed Colesberg–Norval's Pont railway line.

A portion of the Boer forces, their retreat cut off by Roberts's move on Bloemfontein, took a detour via Fauresmith and Modder Rivier, while the other, more numerous portion set off in an easterly direction to Smithfield to join up with the commandos retreating from Stormberg and Dordrecht.

All these units were concentrated at Rouxville and Smithfield under the command of General Olivier …

On 7 March, Roberts's offensive resumed. In all his subsequent encounters with the Boer commandos that tried to block his way to Bloemfontein, one could observe the widespread use of new offensive tactics developed by the British commander-in-chief …

Instead of the frontal attacks of Methuen and Buller, who had operated almost entirely with packed rifle lines supported by closed infantry columns, Roberts employed new tactics, the most typical example of which is the battle of 7 March.[7] Roberts, contending with the peculiarities of an enemy who almost always occupied a strong position that was hard to reach from the front, assigned a purely demonstrative role to the infantry and artillery; their fire drew all the attention of the enemy, while the leading responsibility fell to the cavalry and a new type of weapon, the mounted infantry, that advanced far ahead and had to cover the Boers' flanks and rear.

This tactic was mostly successful, thanks, firstly, to the numerical superiority of the British and the terrible strength of their artillery fire, which could engulf entire stretches of territory rather than just hitting individual targets, and although the results were not commensurate with the quantity of wasted shells, the effect was always impressive. Secondly, for lack of reserves, and especially of cavalry, the Boers were powerless to offer any resistance to these engagements; their mounted troops fell far short of the demands usually placed on cavalry in the generally accepted sense of the word.

But the British cavalry, and especially the mounted infantry that had been hastily organised during the war itself, also left much to be desired. Worst of all was the reconnaissance service. These units, operating in isolation from each other, were forever getting into trouble; they never carried out the pursuit of a crushed enemy to its conclusion, and the patrols by the regular cavalry and mounted infantry often lost contact with the retreating enemy. With the passing of time these shortcomings naturally faded away; the horsemen and yeomanry, who had not been trained in peacetime, were able to turn into fine soldiers during the war. But England had to pay dearly for the lack of peacetime training of its troops; such shortcomings are only eliminated after heavy defeats, and have to be paid for with unnecessary sacrifices and rivers of blood.

When analysing the Boers' actions during the battle of 7 March, one is most struck by the fact that the defensive fighting was fought by separate commandos, each of which occupied separate positions without a prior plan, without communication between the units and without any overarching leadership. De la Rey's units, reinforced by Boers transferred to the Free State from Natal, were operating on the right flank, north of the Modder River; De Wet was in charge of the left flank.

The Boers' position, stretched out over ten versts [10.6 km], consisted of a series of disjoined hills; each of these kopjes was occupied by the burghers of a separate district, whose field-cornets acted at their own discretion, completely oblivious of aiding each other. There could be no semblance of higher leadership or a systematic defence plan against the background of an utter decline in the fighting spirit of the men. Under such circumstances, the outcome of the battle was a foregone conclusion.

◆

There are quite a few dreamers in our country who argue that it is possible to replace a permanent regular army with a militia or simply a volunteer corps of the people. They cite examples from the French Revolutionary Wars, the North American War and the last Anglo-Boer War...

The defenders of militias and volunteer corps have become far more vocal, especially of late. 'A small, hitherto almost unknown nation of peaceful farmers has been struggling successfully against the formidable regular army of the mistress of the seas...' This is a much-vaunted phrase, but its frequent use distorts the true nature of 'the absurdities carried out by the English in South Africa', as our military authority, General Puzyrevsky, so aptly put it.[8]

The outcome of the war is unquestionable: the Boer republics have been wiped from the face of the earth; like the Russians in the Caucasus and the French in Algeria, so the British will remain victorious in the end. The unparalleled courage and self-sacrifice of the Boers have merely served to ensure that the flawless guerrilla operations of De Wet, De la Rey and Botha will make their way into tactical handbooks. The British have long since reduced the war to double-entry bookkeeping, to calculating how many Boers remain and how much time and money will still be required to deal with the handful of partisan units scattered across the country.

There is an enormous difference between the Boer units that today still defend their freedom and independence, and the disjointed militias of my day that confronted Roberts on his way to Pretoria. All that now remain are young men – desperate daredevils – who hurl themselves against the British in hand-to-hand combat with revolvers, using their rifle butts for want of bayonets. This did not happen in my time. Now they have at last, but alas, too late, realised the necessity of submitting to harsh military discipline, and field-cornets now impose the death sentence on disobedient subordinates.

When I read the telegrams concerning the latest events in South Africa, a feverish excitement grips me again. I hear again the ominous buzzing of lyddite bombs, the whistling of bullets and the hoarse groans of the wounded. I see the peaks of rocky hills, covered in a haze of shrapnel; in the distance the yellow shapes of khakis clamber over the rocks, higher and higher...And I long to go back there, I long with my whole body and soul to return to the distant, sweltering Transvaal, forgetting that I am bound by my word of honour...

The Boers paid a heavy price to redeem their blunders – the destruction of their state, the devastation of their farms and property, the suffering of the women and children languishing in captivity in the concentration camps.

Such shortcomings are inevitable in national militias, where in the absence of military discipline, the citizen soldier sees only petty personal considerations and motives as the goal of the war, rather than attaining and protecting the highest interests of the nation and the state.

Had the Boers fought as they are fighting now, the outcome would have been different. Buller and Methuen would not have envied the laurels of Lord Roberts then.

I have given a brief outline of the battle of 7 March, noting that neither the pleas nor the persuasions of the venerable President Kruger enjoyed any success; the Boers trembled under the heavy fire of the British artillery and one by one started creeping away from their positions.

Here is an episode related to me by Major Van Dam, the commander of the Johannesburg Mounted Police, under whose leadership I subsequently had the privilege of serving.[9] He had participated in the battle of 7 March, and after noticing an outflanking manoeuvre by British mounted infantry, ordered a subordinate, a field-cornet of the Kroonstad district, to occupy a hill with his men from where they could cover the outflanking column with flanking fire.

The esteemed field-cornet looked at the mountain and the English shrapnel exploding above it, looked some more and fell into deep thought.

Van Dam told the field-cornet to hurry. The barrage of English volleys grew stronger.

'No, major. You go if you want to. I'm not going,' the field-cornet answered. Van Dam asked, urged and ordered the man. All to no avail. The field-cornet and his men did not have the slightest intention of moving.

One can cite many such cases, as I also mentioned earlier when I described combat life on the Tugela. They all perfectly depict the morale of the Boer troops following Cronjé's surrender.

Roberts's subsequent advance on Bloemfontein, followed by his march on Pretoria, was marked by a series of similar battles.[10] The British emerged victorious from almost all these encounters, not only because of their numerical superiority, and not only because the organisation of their troops, their battle formations and their very conduct in battle were skilfully adapted to the enemy's tactics and the terrain conditions, but also because the martial spirit managed to be stronger in the British Army than in the Boer commandos. Such spirit manifests itself both among enlisted and mercenary troops, depending on the extent to which each soldier's sense of self-preservation and willingness for self-sacrifice is overcome by his sense of duty, his feeling of camaraderie, of belonging to the greater whole of the army, and the authority of his commanding officer.

A soldier does not need loud words about love for his fatherland, honour or glory, nor does he even understand them. Even without such words, he will fight, starve, suffer and die splendidly, sometimes because dying among men is noble, sometimes because he instinctively, unconsciously follows the example of an officer, and most often simply because he was 'ordered to do so'.

There has been much criticism of the British Army, and it has been heavily criticised in the pages of newspapers and satirical magazines, but it has martial spirit, as has been proven at Waterloo, Balaclava, Lucknow and Ladysmith.

I know the British Army not only from caricatures in the *Journal amusant* or the *Alarm Clock*;[11] I have felt on my own skin what it means to fight Tommy Atkins on active duty.

As I lay in the trenches tightly gripping my rifle butt, I sometimes accidentally forgot to hold my rifle sight even as I stared at the pale faces of the soldiers slowly crawling up the steep incline to the peak of the hill from where their invisible enemy showered them in a rain of fire from behind a cover of rocks. They just went on and on, without generals galloping ahead, without fluttering banners, to certain death. This was on the Tugela, on the bloody day of the Pieter's Hill assault.

Again I hear the Boers asking the captured Scotsman: 'How long are you still going to hold out in Ladysmith?' And again I hear the proud reply of the soldier, exhausted by hunger and deprivation: 'For as long as we have enough rounds!'

I saw a platoon of Dublin Fusiliers caught unawares by a cavalry detachment, fighting back with bayonets and rifle butts, without even thinking of surrender. The wounded, bleeding officer was shouting in a hoarse voice to the soldiers: 'Fixed bayonets! No surrender!'[12] Only two of the twelve men surrendered to us.

One should be very cautious about using the experience of the South African war to draw conclusions about the strength of militia armies on the one hand, or the fighting qualities of the British soldier on the other.

The British need only abandon their obsolete system of recruitment and organisation by introducing compulsory military conscription, and, most importantly, by improving the make-up of their officers, and their army will be as good as any on the Continent.

◆

Sooner or later, Russians will have to cross swords with the British. It is now more important than ever for us to study the organisation of their army, and all its weakness and strengths.

After centuries of persistent struggle, and after a whole series of unceasing wars and campaigns deep into the Asian steppes, the two-headed eagle has reached the snowy peaks of the roof of the world, and its keen eyes pierce the misty distance where the decorated domes of pagodas rise in silent grandeur and the quiet waters of the holy river flow among the banks of emerald.

Millennia have passed, have flashed by like a dream, since the warriors of Alexander the Great, Nadir Shah and Genghis Khan watered their horses in the rivers of Hindustan.

A day will come when those same shores resound with the neighing and clattering of Cossack horses.

The British flag now flutters over Hindustan, from sea to sea. Trains are rumbling through the virgin forests, through previously impenetrable jungles; the sacred lotus flowers have wilted under the soot of steam engines, and in the squares and bazaars of ancient cities the white helmet of an Englishman stands out imperiously amid the crowd of dark-skinned Hindus and fakirs in nirvana. Gilded shop and office signs gleam next to a neglected, empty temple of Buddha.

The fabulous sumptuosity and splendour of the former royal dynasties has been replaced by the feverish exploitation and cold, soulless regime of the English. The winner triumphs. The proud Aryan's gaze has faded. He has recognised the power of the newcomers with the resignation of a fatalist; and while he himself is dying of hunger and disease, he has given the foreigners all the riches of his country, without resistance and almost without a struggle. But deep in his soul there lurks a faint hope that the words of the unknown prophet will one day come true: 'The warriors of a white Emperor will come down from the north and free us from the yoke of the foreigners!'

Who among the Russian people does not know that Russia's century-old desire for warm seas, for India, is blocked by the armed forces of Afghanistan, the British vanguard, and behind them stands the whole of Great Britain? ...

Russia's movement forward is not only driven by political considerations or tactics; that movement is chaotic, driven by fate, and caused by the same uncharted, immutable laws that drive the life and historical evolution of every people.

We must fight our way to the warm sea.[13] ...

Decades, perhaps even centuries may pass, but sooner or later the snowy caps of the Himalayas and the endless plains of Hindustan will resound with the roaring of cannons. Russian bayonets will glitter at the walls of imperious Varanasi.

The British know this. The looming spectre of a Russian invasion of India has haunted them for many years, and through the centuries England's entire policy towards Russia has rested on hatred and treachery alone.

England has drawn many valuable lessons from the South African war. She now knows that with the current way in which she recruits, organises and trains her troops, she will not withstand any struggle against a continental power. If armed conflict with Russia should break out in Asia, where the pride and hope of the English navy, her fleet, will play only a minor role, she will only be able to save herself by creating a new army, capable of resisting a Russian onslaught. Based on her experiences in the Anglo-Boer War, one can judge whether today's British army is capable of repulsing even a raid by an irregular native cavalry, which, according to Skobelev's thinking, should be thrust as an advanced guard at India '*sous la bannière du sang et de l'incendie*' [under the banner of blood and fire]...[14]

◆

Almost every train arriving in Pretoria brought new volunteers.

Apparently, the Transvaal government was now treating them with more consideration and courtesy than at the beginning of the war, when they were received without ceremony and the venerable burghers looked down on them with a touch of contemptuous good nature.

Seen from their point of view, the Boers were certainly entitled to be suspicious about the ragtag rabble flooding all the hotels and boarding houses in Pretoria and offering their services as self-appointed saviours free of charge.

The simple psychology of the average Boer found it impossible to solve the seemingly insoluble riddle as to why people of completely alien aspect and language, who had no farms or cows or sheep in the Transvaal, could be coming here from far across the sea to engage in mortal combat.

Back at the Tugela I had already often been asked: 'Why did you come here? We don't need Uitlander teachers: we can manage the English ourselves.'

On such occasions I would humbly respond with my standard phrase: 'I didn't come here to teach you, but to learn from you!'

At this a grin would creep over the Boer's bearded face and he would stretch out his broad, calloused paw: '*Baie goed, jong. Allakragtie!*' [Very good, young man. Good gracious!]

All the volunteers who reasoned in the same manner earned the respect of the Transvaal people. There were quite a few such men. At Graspan, the Scandinavian corps, consisting of Swedes, Danes and Norwegians, perished to the last man when they tried to fight off a British bayonet attack with rifle butts and revolvers.[15] The Germans of Major Schiel fought like heroes at Elandslaagte when they were caught off-guard by French's Lancers. Count Zeppelin, a former Prussian cavalry officer, was another volunteer who died. A lady's man and a carouser, the kind of officer whom superiors describe in their evaluation reports as 'insufferable in peacetime and unusable in war', he was expelled from the service, and that is how he ended up among the German volunteers. At the battle of Elandslaagte, the wounded Zeppelin was surrounded by Lancers and the British officer told him to surrender. The Count's response was a lash of his whip across the face of his triumphant vanquisher. The next moment a dozen lances pierced his body.

The Krugersdorp district, to which the defence of the Tugela at Colenso fell, also earned an honourable reputation in battle. European volunteers who served in the Krugersdorp Commando only had to say they had fought under Field-Cornet Van Wyk for people to look at them with different eyes. ...

The *Krugersdorpsche Mannschaften* [Krugersdorp men], the Lichtenburg Commando and subsequently also the Johannesburg Mounted Police were as popular with the Boers as the 32nd demi-brigade had once been in *la Grande Armée*.[16] The Europeans who accidentally ended up in one of these famous units gradually developed from amateurs into true fighting partisans, shook off their parade-ground manners, became as one with the Boers, as gruff and unwelcoming as the latter may have appeared, appreciated them and were in turn appreciated and treated with kindness by the Boers.

One result of this changed attitude to foreign volunteers was a government order to grant them rights of citizenship of the Transvaal Republic as a reward. Kruger finally realised that the volunteers who fought under arms for the freedom and independence of the Transvaal were different from those Uitlander exploiters, merchants and rogues who had come flooding into the country after the discovery of gold and who actually caused all the trouble. Kruger proposed a bill to the Volksraad according to which every volunteer who swore an oath before the field-cornet of his district or a Pretoria magistrate would be granted citizenship rights in the free republic.[17]

To become the citizen of a republic with the right to vote and to choose, with a land allotment... How tempting it sounded, especially in the event of a successful outcome for the war. A fully fledged citizen of an independent republic, and not just any republic but the South African Republic!

During our stay in Pretoria, my comrades-in-arms took advantage of the government's offer; they sought out the Magistrate's Office and completed all the necessary formalities.[18] With one stroke of a pen, they became the owners of the fateful *stemrecht* [right to vote] that Chamberlain had been seeking since 1885 and that had served as the pretext for the war.

Diatroptov pestered me. 'What is up with you?' he asked. He had already forgotten his unexpected meeting with the 'secret political agent' and had returned to his former carefree air of a 'free-thinker'. 'What is brewing in that head of yours? Have mercy on me! Are you thinking of becoming an independent burgher? A republican? Just think! You can vote, maybe end up in parliament somehow, maybe even stand for election!'

'With time I might even become president,' I answered, deep in thought. 'No, the oath I gave De Souza in the parliament was enough; that was a soldier's oath. I was ashamed to refuse that oath, which asked if I was prepared to fight for the Boers. Becoming a citizen of the Transvaal Republic is a different matter. It would mean renouncing, forgetting everything that binds me to my distant country forever.'

Here, under the sultry sky of a foreign country, a new life is smiling at me. I am here at the very heart of an awe-inspiring and rivetingly terrifying struggle. Oh, to shake everything off and rush headlong into this maelstrom of human passions, anger and despair... God only favours the brave!

I remembered a warm day in May, the quiet rustling of our battle-worn regimental colours, and the murmur of a hundred voices repeating the words of the old Peter the Great oath after the priest: 'By sea... and by land, battles and in sieges... faithfully, not deceitfully... without sparing his life... as it behoves... a gallant and brave warrior.'

I remembered the abandoned cemetery. Age-old pine trees press around the collapsed fence. Grasshoppers chirr in the tall grass. A caressing breeze fills the air around me with the honeyed scent of buckwheat and wild rosemary... No, I will not trade the quicksand and the forests of my homeland, where the bones of my grandfathers and great-grandfathers lie, for the hills and oleander groves of the Transvaal.

As I mentioned earlier, we had been joined by Lieutenant Dreyer, a new volunteer from one of the infantry regiments of the Warsaw

Military District. He quickly won everybody's sympathy with his cheerful simplicity. He was forever laughing out loudly or singing some tune from an opera in his sonorous baritone. He left us in stitches with his stories of regimental life, or how he diddled his mummy out of 600 roubles for a trip to Paris, but instead of Paris ended up in Pretoria. It was only with Colonel Maximov that he somehow didn't get along. The two cautiously sidestepped each other on the stairs or in the corridors of the hotel.

'What happened between the two of you?' we asked him.

'Oh for goodness sake! He's a very confident man who can't do a thing wrong,' Dreyer responded. 'So the two of us are sitting all good and proper in the smoking room, that's now before you received your order, and he's telling me his whole biography. About Serbia, Kerim Pasha, the storming of Aleksinac, Đunis… I'm thinking to myself – now that's a hero! "So where were you on duty afterwards, in 1877?" I ask. "At Plevna or Shipka probably?" No, as it turns out he was somewhere in Romania, far away, at the very rearguard of operations, either as a way-station commander or a station commander. And he stayed like that until the Treaty of San Stefano.[19] Then he started telling me about the storming of Geok Tepe.'

'How could Colonel Maximov not have participated in the 1877–1878 war?'

'Beats me. He said it was because of the scheming of some high-ranking officials. Well, his Geok Tepe story was also full of fancy stuff. In the end I couldn't control myself any longer and started arguing with him, because I know the details of the assault from my old battalion commander who participated personally in the campaign and received a medal for it. Even then Maximov wasn't a combat officer, but only a Red Cross commissioner. At this point we got at each other's throats, until he fired off his last defence: "I would request you not to forget who you are! I would request you to remember that I am a staff officer, and you are just a mere lieutenant or something!" Nice fellow, heh? And in the Transvaal of all places that a volunteer, just like me, is reminding me of respect for ranks! Ha-ha-ha!'

To-re-a-dor… To-re-a-dor…?[20]

Ganetsky beamed as he listened to Dreyer's account of the skirmish between him and the colonel. Misunderstandings like these played right into his hands. The rumours about Maximov's mysterious political mission that had so startled the poor Diatroptov, and especially that last scene, had considerably reduced Maximov's chances of ever taking over command of the Russian corps in place of Ganetsky.

Maximov was not despondent, however. He somehow managed to acquire the trust of Transvaal government men, began paying visits to President Kruger without any trouble, became old Reitz's man, established relations with Steyn and no longer quarrelled with Ganetsky. For us, mere mortals, who could never even imagine of being so honoured as to drink tea with Kruger or Reitz, his activities seemed highly mysterious. A great ship requires deep waters, as the saying goes.

Just before our departure from Pretoria, we learnt that if Colonel Maximov failed to carry out the plan he had conceived here, he intended to travel to Glencoe and for the last time raise the question of electing him or Ganetsky as commander of the Russian corps, as by then we would have had enough time to come to our senses. We began to hurry up with our departure. It was time to say our farewells to the hotel's table d'hôte, and we were tired of the repetitive lunches, the sleek bellboys and the red-nosed, shaven faces of the gentlemen dining with us; all in all, we felt out of place here. We needed to get out of this place, where we bumped around every corner into contractors, sales agents, commission agents and other devotees of fishing in muddy waters.

Only the volunteers who were recovering from their wounds or sickness, or who were busy organising new units, felt fine here. A couple of these types became stuck in my memory. One of them, Jonkheer van der Neer from Holland, placed daily notices in the *Volksstem*, a government-sponsored newspaper, in which fervent appeals were made to all foreign volunteers to gather at the Union Club for the formation of a unit. With the modesty behoving a true hero, Van der Neer proposed himself as the commander.

Another fellow, whom I must proudly acknowledge as a compatriot, went so far in his modesty as to declare himself incapable of fighting any further, as he had been dangerously shell-shocked by a lyddite bomb fragment in his side. This Captain Kopeikin, who once had been the pride and joy of one of our infantry reserve regiments, obligingly displayed this battle relic to anyone who expressed an interest. And yet the fatal hole in his jauntily tilted hat suggested, somewhat incongruously, that his skull should at least have suffered to some extent. Our hero, without the least embarrassment, explained this misunderstanding away with a treatise concerning the peculiar, as yet little-studied trajectory of English dum-dum bullets, and to put a final end to this uninteresting topic, suggested a little game of *stuss*.[21] A familiar deck of cards appeared, bearing the stamp of an orphanage.

'Trumps!' 'I'll double my stakes again!' 'Triple it!' The ringing of shillings, the rustling of greasy pound notes. Jacks, diamonds, threes flashed. The players' eyes flared, their fingers trembled. The stakes grew higher and triple, new stakes were laid …

In the stuffy boarding-house room filled with exotic flowers, our gracious host provided us with the opportunity to relive again those thrilling, terrifying and yet immeasurably sweet sensations of gambling that we relentlessly used to indulge in on the 20th day of each month in the regimental assembly.

Mind you, our card games at the hospitable Arnoldov[22] were more of an innocent pastime; what was there to be had from us ragged Krugersdorpers? Later, when new aristocratic volunteers, Count Bobrinsky, Count Komarovsky and Cornet Biskupsky,[23] arrived in Pretoria, and when our gallant Arnoldov's admirers came to include some Jewish mercantile agents with fat wallets, the games took on more exalted, grandiose proportions. In the end, along with the defeat of the Transvaal Republic, candlesticks, tables and chairs were sent flying at our croupier with the bullet hole in his hat. The final act of that saga only played itself out at the Lourenço Marques police station.

Lieutenant G***no[24] of the mounted riflemen, a worthy representative of our ally France, also put down roots in a cosy and tastefully furnished room of the Grand Hotel. Every day I had the pleasure of seeing his courageous figure as he entered the common room with his spurs a-jingle. 'If you want to be handsome, join the hussars,' I recalled the words of the wise Prutkov,[25] but frankly speaking,

my interest was piqued not so much by G***no's stately comport-
ment (his profile bore a strong resemblance to caricatures of Paul
Déroulède) as by his female companion, a French lady, quick-eyed,
powdered, wearing an enormous hat with triumphantly fluttering
feathers. How had this *grisette* [young working woman] from the
Parisian boulevards ended up *chez les vaillants boers* [among the
brave Boers]?

At lunch she usually sat not far from my table. I could hear the
rustling of her silk skirts, inhale the provocative scent of her perfume,
and in those rare moments when she let her eyes fall on me amid the
crowd, I tried to catch her languid glance. The steak I was chewing
would get stuck in my throat whenever her long tinted lashes fluttered in a kind of perplexity as her gaze paused on me, as though she
were divining that I had been deprived of female companionship
for two whole months, apart from the occasional goat or antelope –
and this despite my diet of meat and the rugged life of a horseback
combatant!

I will end this series of scenes from the peaceful life of volunteers
away from the battlefield with another sketch. Among the foreign
military agents there was a Captain Demange of the French General
Staff, who had brought an orderly, a *brigadier* of a hussar regiment,
with him.[26] Demange departed for the Orange Free State front but
left his batman behind in Pretoria. The dashing hussar took advantage of the absence of his officer to don his *tenue de parade* [dress
uniform] – scarlet pantaloons and azure dolman[27] embroidered
with black cord and decorated with the golden chevrons of a non-
commissioned officer – and hitch his sabre, and thus went strolling
through the streets and gardens of Pretoria.

I saw him the first time in the parliament building where I had to
receive some orders for the squad. Grey-bearded Boers and ministry
officials thronged around the sprightly hussar, frantically trying to
make out every word uttered by the French 'military attaché' in his
broken German: 'I sent the captain to the Free State. I will soon receive his report and let your president know by cable, but for now,
keep going at it. Do not be despondent. France will not betray you!'

I could not contain myself, pushed my way to the hussar and slap-
ping him rather unceremoniously on the shoulder, interrupted the

self-styled military attaché with the words: '*Dites donc, mon brave, vous êtes de Gascogne, sans doute?*' [Tell me, old chap, are you perhaps from Gascony?]

The gallant hussar did not skip a beat, but with unparalleled aplomb took my hand away and declared with the most amiable smile that he would be happy to talk to me in half an hour, but that he now had '*des affaires très importantes*' [very important business]. The Boers seemed highly outraged at my brashness and familiar treatment of an official French representative.

Later I learnt that the deft *brigadier* had managed to persuade not only the respectable burghers of his political mission; he had also won the heart of one of the town beauties. It had taken two or three days to make her acquaintance, propose and obtain the consent of her gratified parents. But then thunder struck. Captain Demange suddenly returned to Pretoria. He was still on his way when he was informed that some new French military agent had arrived in the Transvaal. With fear and trepidation, the rakish hussar reported to his commander, received his well-earned punishment and, ruing with a heavy sigh the loss of a happiness so close within his reach, carefully packed his scarlet pantaloons and his blue dolman back in his trunk. Naturally, the marriage plans fell apart. The parents were furious to learn that the dashing French officer was none other than Captain Demange's baggage handler. As for the blue-eyed Boer maiden, when she accidentally ran into her beloved and saw him attired in the coarsest of trousers and a straw hat instead of red pantaloons and an embroidered cap, she almost fainted. The government officials who only a few days before had been at a loss as to how to address or attend to such an important personage, just threw up their hands with mouths agape.

◆

This episode was a harmless piece of vaudeville. A greater disappointment was to befall the Boers, however. News had reached Pretoria that one of the European monarchs on whom the Boers had, since the start of the war, pinned their most fervent hopes, Kaiser Wilhelm, had sent Queen Victoria a heartfelt congratulatory telegram on the occasion of the latest British victories, the capture of Cronjé and the relief of Ladysmith. The kings of Portugal and Italy immediately followed his example. The London press was jubilant: it was now clear that the sympathies of the world were on the side of the nation who would spare no sacrifices to bring enlightenment to the dirty, uncivilised Boers, and make all the benefits of 'progress and civilisation' available to them.

The 'uncultured, dirty Boers' – who incidentally had won a gold medal at the 1900 Paris exhibition[28] for their rational organisation of public education – were seriously crestfallen. Everyone still remembered the telegram President Kruger had received [from Kaiser Wilhelm] in 1896 on the occasion of their defeat of the rapacious Jameson Raid. The Germans were especially favoured in the Transvaal. On Emperor Wilhelm's birthday, a special service attended by the president and members of the Volksraad was held in Pretoria's main church. From the first day of the war, talk had been that armed intervention by the Germans was just a matter of time, but suddenly the Emperor remembered the ties of kinship that bound him to Queen Victoria, changed his policy and turned his back on the unfortunate Boers who had looked upon him as their defender. Newspapers containing the text of the telegram were passed from hand to hand and everywhere – in hotels, on the streets and in government agencies – it created a sensation of dumbfoundedness.

◆

Nonetheless, the Boers had not yet abandoned all hope of armed intervention, or at least of mediation by the great European powers.

At a conference between presidents Kruger and Steyn (Colonel Maximov was one of the few selected invitees), it was decided to make a new attempt in this direction. Dr Leyds, the representative of the Transvaal Republic's interests in Europe, had still not achieved any positive results; all his activities amounted to fruitless trips to the European capitals and conversations with journalists. It was clearly necessary to find another way of drawing the foreign powers' attention to the critical situation in the South African Republic.

Then Colonel Maximov came forward with his plan, which

consisted of sending a special embassy, with the widest possible powers, to Europe. Thanks to Maximov's eloquence and energy, his plan met with general approval.[29] The leaders of the Boer nation knew that their heroic six-month struggle for freedom and independence was nearing its inevitable end, and that they did not have enough strength to resist the enemy, who were already flooding the Free State with their troops. They were unable and unwilling to accept the thought that the highly cultured and humane nations of Europe would ignore the cries of bleeding victims, or that the rulers of these nations, who had millions of bayonets and cannons at their disposal, would not put an end to this merciless slaughter of one nation by another by just speaking a single word.

The choice of the presidents fell on Fischer, Wolmarans and Wesselman, men well known throughout the Transvaal.[30] Intelligent, ardent patriots who had held prominent positions of public office before the war, they unslung their bandoliers and rifles, bade their fatherland farewell and set off on a journey around the world to seek protection and justice from the high and mighty.

The members of the mission were, of course, provided with filthy lucre. For all their naivety, the Boers understood perfectly well that even if they went 'in search across the world for but a nook where injured sense can mend', they required fat wallets more than anything.

The delegation, bearing with them universal wishes for their safe return, departed for Lourenço Marques in early March 1900. The results of their journey are known, of course, to all readers from the newspapers ...[31]

But the Boers, incorrigible idealists that they are, did not doubt back then that the delegation would obtain a veto from one or more of the European powers, and that such a veto would stall the further advance of the British and force them to make peace on honourable terms. Even Kaiser Wilhelm's telegram did not seem so portentous to them any longer. 'Our cause is right before God and men; they will not forsake us now, when we are begging them for help.'

The poor Boers! They did not even suspect that European society was fully immersed in crude materialism and would callously abandon them to their fate. It had sent them a couple of hundred madcaps, organised charitable collections for the Boers during concerts and theatre performances, and had vilified Chamberlain and John Bull in the caricatures of their satirical magazines, but further than that it could not go.

And indeed, what circumstance could impel any of the continental powers to intervene in England's domestic dispute with the South African republics? Politics should not be driven by impulses of sentimentality. That fabled time when Christian kings mustered troops and marched off to unknown countries to liberate the Holy Sepulchre is a thing of the past. But as little trust as the Boers could place in diplomacy, which under different conditions might willingly have taken advantage of Great Britain's constrained position and at least have provided some indirect aid to the Transvaal, they could count even less on the sympathies of the masses, which by itself would never have been capable of providing positive results.

What, in essence, had attracted the sympathies of the 'average' educated man to the cause of the Boers? To be honest, it was not only because he experienced a feeling of indignation at the violence, and not only because he recognised and enjoyed the aesthetics of a struggle for freedom and independence, but more likely as a result of the breathtaking, titillating spectacle of war unfolding before him, just as at a bullfight where one has to place a bet on either side. And the spectacle of a bloody war is excruciating and yet so agreeable to observe that we fret and tremble as if experiencing the sensations of war for ourselves. The Dreyfus affair had become boring, and the Anglo-Boer War introduced some pleasant variety to everyone's newspaper reading.

I think it was in *Faust* where Goethe pointed at this trait of human nature when he depicted a complacent philistine reading the papers in order to aid his digestion:

> *Wenn hinten, weit in der Türkei,*
> *die Völker aufeinander schlagen!*

> [When down in Turkey, far away, / The foreign people are a-fighting][32]

◆

The Boers possessed a more effective means than all the appeals, diplomatic notes and cries for help to make Europe pay more heed to the outcome of the war. In the event that the English invaded the Transvaal, they could blow up all the mines of the Witwatersrand. Economic considerations are the strongest lever in politics, and the majority of the capital stolen through shares in the gold mines of South Africa belonged to the French, Germans and Americans, and not to the British. The mere threat of such an action would have been enough to trigger the Great Powers to intervene. The Boers knew about this but reasoned as follows: if we were to destroy the mines, whose equipment cost foreign capitalists millions, that would lead to a financial crisis in all of Europe, the delegation would meet with a cold reception and be forced to return empty-handed. Fear of 'What will Europe say?' played a significant role in the activities of the Boer government.

On the whole, and even in the most critical moments of the war, the Boers treated the property of not only private individuals but also the enemy with a chivalrous generosity that sometimes bordered on inexcusable naivety.

Just take the humanity with which the government treated the 3 000 British prisoners of war held at Wonderfontein, north of Pretoria. The prisoners were amply housed in tents, some of them in wooden barracks. Food (meat, fresh or canned, two kilograms of wheat bread, jam, tea, sugar and coffee) was handed out in abundance.[33] Boer commissioners oversaw the distribution of the food, which was then handed out among the prisoners by delegated mess officers enlisted from among the English themselves. The entire camp was fenced in by barbed wire and guarded by a small detachment of the Pretoria police.

Captured officers, whose number at the time of my stay in Pretoria did not exceed 70, were held in the city itself, in the Model School building. Of course, they enjoyed much better amenities and comforts than the lower ranks. À la carte dinners, musical instruments – all this was magnanimously provided to them by the government, while Boer commandos themselves often lacked the bare essentials.

The prisoners were in tremendous spirits; they had escaped all the deprivations and hardships of camp life and felt splendid under the protection of the policemen in their white helmets, and with a sense of fulfilled duty spent entire days at their beloved lawn tennis, leaving it to their happier compatriots to engage in the difficult task of coping with those 'bloody fools and buggers', the despicable Boers, and of liberating them from their captivity.

During all the time that the prisoners were held in Pretoria, there was only one escape, not of the lower ranks, who balked at the very thought of exchanging their well-fed, indolent life at Wonderfontein for the turmoil of war, but of two officers from the poorly guarded Model School premises.[34]

◆

At long last, the memorable day arrived when the Russian corps would be leaving Pretoria.

We were to take the evening train, with the difference that additional wagons for the horses and heavy equipment of the unit were to be attached to it, at Ganetsky's request. It must be said that the management and all the employees of the Zuid-Afrikaansche Spoorwegmaatschappij operated with the utmost dedication and consistency throughout the war and right up to the final occupation of the country by the British. This was aided, firstly, by the fact that the sympathies of the administration and employees, almost exclusively Dutch, lay entirely on the side of the Boer government; and, secondly, by the good working condition of the equipment. Finally, and importantly, there was almost never a palpable shortage of rolling stock; the Boer units retreating by rail from Natal and the Free State always got the locomotives and wagons out in time. At the Pretoria station, locomotives bearing the names of 'Queen Victoria', 'Prince Albert' and 'Hercules Robinson' (captured by the Boers in the Cape Colony and Natal) manoeuvred alongside locomotives from the Dutch company: 'President Steyn', 'Pretorius', 'Piet Maritz', 'Vryheid' and others.

The important services rendered to the Boer government by the Transvaal railway, which belonged to a private Dutch company, subsequently served as a welcome pretext for Lord Roberts to confiscate the railways and declare them the property of the British government without any compensation.

◆

Loading the horses and effects into the wagons was no easy task. Our black servants worked reluctantly and clumsily; we could not reckon on the assistance of the railway employees, and had to roll the heavy wagons onto the platforms and drive the mules and horses into the carriages ourselves. Dealing with the mules in particular created a terrible fuss: these stubborn creatures kicked, thrashed, broke free and ran between the rails of the station with their tails in the air. It took quite a while to chase them back into position.

At last the job was complete, the wagons were hitched to the train and we returned to the passenger station, where an extraordinary number of people had turned out that evening. Around 20 Boers from Pretoria whose *verlof* [leave] had come to an end were heading for the front with us, as was the newly formed American corps, consisting of Dutch and Irish. These volunteers had, according to American custom, managed to get quite drunk and were in high spirits. The Ariston organette standing in the canteen had already played 'Yankee Doodle' for the hundredth time, but the volunteers could still not get enough. Finally, a pin cracked with an awful screeching sound, and then the Americans demanded a new cylinder with 'Het Volkslied'.[35] There was no such cylinder, and the bewildered pantryman accidentally slipped in another cylinder with the title 'Rule, Britannia!'

'Damn that! Damn that!' the Americans roared, and the poor cylinder was smashed to smithereens.

The children seeing their fathers off clutched their mothers' skirts, their blue eyes wide open, and stared at them in fear. There was a big contrast between the taciturn, gloomy-looking Boers surrounded by their families and children, and the noisy, drunken Uitlander volunteers. For extra show, some of them had donned cavalry sabres they had picked up who knows where. A red-haired, unkempt man who could hardly stand on his feet waved a Stars and Stripes and tried in vain to bawl out the popular Boer song:

'Kent gij dat volk vol heldenmoed ...' [Do you know the folk full of heroism ...?][36]

But nobody joined in. Close by, I could hear muffled sobs, convulsive weeping and a subdued male voice. I turned around and saw a group of people standing in the light of an electric lantern. A young Boer, dressed in city clothes but with a bandolier slung over his shoulder, was apparently trying to calm down a crying woman. She clung to him, buried her head in his chest and sobbed uncontrollably, bitterly, shuddering with all her body. A boy and girl, dressed as neat as pins, stood sedately to the side and held the father's rifle (the boy) and his water flask (the girl). The children did not seem very sad at their father's departure; this was not the first time they were seeing him off and they expected him to return soon with toys – shiny English bullets – and many, many funny stories to tell. The mother, who was with child, was unable and unwilling to calm down; her heart could sense that she was seeing her husband for the last time, that he would not return to her again, but maimed by an enemy bullet would perish far away in the mountains of Natal. And she would be left alone with the defenceless children.

My heart became heavy, unspeakably heavy. I pushed my way through the crowd of shouting and clamouring people, drunken volunteers, black porters and grim-faced Boers and found myself at the very end of the platform. Slowly our steam locomotive puffed past me, giving off shrill whistles as it spewed out clouds of fiery smoke: the buffers thudded desolately, the couplings clanked and everything was quiet again. I looked up. A full moon shone high in the sky above the station, above the city and above the dark hills in the distance. Light whisps of cloud glided across its face like a dim, shimmering shadow. Each time a cloud would light up brightly, then fade away and disappear into the dark sky.

And I remembered that the same mysterious, cold light of the moon had shone over fabled Troy, and over the helmets and swords of Alexander the Great. Hannibal's and Caesar's legionaries had glimmered in rays of that very same light. The moon had stared with the same cold indifference at the fires engulfing the Eternal City and the ashes of the great cities of antiquity. For as long as the world has existed, that silvery disc has heard the groans and cries, curses and sobs of people and been looked upon by the fading eyes of the dying. Mighty kingdoms arose, great cities were built and then everything was destroyed again until the last traces of glory and grandeur were scattered into ashes. One age followed another, and all of that ungraspable, incomprehensible vastness now seems a single, fleeting dream while people remain willing to suffer and struggle, as still the moon casts its light on this ant hill of human malice, longing and despair. Why live? Why struggle?

'And where have you been hiding? Not good at all! I told you I'd be at the station. Please come with me! There is a nice surprise for you!'

'What? Huh? Isaac Petrovich!'

Before me stood the highly esteemed Isaac Petrovich Abrahamson, one of those kindly and enlightened Jews, a millionaire with whom I had made my acquaintance in January during my first visit to Pretoria. He had arrived here from Russia with a samovar, his wife and 15 roubles in his pocket, but now, after living in the Transvaal for 20 years, he was the owner of seven-storey buildings and shops in Johannesburg. He regarded the Russian volunteers like a true patriot to his homeland, of which, despite the Pale of Settlement,[37] he had retained the fondest memories. He had tried to help us wherever he could, and his only regret was that he could not entertain us at his home in Johannesburg.

Isaac Petrovich grabbed me unceremoniously by the arm and we went into one of the station rooms together. I was blinded at first by the sudden passing from semi-darkness into the bright light of electric bulbs.

'*Voyons!* [Let's see!] Show me your volunteer!' It was the sing-song voice of a woman.

I dare say that if a lyddite bomb had suddenly burst through the ceiling and exploded with a deafening crack right under my nose I would not have been at such a loss as I was then. Before me stood a voluptuous woman with eyes that laughed provocatively and a light down above her upper lip.

'Monsieur Abrahamson told me a lot about you. I wish to make your acquaintance. Are you off to that unbearable war again?'

I blushed, turned pale, speechless.

She continued talking, walked up close to me and suddenly knocked my pince-nez off and burst out into raucous laughter, revealing a row of teeth as white as pearls.

'*Ah, comme c'est drôle* [Ah, how funny that is], a Boer hat with a pince-nez! You're better off without those silly pieces of glass! And what a tiny moustache you have! You're still a boy!'

In my confusion I muttered something like: 'Madame… mademoiselle … *je dois partir* [I must leave] …'

'Ta, ta, ta! *Mon petit pion-pion!* [My little boy!] There's still half an hour before the train leaves. You won't miss it! *Tenez!* [Take it!]

The French woman took out a miniature watch and showed me a gold-rimmed velvet locket converted into a bracelet charm.

'Do you recognise it?'

I recognised it. It was a medallion taken from the dead officer after the battle of Spion Kop.

The Boer who had plundered the corpse had presented it to me, and I, touched by the dinner Abrahamson had given me and my comrades a few days earlier, had given him the medallion as a keepsake.

'I hope you do not mind, you bloodsucker, that I have the medallion now?'

'*Mais, je suis enchanté,*' [Well, I'm delighted] I stammered.

'Anshante, anshante!' she mocked my pronunciation. 'Sit down! Let's have a chat!'

I found myself sitting beside her on the oilskin couch of the station room. Abrahamson had disappeared somewhere. The Frenchwoman had by now quite taken possession of me and kept chatting incessantly. I stared at her, unable to take my eyes off her; I had quite forgotten that my comrades were waiting for me, that the train would be leaving any minute now. It felt as if I had known this woman for a long time already, that I was seeing the incarnation of my hazy reveries and dreams before me. Why had she come to this meeting? Why was she caressing me? There was something intoxicating, something thrilling my entire soul and all my thoughts in the sound of her voice, in the curves of her body, in the enchantment of her smile and in the mischievous gleam of her eyes.

All of a sudden she leaned close, so close, to me, that I could feel the silky curls of her hair touching my flushed face, and said in a quiet voice: 'I feel sorry for you. Leave this nasty war! You're just like a schoolboy who's read too much Mayne Reid. It's actually quite funny! Come to Johannesburg, to Abrahamson. Do you hear me?'

There was no time to answer.

Diatroptov, out of breath and agitated, burst into the room.

'There you are! We searched the whole station! Even sent for you at the hotel. Pardon!' Only now did he notice the lady and gallantly bowed and scraped.

'Ganetsky is waiting for you. The train is leaving. Come quickly!'

The Siren had guessed from my bewildered look that I was required 'on business'. She rose and began saying her goodbyes to me.

'Well, so be it. Go off to your Boers. But I'm waiting for you in Johannesburg! Do you hear me?'

At the station Ganetsky pounced on me.

'Gentlemen, all hell has broken loose! The blacks have scattered in all directions. Kaplan and the Italian have vanished into thin air. The mules and horses need feeding, and to cap it you've disappeared. My head is spinning! When is this going to end?'

We somehow managed to sort things out. Blanchetti and Kaplan appeared just before the train's departure, both quite tipsy and in the company of some fishy-looking friends.

We found the blacks and accommodated them on the platform with the wagons. We fed the horses and mules by pouring some maize right onto the floors of their wagons. We took our places in the passenger carriages, in the first-class compartment, where we had dragged in our saddles and ammunition. Everything was cramped and uncomfortable. The compartment reeked of tobacco smoke. The Americans hoarsely cried out their 'Hip hip hurrahs' as they took their leave of the public, who roared back the same to them in reply. The engine driver blew the whistle repeatedly to hurry the late passengers on. On top of this, Kaplan, our brave dragoon, had got into a fight with a drunken Irishman in the carriage aisle. The seats rattled and broken windowpanes rang as they grabbed each other by the throat and tussled on the floor. The fellows barely managed to pull them apart and get them to cool down. At last the train started moving and rattled along the tracks.

I huddled up in a dark corner of the train. All these wild, discordant sounds came to me as if from afar, like the distant, indistinct rumble of the surf.

I was still very much under the influence of that unexpected encounter. I could still hear the music of her voice in my imagination, could still picture her gaze so filled with the promise of tenderness, bliss and happiness.

'Hey, you lustful insect! I had a devil of a time finding you!' I heard the voice of Lieutenant Dreyer, and he stepped over the people stretched out on the floor towards me. 'Here's a basket of fruit from Abrahamson. You'd better help yourself while you can, or I'll have gobbled them all up by the morning. So was the Frenchwoman pretty? She's probably an ex-singer from the Moulin Rouge in Paris? They say there are a lot of them in Johannesburg.'

'Don't ruin my illusions!' I pleaded, pushed the fruit basket away and surrendered myself to my dreams again.

◆

This is the end of Yevgeny Avgustus's memoir of the South African War. The last instalment appeared in print in June 1902.

Notes

[1] Ivan Gringof, a Saratov civil engineer of Lithuanian extraction.

[2] The author of the article not only points to the possible Jewish ancestry of Gringof but also implies that he could be a fraud. It was a well-known turn of phrase from the high-school textbook of Russian history by Professor Nikolay Ustryalov (1805–1870). Commenting on the origin of False Dmitry II (?–1610), Ustryalov suggested that the pretender to the Russian throne was 'most probably, a Polish agent and pretty well a yid'; see Ustryalov, NG, *Russkaya istoriya do 1855 goda, v dvuh chastyah*. Petrozavodsk: Folium, 1997, p 294.

[3] Lieutenant Boris Strolman (1872–1900), a Russian naval officer, continued to fight with the Boers after the fall of Pretoria. He was killed in action near Lindley in July 1900. *Anglo-burskaya voyna 1899–1902 godov…* Vol 8 (2012), pp 277–282.

[4] Second Captain (*shtabs-rotmistr*) Count Georgy Komarovsky (1865–?), a Russian cavalry officer. On his return from South Africa, he took part in the crushing of the Boxers in Manchuria (1900–1901) and in the Russo-Japanese War (1904–1905). *Anglo-burskaya voyna 1899–1902 godov…* Vol 8 (2012), pp 277–282.

5   Second Lieutenant *(podporuchik)* Ivan Nikitin, aged 28, was wounded in action at Doornkop, near Johannesburg. *Anglo-burskaya voyna 1899–1902 godov...* Vol 8 (2012), pp 277–282.

6   Major General Ralph Arthur Penrhyn Clements (1855–1909) commanded the 12th Brigade of the 6th Division, which took Colesberg on 28 February 1900. General Hendrik Jacobus Schoeman (1840–1901) eventually surrendered to the British in July 1900.

7   The Battle of Poplar Grove, which took place after the surrender of General Cronjé.

8   General Alexander Puzyrevsky (1844–1904), a Russian military historian. He was Assistant Commander of the Warsaw Military District, where Avgustus's regiment was based.

9   Gerard Marie Johan van Dam (1855–1940), a Dutch immigrant, was the leader of the Johannesburg Police Commando.

10 The British captured Bloemfontein on 13 March, Johannesburg on 31 May and Pretoria on 5 June 1900.

11 Satirical magazines from France and Russia.

12 An episode from the Free State campaign (a note by Avgustus).

13 In 1907, Russia and Britain became allies. Russian troops almost reached the Persian Gulf after their advance through Transcaucasia during the First World War. In 1917, Russia became a republic, and the imperial dream of having a port in Persia remained unachieved.

14 An expression attributed to General Mikhail Skobelev. In 1876, as the governor of the Fergana Oblast in the newly conquered part of Turkestan, the Russian general proposed to occupy Afghanistan, establish relations with Indians who were discontented with the British rule, organise the inhabitants of Central Asia into irregular cavalry units and launch an all-out assault on India; see Lebedev, VL, *'V Indiyu': Voyenno-statistichesky i strategichesky ocherk. Proyekt budushchego pokhoda.* Saint Petersburg, 1898, p 10.

15 The Scandinavian corps was wiped out at Magersfontein on 11 December 1899, not at Graspan on 25 November 1899.

16 The army commanded by Napoleon Bonaparte during the Napoleonic Wars (1803–1815).

17 Normally, applicants took an oath renouncing their allegiance 'to any other state or prince' and waited for five years to get their full burgher rights. However, foreign volunteers could acquire full burgher rights with the Letters of Naturalisation for their service to the South African Republic.

18 The following Russian volunteers used this opportunity: Alexey Diatroptov, Fyodor Guchkov, Vasily Nikitin, Leo Pokrowsky and Vasily Ruckert; see *Subjects of European nations (other than British subjects) who have taken full burgher rights under the Transvaal Government since the commencement of war: arranged under their different nationalities.* Pretoria, 1900, p 14.

19 The 1878 treaty that ended the Russo-Turkish War.

20 The refrain from the 'Bullfighter Song' in the opera *Carmen*, composed by Georges Bizet (1875).

21 A popular card game.

22 Second Lieutenant Fyodor Arnoldov (1876–?) was wounded during the Battle of Spion Kop. *Anglo-burskaya voyna 1899–1902 godov...* Vol 8 (2012), pp 277–282.

23 Count Pavel Bobrinsky, a landowner from the Tambov Governorate, was on

the staff of the Russian Red Cross ambulance. Cornet Biskupsky had served in a Russian dragoon regiment. *Anglo-burskaya voyna 1899–1902 godov ...* Vol 8 (2012), pp 277–282.

24 Lieutenant Ernest Galopaud.

25 A fictional writer invented by Aleksey Tolstoy with Alexey, Vladimir and Alexander Zhemchuzhnikov. The authors produced works of fiction using this pen name in the 1850s and 1860s.

26 Captain Marie-Georges Demange (1860–1941), a French military attaché with the republican armies. He was accompanied by an adjutant and interpreter, Lieutenant Roger Raoul-Duval; see De Jong, C, 'Reports of neutral military observers on the Anglo-Boer War 1899-1902', *Scientia Militaria: South African Journal of Military Studies*, 1976, vol 6, no 1, pp 52–53.

27 A short hussar jacket decorated with passementerie.

28 The 1900 Paris Exposition.

29 Maximov had an audience with President Marthinus Theunis Steyn in Bloemfontein on 4 March. According to Maximov's diary, the Russian officer convinced him that Russia, France and Germany might intervene on behalf of the Boers. He suggested that the republican governments ask the Russian Tsar, as the initiator of the Hague Conference, to defend their rights to independence and self-defence. When, a few days later, the governments of the South African Republic and the Orange Free State decided to send a joint diplomatic delegation to Europe and the United States, Maximov believed that it was a result of his conversation with Steyn. *Anglo-burskaya voyna 1899–1902 godov ...* Vol 6 (2012), pp 6–10.

30 Abraham Fischer (1850–1913), member of the Executive Council of the Orange Free State; Andries Daniel Wynand Wolmarans (1857–1928), member of the Executive Council of the South African Republic; Cornelius Hermanus Wessels (1851–1924), president of the Volksraad of the Orange Free State.

31 None of the Great Powers intervened in the conflict on behalf of the Boer republics.

32 Translated by Bayard Taylor.

33 The prisoner-of-war-camp north of Pretoria was not at Wonderfontein but at Waterval. The food given to the British prisoners was not of such a high standard as Avgustus claims, and there were many complaints.

34 Captain Haldane, Lieutenant le Mesurier and Sergeant Brockie escaped from the Waterval camp on 16 March 1900. More notably, Winston Churchill had escaped earlier, on the night of 15 December 1899.

35 'Die Volkslied van Transvaal', the national anthem of the South African Republic.

36 The first line of 'Die Volkslied'.

37 The western region where permanent residency by Jews was allowed in Imperial Russia.

A soldier's life – Yevgeny Avgustus
(1874–1914)

◆

Avgustus's memoir ends rather abruptly with the leadership crisis in the Russian corps and the departure of this unit for Natal. It appears that the available text was intended to be the first volume of his war memoir. A copy of his book at the Russian State Library in Moscow contains an inscription 'Part I' in Avgustus's handwriting. However, the manuscript has not been found, and it is unknown if he ever finished his account.

◆

In the Russian corps

The unit was formed in March by Avgustus and his compatriots on the republican side. Their commandant, Alexey Ganetsky, was 'a well-known personage' in Russian society.[1] In the early 1890s, he left active duty as a dragoon officer in a Guards regiment to become an assistant to the Minister of War. A son of an illustrious general, Ganetsky married a rich divorcee and rebuilt the Sandunovsky Baths as a palatial structure for the business and cultural elite of Moscow with state-of-the-art equipment and 400-strong personnel. The Russian and the European press covered his departure for Africa to 'place his sword at General Joubert's service'.[2]

The other contender for the leadership of the newly formed Russian corps was Lieutenant Colonel Yevgeny Maximov, who claimed that he deserved to be in charge of the unit more than the upstart second captain. During the South African War, the 50-year-old Maximov was the most senior Russian volunteer in terms of age and military rank. A veteran of the Herzegovina uprising, the Serbian-Turkish and Russo-Turkish wars and the Russian conquest of Turkestan, he had broad experience in guerrilla warfare and commanding volunteer units.[3] The concept of a Russian corps was familiar to him from the Balkans, where most such units were multi-ethnic, with Russians often occupying most of the officers' positions.

Maximov went to the Transvaal as an observer and war correspondent. With his travel expenses met by the Russian Ministry of War, Maximov sent his reports from the republics to the General Staff in Saint Petersburg. He probably had been given a secret assignment by the ministry.[4]

In late February 1900, Maximov and Ganetsky began to organise a Russian corps in Pretoria to conduct raids behind enemy lines. Ganetsky seemed to be willing to become his lieutenant but later took the initiative, bypassing the lieutenant colonel. In early March, Ganetsky travelled to Glencoe, where Commander-General Piet Joubert had established his headquarters after the retreat from Ladysmith. Avgustus and other Russian volunteers also gathered in that town, and Ganetsky tried to recruit them. Although he had not yet participated in the war, he was elected to be commandant of the newly founded Russian corps as a senior officer among his compatriots at Glencoe and the idea's originator.

When members of the newly formed corps went to Pretoria, they met Maximov, who confronted Ganetsky in front of his men and demanded that the second captain relinquish command of the unit in his favour. However, the Russian volunteers backed their elected leader.

Maximov had not yet had an opportunity to prove his ability to lead his men on the battlefield in South Africa. He was known there as a reporter for a Russian newspaper (his official status) and as a good shot. This was not enough to persuade his compatriots who had taken part in some of the bloodiest battles of the war that he should replace Ganetsky. Besides, the Russians found out that Maximov had been a policeman. Indeed, he was made lieutenant colonel while serving in the Special Corps of Gendarmes. This and his close relations with Boer leaders suggested that he was on a mission from the Russian government. Members of the Russian corps believed that Maximov was spying on his compatriots, but they were probably wrong because he had resigned from the security police 16 years earlier.[5] Yet Maximov had no chance of becoming the leader of the Russian corps: its members resented the prospect of being commanded by an 'undercover agent'. Avgustus's memoir ends with the departure of the Russian corps for Natal. Soon after their arrival, on 17 or 18 March, Maximov also went to Glencoe, tried to reason with them and was rejected again. The matter seemed to be settled.

The Russians and the demise of the international legion

The Russian corps reconnoitred between the British patrols and the Sundays River, north of Ladysmith.[6] They did not take part in major engagements with the enemy because the unit was transferred to the southern front before the burghers began their offensive from Glencoe. In late March, the new commander-in-chief, General Louis Botha, ordered the Russian corps to proceed to Kroonstad, 500 km west of Glencoe, where units of foreign volunteers were to be incorporated into an international legion. Kroonstad became the new seat of the Orange Free State government after the surrender of Bloemfontein.

Botha had urged commanders of foreign volunteer units to organise and elect a leader who would direct and coordinate their missions. However, the commanders preferred to remain autonomous. At the historic council of war of 17 March 1900, George de Villebois-Mareuil, a retired French colonel and veteran of European and colonial wars, was authorised to set up and command a formation that would encompass the various foreign volunteers and units on the Boer side. He was also given the rank of general in the republican forces.

On 23 March, De Villebois met Maximov, the second most senior foreign officer with the burghers, and invited the lieutenant colonel to be his second-in-command.[7] Maximov accepted the proposal: the new position matched his ambition and experience. By the time the Russian corps reached Kroonstad, De Villebois had entrusted his international legion to the deputy and departed with his trusted men to carry out raids near Kimberley.

Most legionnaires did not see Maximov as an inspirational leader, and his position was precarious. His credibility rested on the French general's confidence. Republican politicians valued his opinion, regarding him as an emissary of the Russian government. However, without combat experience in the war, Maximov had yet to earn the respect of Boer generals and his own subordinates.

The Russian corps refused to join the international legion: they had not changed their minds about Maximov and did not want to follow his orders. Their disrespect was imparted to other foreign volunteers, bolstering opposition to De Villebois's deputy. The Russians spread rumours about Maximov that he was unable to dispel, having no one to vouch for him. A French volunteer recounted that Maximov's compatriots 'could not pardon his position as a police officer and even professed a certain contempt for him'.[8] Their mistrust reinforced the prejudice against him in the legion. Commandants of other volunteer units, who viewed Maximov as an unnecessary intermediary between themselves and De Villebois, did not rush to dispel these rumours.

The defiant Russian corps put itself at the disposal of General Philip Botha south of Brandfort. New Russian volunteers augmented their ranks: Vladimir Roubanov and Vladimir Semyonov, graduates of the Saint Petersburg Institute of Civil Engineers, and second lieutenants Ivan Nikitin and Prince Mikhail Yengalichev. The size of the unit in April 1900 was roughly 25–30 members.

Maximov was unable to resolve conflicts among his subordinates in Kroonstad and moved his units southwards. After De Villebois was killed by the British at the Battle of Boshof on 5 April, resistance to Maximov grew. The Russian officer remained commandant of the international legion for just a few more days. Since no other foreigner seemed to have the backing of most volunteers, Maximov was superseded by a Boer officer, General Koos de la Rey's brother. By 13 April, when th e new leader was appointed, the legion had practically broken up. Only the Dutch corps, comparable in size to the Russian corps, remained under Maximov's command.[9]

The Russian corps disbands

Until late April, the Russian corps camped south of Brandfort, carrying out raids and reconnaissance in the direction of Bloemfontein in coordination with General Philip Botha. Michael Davitt, an Irish politician and war correspondent on the Boer side, commented on the work of Russian scouts in that area: 'On one occasion, three of them actually penetrated into the British lines near Bloemfontein and returned with a most accurate plan of Roberts' great encampment near the Free State capital. Philip Botha, who was himself an ideal chief of scouts and Christian de Wet's right-hand man during his most successful enterprises in the Free State, had a very high opinion of his Russian pupils and placed great confidence in their reports.'[10]

The Russian unit remained south of Brandfort for nearly a month. Members of the corps recounted that, despite Ganetsky's eagerness to engage the British, they spent most of their time in idleness. They blamed it on Botha's 'indecisiveness'.[11] The republican leaders were still recovering from the shock of the British victory at Paardeberg, the relief of Kimberley and Ladysmith, and the abandonment of the Free State capital. The enemy was not spoiling for a fight either: after the capture of Bloemfontein, the British army stalled because of a shortage of supplies and an outbreak of enteric fever.

In late April, Ganetsky ordered his men to move to the western front, towards Fourteen Streams, where intermittent fighting was taking place. Ironically, once the Russian corps left the Free State, skirmishes with the British intensified, which resulted in serious hostilities. When Ganetsky and his men reached Johannesburg, he read his own obituary in a newspaper: it was announced that the Russian officer had been killed in action on 30 April.[12] Evidently, the journalists had confused Ganetsky with Maximov, who displayed dauntless courage and sustained severe wounds when the Dutch corps under his command held the Tobaberg Hill, defending the road to the burgher position at Houtnek. It was the highlight of the Russian officer's two-month career with the Boer forces. Several commandos elected him as general. Yet it turned out to be his last battle on the republican side. Being no longer fit for active service because of his injuries, Maximov had to relinquish command of his unit and returned to Russia to recuperate.

'Captain Towse at Mount Thaba 1900' by Stanley Berkeley. The man being shot is Russian Colonel Yevgeny Maximov (MuseumAfrica).

In Pretoria and Johannesburg, the Russian corps obtained equipment and ammunition, but their morale was so low that their own men stole their horses. Meanwhile, on 3 May, the British resumed their advance and captured Brandfort. The Russians were ordered to return and help delay the progress of the British troops.[13] At that point, the unit disbanded because of a disagreement between the commandant and his men. Ganetsky and Shulzhenko returned

227

to the Free State. Avgustus, Diatroptov, Kravchenko, Nikitin and Yengalichev took a train and proceeded westwards.

Near Christiana, about 50 km from Fourteen Streams, they met the retreating Krugersdorp Commando, which was being pursued by the British troops. Four Russian volunteers joined them and headed back to the Witwatersrand. However, Avgustus did not enlist in his old commando, with whom he had fought in Natal two months before. Instead, he became a member of the Johannesburg Police Commando under a Dutch-born officer, Gerard Marie Johan van Dam.[14]

The last months in South Africa

Like other Russian volunteers, Avgustus spoke very basic Dutch. He probably often had trouble communicating with burghers, which was annoying in the camp and dangerous on the battlefield. In their memoirs, Russians seldom mentioned their Boer brothers-in-arms by name, unless those were officers, who apparently could keep up a conversation with them in German or French.

Avgustus was not going to die for the republican cause. It was not his struggle. He came to South Africa to escape from the drills, the drinking, the waiting for his military district to justify its being called an 'advanced theatre'. Avgustus wanted to study war and the future enemy, and to return home to apply his experience in conflicts that Russia was bound to come into. He was certain that those conflicts would not take place in South Africa, where Russia had no political or economic interests.

But he remembered how, together with burgher fighters, he 'suffered from cold, hunger and hardship at camp and in battle, and I learnt to appreciate and love those seemingly austere and stand-offish people, who are hearty and unselfish in the extreme. I could not help being surprised by their courage, calmness and endurance in dangerous situations, their almost fatalistic indifference to facing death … I saw how boys aged ten or twelve calmly and unhurriedly, like old gunners, installed a shrapnel shell fuse and aimed the gun at the yellowish lines of the English infantry in the distance. I saw Boer women who, disregarding the hail of splinters and the buzzing of bullets, brought flasks with cold spring water, meat and rusks to us in the trenches.'[15]

The Russian officer realised that the burghers would soon turn to guerrilla tactics, which had little to teach him about conventional fighting. After the resounding defeats inflicted by the British on all fronts, burgher units were retreating steadily, and there was little hope of protecting towns and cities. Still, Avgustus had taken an oath that he would do his duty to the republic and remained on commando even when many disheartened Boers abandoned their positions and returned home without leave.

His sympathy for the burgher soldiers did not blind him to their faults, which he criticised at length in his memoir. Avgustus and other formally trained Russian officers on the Boer side organised their own corps because, among other things, they wanted to 'set the Boers an example of correct organisation' and discipline, as he remarked in his war account. When he arrived in South Africa, the Boers were besieging Kimberley and Ladysmith, and the British offensive had failed on all fronts. But the burgher leaders did not use their victories to their advantage and lost the initiative. The British, on the other hand, soon learnt from their mistakes, adapted their tactics and brought in reinforcements, which is why their next offensive succeeded. The Boer sieges were raised, and the drilled and obedient British soldiers began their march to Pretoria.

But a change was coming. Younger, more talented and often better-educated burgher generals such as Louis Botha, Jan Smuts, Koos de la Rey and Christiaan de Wet became particularly prominent during the transitional phase of the war, replacing more cautious commanders such as Piet Joubert, Lucas Meyer and Piet Cronjé. The progressive commanders largely abandoned outdated methods of waging war and organisation. Their preferred style was mobile warfare. They got rid of the large wagon laagers. They also asserted their authority over their men and established firmer discipline.[16] Under their leadership, the burghers continued to mount an unrelenting struggle for almost two years during the guerrilla phase.

Avgustus served in the Johannesburg Police Commando from early May 1900 until the British capture of Pretoria. He was wounded during the battle for the capital on 4–5 June. British orderlies picked him up.

Going home

'After I became a prisoner of war, dirty, ragged and hungry, as I was being escorted to jail by English bayonets,' he recounted, 'in the street, I saw Boers that I knew, who remained in Pretoria under the English occupation and had already taken the oath of allegiance to Queen Victoria. They pretended not to recognise me, turned away and did not greet me. But the attitude of those cowards could not affect my sympathies for this people, with whom I had grown close in the trenches by the Tugela, near Bloemfontein and in the fields near Wolmaransstad. Having elected me as their corporal, and later as their lieutenant, they always treated me with courtesy, readily listened to my opinion and shared their last sip of water, their last piece of rotten biltong.'[17]

As a prisoner, he met the man to whom he dedicated his memoir of the war: the Russian attaché with the British troops, Colonel Pavel Stakhovich. Thanks to the colonel's intervention, Avgustus was released after he promised to stop fighting. He was allowed to return to his homeland although some other members of the Russian corps were sent to Ceylon and remained in confinement there for another couple of years. Perhaps Avgustus was treated differently because, unlike his compatriots and brothers-in-arms, he had not obtained full burgher rights. He had only taken the oath of allegiance to the people of the Transvaal in their war for independence. Stakhovich vouched for Avgustus and a few other wounded Russian volunteers so that they were permitted to board a ship for Europe at Cape Town in July 1900. Before their departure, the British helped them to recover and arranged free passage home for them.[18]

The following month, Avgustus was already in Poland. He was restored to duty and assigned to the 192nd Wawer Infantry Regiment, stationed near Warsaw. Later, he recounted: 'Having experienced the horrors, suffering and deprivation in combat and on the march, broken physically and morally, I returned and rejoined the ranks, adorned with the cheap laurels of a Boer War hero.'[19]

But, officially, Avgustus was not a war veteran: in his record of service, nothing indicated that he had spent six months in South Africa. According to that document, Avgustus 'took no part in [military] campaigns and engagements with the enemy'.[20] It was typical of the

Colonel Pavel Stakhovich, the Russian attaché with the British troops (top row, middle), with military observers from other countries.

records of service of Russian volunteers: they were in South Africa in their personal capacity. It was their private matter and had nothing to do with the Russian Imperial Army.

Colonel Stakhovich continued to favour Avgustus. In a report to the War Minister, he pointed out that the participation of this 'brave, very enterprising' second lieutenant in the South African War had not been recorded as part of his total active service. The report was presented to the Tsar, who ordered not only that the missing months be taken into account but also that Avgustus be paid for his maintenance during that period, so that the officer could repay the large debts he had incurred to raise money for his trip to South Africa.[21]

Writing his memoir

Avgustus wanted to share his war experiences with his compatriots, particularly with other military men. Although parts of his memoir appeared in popular Russian newspapers, the longest version was published in the *Varshavsky Voyenny Zhurnal* (Warsaw Military Journal). According to another contributor to this publication, Russian soldiers found the war in remote South Africa instructive because 'it gives us the opportunity to learn about one of our future adversaries, to familiarise ourselves with his strengths and weaknesses'.[22]

The new official monthly of the Warsaw Military District was edited by officers, and most articles were written by them as well. They encouraged their colleagues to read about modern approaches to strategy and methods of warfare, the latest technical innovations in their field and the future of the armed forces in their country. Their writing was usually factual and dispassionate. In nearly every issue, starting from late 1899, the journal ran a chronicle of the South African War, with descriptions of the important battles and an analysis of each stage of the military campaign, by Nikolai Monkewitz, a future lieutenant general and chief of staff of the 4th Army during the First World War.

The professional military literature on the South African War, which came out in Russia during the conflict and shortly afterwards, was voluminous. Apart from translations of works by experts from other countries, there were hundreds of published works by Russian officers, mostly articles in military journals, often illustrated with battle maps of their own design. These were utilitarian texts, with technical data and calculations, issued in the specialised media for soldiers. Unlike journalists, Russian military authors were not preoccupied with moral and ethical questions. It was beside the point whether the struggle of the burghers against the British was fair and just. The audience of the professional publications did not need another condemnation of 'perfidious Albion' or praise for the 'valiant Boers'. They wanted a thorough and critical assessment of the warring parties. The commitment to objectivity and the practical approach set the texts by military men apart from other Russian writing on the war.[23]

Avgustus arrived in Warsaw in August 1900. His first article on the South African War, with his appraisal of the burghers' ability to continue their resistance, appeared in a Warsaw newspaper the following month.[24] A prolific writer, he contributed several essays to the *Varshavsky Voyenny Zhurnal* shortly after his return, such as his essays on the Paris Exposition and the former Royal Prussian Armoury, which he visited when returning from South Africa. The first chapter of his war memoir came out in the November issue and subsequent chapters were published once every two or three months, but he took his time working on the project.

The officer was not satisfied with recording his memories, because, according to him, 'personal impressions of the battle are unlikely to seem interesting'.[25] Avgustus took trouble to study official data and analysis by leading military experts, so that he could put his own experiences into context. He dedicated pages to explanation of the operations, citing information that he could only have learnt from literature on his return. He described the movements of British troops, indicated their numbers and the names of their regiments, which he could not have known in the field. The journal even reproduced a map of Lord Roberts's operations in the Free State drawn by Avgustus.

He spent much time and effort finding and processing such material, which slowed down his output. By mid-1902, Avgustus had managed to describe in his articles less than two months out of the six that he had spent in South Africa. He also brought out a self-published book on the South African War, consisting of the texts that he had published in the journal by September 1901.[26]

The last instalment of his South African War memoir, which came out in the *Varshavsky Voyenny Zhurnal* in June 1902, ended with the usual phrase, 'To be continued'. But there was no sequel, although Avgustus's articles on other topics continued to appear in that journal in 1903–1904.

Why the abrupt ending?

It could be that Avgustus decided not to publish the following chapters because he did not want to revive his painful memories and show the Russian volunteers in a bad light. In the published chapters, he had hinted at his disappointment with the Russian corps. The story ends abruptly after the unit leaves Pretoria for Natal. If Avgustus had continued, he would have had to recount how members of the corps discredited Maximov in the international legion and how Ganetsky's poor leadership resulted in the disbanding of the Russian unit, which never had a chance to take part in anything bigger than a skirmish. Avgustus could not skip the period from late March to early May.

Despite the intentions of its founders, the Russian corps did not 'set an example of proper organisation for the Boers'.[27] Maximov predicted that sensible volunteers would be disappointed in their commandant. Ganetsky and the other Russians misjudged the lieutenant colonel. With hindsight, Avgustus admitted that Maximov fully deserved to command their unit.

The Russian corps was not an embarrassment but a missed opportunity. However, a story of their failure could be used by British wartime propaganda, which presented foreign volunteers with the Boer forces as Anglophobe adventurers. The scandalous interview with a Russian who alleged that his compatriots on the Boer side were thieves and dodgers, which Avgustus quoted in his memoir, was carried by the press in the United Kingdom. Based on that claim, the British public was told that 'the Russians were never in the front of an attack or defensive action'.[28] Avgustus would not want to support that distorted view.

Although Avgustus's memoir appeared in a local specialised journal, it was noticed in various parts of the Russian Empire. Avgustus gave a lecture at the Society of Military Science Enthusiasts in Saint Petersburg, in a series that featured the Russian military attachés during the South African War, colonels Gurko and Stakhovich.[29] Papers in Odessa and Reval (now Tallinn) reproduced slightly modified excerpts from his memoir.[30] The organ of the Ministry of War praised Avgustus for his powers of observation and expressed a hope that a full version of his reminiscences would be available in wide distribution.[31]

The memoir also became known abroad. British papers quoted the story of a brave Scottish infantryman who told his captors during the siege of Ladysmith that he was hoping to see every Boer chased out of Natal.[32] In 1901, *La Revue hebdomadaire*, a popular Parisian magazine of arts and history, translated and published several chapters from Avgustus's account as it had appeared in the *Varshavsky Voyenny Zhurnal*. The editors believed that the author's 'Slavic intelligence, with its flexibility and finesse', had helped him to understand the strengths, the weaknesses and the strategy of the Boer forces: 'Better than any theoretical explanation, these sketches and stories will allow you to learn about this very special army.'[33]

The following year, a Polish translation of the French version was brought out as a supplement to a Warsaw conservative daily.[34] It seems as if the editors did not know that these chapters had already been published twice in their city (in the Russian military journal and as part of Avgustus's book). One thousand copies of the Polish edition were printed, which was also the exact number of copies of the Russian book that Avgustus had produced at his own expense in 1901.[35]

It appears that the author was not keen on promoting and selling his book. After he placed the order with the printers, he moved to Saint Petersburg. His roommate in Warsaw, Kārlis Goppers, settled his bill and brought the boxes home. A Latvian officer like Avgustus, Goppers had studied with him in Vilna, where they became friends. After Goppers returned from the Russian Civil War in 1920 with the rank of major general, he still had two boxes of Avgustus's unsold books in the attic.[36]

The lack of commercial success could have discouraged Avgustus from bringing out the rest of his memoir. Then again, the whereabouts of the original manuscript is unknown, so it cannot be established if any part remained unpublished.

It is possible that he never finished his war memoir. Avgustus did not need to write about the distressing period in his life. From Yevgeny Maximov, he would have known that Sophia Izedinova, a nurse with the Russo-Dutch Ambulance in South Africa, was working on her war memoir. In 1903, her book was issued by Alexey Suvorin, the publisher of the *Novoye Vremya*, the newspaper that had published Avgustus's articles from Pretoria.[37] Izedinova described the formation and disintegration of the international legion and sharply criticised the activities of the Russian corps and its leader. The nurse did not witness those events because she was working elsewhere at the time.[38] It seems that her main source of information on the legion and the corps was her friend Maximov. His opinion of the events, as expressed in his surviving writings, corresponded to the attitude that Izedinova assumed in her book. It was convenient for Avgustus: the story of the Russian unit was written by a disinterested party from the words of Maximov, an officer that he respected.

Imperial delusions

In writing his memoir of the South African War, Avgustus envisioned a moment in the near future when the Russians would cross swords with the British in India, and the shores of the Indus would 'resound with the neighing and clattering of Cossack horses'. He dreamt of being in the vanguard of the Russian army that would invade Hindustan to clear a path to the Indian Ocean. Such a dream did not seem wild to Russian officers of nationalist and conservative convictions. Throughout the second half of the 19th century, Tsarist strategists conceived plans for an Indian campaign. In the 1880s, General Alexey Kuropatkin, the Russian War Minister during the South African War, and other members of the General Staff devised an elaborate scheme for an attack on British troops by reaching India through Afghanistan and the Pamirs. The aims of a Russian invasion were to expel British armies from the Middle East, gain control over the lines of communication between Europe and Asia, and obtain a port on the Indian Ocean.[39]

Some of the points that Avgustus vigorously, even feverishly, defended in his memoir were hammered home by the Russian nationalist press to their readers before, during and after the South African War. They asserted that continuous expansion was Russia's 'historical mission'. Britain's hold over India was weak, they claimed, and if Russian troops were to advance, Indians would welcome their new 'liberators'.[40]

The intentions of the Tsar, an absolute monarch and ultimate Russian nationalist, in Asia were even bolder. In 1903, Kuropatkin recorded in his diary that his sovereign wanted 'to take Manchuria for Russia, to move towards an annexation of Korea by Russia. He dreams of bringing Tibet under his power. He wants to take over Persia, to capture not only the Bosporus but also the Dardanelles.'[41]

Avgustus's ideas had much in common with the aggressive ambitions of his emperor. The Russian people, wrote the young officer, 'expanded Russia's confines from the icy seas to the torrid South; they are the source of our greatness and glory; they will keep themselves occupied in the future, too.'[42]

From 1901, thoughts of Asia crossed his mind far more often than his memories of Africa. In a report for the War Minister, Colonel

Stakhovich remarked that Avgustus's 'cherished dream' was to serve in Turkestan, a Russian territory in Central Asia, bordering on China, Persia and Afghanistan.[43] British India was a few dozen miles southwards, across the mountainous strip known as the Wakhan Corridor. Diplomats and the military personnel in Turkestan collected intelligence from Hindustan. Officers at the headquarters of the Turkestan Military District prepared reports on the attitudes of the local population and political events in the region, looking forward to occupying the Wakhan Corridor and crossing the mountains into India.[44]

To be transferred there, Avgustus had to speak local languages. Officers could enrol in the courses in Asian languages in Saint Petersburg, but only up to five students a year were admitted, graduates of military academies exclusively. Avgustus did not meet this requirement: he had finished a cadet school only. The War Minister presented Stakhovich's report to the Tsar, who 'expressed an opinion' that Avgustus ought to be allowed to do the entrance examination.[45]

The sovereign's opinion was taken as an order, so Avgustus was granted special permission to take the test. He succeeded, and it was the end of the 'gloomy, tedious life' at the regiment for him. From 1901, Avgustus was a student at the Ministry of Foreign Affairs Courses in Oriental Languages for military officers in the Russian capital. He was excited: 'As a child, did you ever dream of the magical palaces, the pointed minarets crowned with golden crescents, the murmur of marble fountains under shady Oriental planes, the swaying of solitary broad-leaved palms that tower above the vast desert, caravans of striding camels – all those vivid and uniquely delightful images of the Orient, inspired by the tales of Scheherazade? To me, the exploits of the brave characters of Mayne Reid or Cooper novels paled in comparison with Aladdin's wonderful lamp, with the adventures of Caliph Harun al-Rashid or the fearless Sinbad the Sailor.'[46]

Studying languages (Arabic, Turkish and Persian), as well as Muslim law, helped him to understand the East better. But Avgustus was an imperial soldier who wanted to contribute to the expansion of Russian territory. He had had it in him since childhood: 'In wide-eyed wonder, I listened to my nurse's tales of the Muslim invasion of the Holy Land and of the distant Constantinople where the valiant men of [Russian] princes Igor and Oleg sailed to in their light vessels. The brave fellows from the remote, sullen North were driven not only by their lust for blood and plunder; they were lured there by the bright sun, the azure sky, the bliss and luxury of the sultry South. And soon, the guns of Zaporozhian Cossacks thundered over the exuberant shores of Anatolia: the carnage raged, and the smoke from burning villages veiled the bright sky ...'[47]

Eyeing the Bosporus

Avgustus's fascination with Central Asia, reinvigorated by his entry into the school of languages, left little time for his other interests. In March 1902, while the last chapters of his South African War memoir were coming out, the same *Varshavsky Voyenny Zhurnal* published his first essay on Turkey, a review of a German study of the Ottoman armed forces. Russia, he believed, was destined to take over the straits and gain access to the Mediterranean. In his opinion, a conflict with the Ottoman Empire was inevitable, and Russian officers had to learn about their future adversaries, watching their every move.[48] According to Avgustus, his country would not be able to annex Turkey, but an unequal alliance that enabled Russia to use and control the Bosporus and the Dardanelles would be a natural development.[49]

From the 18th century, Russia had aspired to gain a foothold in the straits leading from the Black Sea to the Mediterranean Sea to ensure a safe and free passage for its merchant and naval ships. Russia without the Bosporus and the Dardanelles was likened to a man in a locked room: he had grown so tall that his head touched the ceiling, so he needed to get out and 'breathe in the free air of the seas and oceans'.[50] There was also a romantic aspect to it: Russian Pan-Slavist poets and thinkers called for a unification of the Slavic peoples around Constantinople (Istanbul), the city where their ancestors had received the good news of the Eastern Orthodox Church. Russia, the leading Slavic nation and protector of the Orthodox faith, had to make Istanbul Christian again, they claimed.

'Yes, the Golden Horn and Constantinople – they will all be ours', wrote Fyodor Dostoevsky. The Russian novelist believed that 'it will happen by itself, precisely because the time has come, and if it has not come yet, there is every indication that the time is near. It is a natural outcome; it is, so to say, the word of nature itself.'[51]

For decades, the ruling elite in Russia had discussed a major operation to seize the Bosporus and Istanbul. The country had used military tools to achieve its goals in the region: four Russo-Turkish wars took place in the 19th century. In the first decade of the 20th century, the government still believed that Russia should 'get the keys to its own house', that is, the straits. However, the Bosporus and the Dardanelles were meant to remain part of a weakened Ottoman Empire, which had to be allied with and preferably controlled by Russia. Plans to occupy the straits and establish full control of them were revived shortly before the First World War, when Turkey joined the German-led coalition and became Russia's enemy. Yet such projects were never carried out. A veteran of the South African War, the Russian War Minister Alexander Guchkov, finally discarded those plans half a year before the Bolshevik revolution of 1917.[52]

After his first year at the school of languages, Avgustus visited Turkey. He summed up the main purpose of his trip in the epigraph to his travelogue in the *Varshavsky Voyenny Zhurnal*: 'Whoever wants to understand the enemy has to go to the enemy's country.'[53] Apart from practising the language and exploring the local culture, Avgustus dedicated his time to studying the training, the attitudes and the combat readiness of Turkish troops. On the very first day, while sailing into Istanbul, Avgustus saw the coastal fortifications of the Bosporus and started ruminating on the most effective way of invading the city.[54]

He arrived in the Turkish capital as a deck passenger wearing a Circassian suit that he had bought in Odessa: a shaggy hat, a *beshmet* with *gazyrs* (a long jacket with chest pockets for rifle cartridges) and a blunt dagger. Avgustus had an ambitious itinerary: to walk all the way from Istanbul to Mashhad in Persia. It was a 3 350 km hike, but Avgustus, who could not afford to travel another way, had to try it.

'Due to the circumstances and conditions of my journey,' he recounted, 'I had to immerse myself in the life of the East, to live and be imbued with the world view of the Turks. Whether in bustling centres of trade, in remote Anatolian villages, in caravanserais, in barracks, in a prison or in conversation with venerable *kaymakams* [the sultan's representatives in the provinces] and Osman Pasha's veterans, or at lunch from a bowl shared with Kurdish robbers and gendarmes, or when sleeping under the same roof with Circassian émigrés and grey-bearded pilgrims, people everywhere treated me not as a respectable foreign tourist but, as I pretended to be, a fugitive soldier, who was brought by fate from the distant Muscovy to the blessed Anatolia.'[55]

It is unknown if Avgustus reached Persia: only the first two parts of his travelogue and an article on the Turkish army appeared in print. Perhaps, like his war memoir, that manuscript remained incomplete. But he certainly reached Erzurum, which lay 270 km west of the Persian border. The Russian consul in that town mentioned Avgustus in his report in September 1902.[56]

To the Far East and Siberia

Avgustus continued his studies in Saint Petersburg for just another year. Having failed the annual exams, he was expelled from the school of languages and returned to his regiment in Poland. It was back to the 'gloomy, tedious living' of a junior officer for him.

But there was hope. In February 1904, the country entered its first large armed conflict in two decades: the Russo-Japanese War. Avgustus's regiment was not sent to the Far East, although he was apparently keen to go. How could he persuade his superiors to transfer him closer to the front line? He decided to use his South African commando experience. From June 1904, Avgustus was put in charge of the regiment's volunteer unit. In the Russian armed forces, such units specialised in reconnaissance, scouting and special assignments that required courage and ingenuity.

Evidently, Avgustus did well at his new job, because he was sent for several months' training to other regiments stationed in Poland. In October, he was transferred to Vladivostok, one of the largest Russian towns in the Far East. From March 1905, Avgustus was a commanding officer with the volunteer unit of the 30th East Siberian Rifle Regiment.

Although his new regiment was stationed thousands of kilometres nearer to the battlefields of the Russo-Japanese War than his previous one, Avgustus never had a chance to take part in hostilities. Throughout the war, his unit remained in Vladivostok, protecting it from a possible attack by the Japanese, which did not take place. Instead of attacking the enemy, the soldiers quelled political unrest in the town in 1905.[57]

The following year, the regiment was relocated nearly 5 000 km northeastwards and stationed in the old Siberian town of Krasnoyarsk. Avgustus commanded a platoon of mounted scouts. He enjoyed training his men: 'We used to march for 70 miles with no bother, swim across the Yenisey in full kit, feed on wood grouses and "wild" chickens; they sang songs so well that even the locals approved, "Fancy that, they're just like proper warriors!"'[58]

In 1908, a crisis emerged near the border with China.

Yevgeny Avgustus (bottom row, fourth from left) and his scouts returning from Uriankhai to Krasnoyarsk, Siberia (1910).

For over a hundred years, Russians had crossed the Sayan Mountains and settled in the fertile valleys populated by nomadic hunters and reindeer herders, Soyots and Uriankhais. In the so-called Uriankhai Territory, Russian immigrants established villages, trading posts and gold mines. About 8 000 Russians lived there in Avgustus's time, with permission from the local rulers as well as from the authorities in Beijing, who regarded Uriankhai as part of China.

Over the years, tensions increased in the territory. Uriankhais accused Russian traders and mine owners of land seizures, unauthorised construction and tree felling, while Russians blamed Uriankhais for stealing, violent attacks and failure to repay their debts.[59] Haidyp, the ruler of the Khemchik Khoshun, the best-developed district, ordered the eviction of Russians who did not have residence permits. In November 1908, he gave Russian merchants three days to sell their businesses and return to their homeland.[60] Uriankhai patrols along the border started preventing Russian traders from entering the territory.

To stop the evictions and protect Russian subjects, Colonel Victor Popov, who had explored Uriankhai and the living conditions of Russian settlers, persuaded his superiors to send soldiers to the area. The expedition was to be conducted by a platoon of mounted scouts under Avgustus's command.

In search of the borderline

'Yes, man is a plaything in the hands of fate, and even more so if he is a commissioned officer!' noted Avgustus. 'It is enough to get an order number so and so, and you must say goodbye to the peaceful garrison life with all its joys and delights: regimental evening dances, tactical training, "loaded marches" … We are on the march, we truly are! Beyond the mountains, beyond the forests, into the blue horizon.'[61]

Avgustus gave his books and a bust of Napoleon to an assistant for safe keeping and set out with his 30 men from Minusinsk in extremely cold weather at the end of December. They covered 640 km riding and walking in deep snow through the taiga, on the frozen Yenisey River and icy ledges of the Sayan ridge.[62] The appearance of the Avgustus scouts in early January took the Uriankhai patrols by surprise. The Russian soldiers captured or scattered the guards. After Popov and Avgustus held talks with Haidyp and Chinese officials, the eviction of the Russian settlers was stopped.[63]

Colonel Popov was among the many Russian officers and students of Russian-Chinese relations who stated that Uriankhai belonged to Russia. He argued that the 18th-century delimitation treaties had been misinterpreted in China's favour. Both Russians and Chinese came to believe that the border between their countries ran along the Sayan Mountains. However, Popov asserted that the 'forgotten border' was located about 100 km southwards, along the Tannu-Ola ridge.[64] Popov saw the attempt at expulsion of Russians from Uriankhai as part of China's strategy to strengthen its influence in the disputed territory. Such attempts might be repeated, he pointed out, unless Russia rectified the historical error and made China accept that Uriankhai was Russian territory.

Russian political and business elites were in favour of solving the 'Uriankhai question', because the area had remarkable economic potential, but they needed evidence that their country could stake a legitimate claim to it. Popov and his faithful associate, Avgustus, were determined to procure such evidence.

Avgustus and his scouts stayed in the Sayan Mountains and neighbouring villages for the rest of 1909. They identified the most favourable route for a road across the ridges, from the mouth of the Buiba River to the village of Turanskoye (Turan), to enhance the lines of communication with the region that the Russian government had set its sights on. The road that was built there shortly afterwards is now part of the Yenisey Highway, the main artery in the region. The platoon also explored the entire border that separated Russia from Uriankhai, searching for the original boundary markers. They found only old gravestones and religious sites, which were, in Avgustus's opinion, usually taken for such landmarks.[65]

The following year, in 1910, research on the Uriankhai question continued. At Popov's request, Avgustus examined old maps, treaties and other documents on the demarcation of the Russian-Chinese border.[66] With his scouts, he joined Popov's expedition to Uriankhai, financed by the Russian government. They explored the southern slopes of the Tannu-Ola and other areas where the border was meant to lie, according to their estimation.[67] They also interviewed Russian settlers to find out when and how Uriankhai came to be regarded as Chinese. By then, Avgustus was confident that the border had been incorrectly drawn by cartographers, with no regard for the 18th-century agreements. While travelling in the Chapchal Pass in the Sayans with his platoon the same year, he let his men cut down a post that was thought to be a boundary marker and use it as firewood.

Chinese officials in Beijing investigated the matter and complained to the Russian envoy.

On the Russian side, the ministers of Finance and Foreign Affairs, as well as the prime minister, took part in the discussion of the Chapchal Incident, as it became known. On instructions from his government, and possibly based on Avgustus's findings, the Russian envoy stated that no archival or other data indicated that there was an official border marker on that site.[68] Chinese and Russian diplomats discussed the matter for over a year.

Russia takes over Uriankhai

By the end of 1910, the government in Saint Petersburg had concluded that Urianchai was indeed a 'disputed territory'. Materials of Popov's expedition, including reports by Avgustus, which substantiated Russia's claim to Uriankhai, were widely cited in books and articles. The Russian Foreign Minister argued that his country could legitimately demand a revision of the demarcation line in Uriankhai, and therefore the Russian representatives in Beijing had to 'query the investigation into the question of the [Chapchal] post'. Accordingly, the Russian envoy, in his correspondence with the Chinese Ministry of Foreign Affairs in August 1911, insisted that the incident caused by Avgustus's platoon could not be considered without reviewing the Uriankhai segment of the border.[69]

Soon, the political situation in the region changed, and Russia was free to act decisively. The Chinese revolution of 1911 ended the 2 132 years of imperial rule. A republic was proclaimed. Meanwhile, Chinese officials were expelled from Uriankhai. Russian influence in the area grew substantially, which caused the rulers of five districts to pledge allegiance to the Russian Tsar. In 1914, Nicholas II agreed to declare Uriankhai a Russian protectorate.[70]

This took place at the end of Avgustus's stay in Siberia. His work of several years helped to prevail upon the public and the authorities in his country to regard Uriankhai as a territory that should rightfully be Russian. In this way, he achieved his goal: to contribute to the expansion of the Russian Empire. An area the size of Greece and Switzerland combined joined the Russian realm voluntarily. Thirty years later, it was formally incorporated into the Russian Soviet

Yevgeny Avgustus (centre, with a beard and glasses) during a visit of Japanese officers to the 30th Siberian Regiment (1912).

Federative Socialist Republic. The region is now known as Tuva.

In 1914, Avgustus was still a staff captain. In terms of rank, his military career was conventional. Promotion of Russian infantry officers was notoriously slow. To become a captain, a staff captain had to be placed in charge of a company, and such appointments were rare. On the average, Russian staff captains waited for nine years for their next rank in peacetime.[71] Avgustus could reasonably expect a promotion no earlier than in 1916.

His participation in the exploration of Uriankhai did not speed up the process. What is even more remarkable is that Avgustus received no accolades for it either. The only award that he held, the Order of St Stanislaus of the lowest grade, was the most common Russian imperial decoration. Every officer and government employee could get it for honourable service after a number of years.

By then, Avgustus had married a Russian woman from Poland. They had no children and no property.[72] But he seemed to have settled down. 'You should not believe the authors of tendentious, laboured articles with complaints and lamentations about the

245

tedium, deadly boredom and material hardship that we experience in Siberia,' he wrote. 'An officer who is fond of his work has many prospects and much freedom in Siberia. Can other Russians even imagine marching, scouting or riding for thousands of miles on the wild bare sides of mountain ranges, through the impenetrable taiga where only bears and elks roam, and across the endless steppes where solitary kurgans of Tamerlane and Batu's ancestors rise?'[73]

A war, at last

In August 1914, Russia entered the First World War. The same month, Russian troops invaded East Prussia, aiming to continue their offensive in central Germany. The month-long operation failed. Fifty thousand Russian soldiers were captured or lost in action. By the second half of September, the Russians had withdrawn from Germany. Morale among their troops sank after this rout, one of the worst in the history of Russian-German conflicts at the time. The tables were turned: Germany advanced into Poland, and Russia had to defend its imperial domain. The country needed to replenish its troops and take the offensive again.

Avgustus's regiment, by then known as the 30th Siberian Rifle Regiment, was transferred to the northwestern front and incorporated into the 10th Army. After a long absence, Avgustus found himself in Poland, which had become an 'advanced theatre' at last. His regiment was preparing to take part in the Augustów operation. The Polish town, whose name uncannily resembled Avgustus's surname, had been occupied by German troops. The Russian army had an advantage in numbers, but the Germans were superior in heavy artillery. To protect their men from the German gunfire, the Russians inveigled the enemy into fighting in forests. The Augustów district also abounded in wetlands, rivers and lakes with hilly shores.

Avgustus's regiment was ordered to march to Augustów and drive the enemy out. Their first skirmishes with the Germans took place along the way. But on 29 September, the commander, Colonel Mikhail Izhitsky, received new instructions: to bypass Augustów, march northeastwards and set up blocks to cover the movement of other Russian troops towards the provincial capital, Suwałki, which was held by the Germans. The following day, moving along the eastern side of the Rospuda River, they noticed, on the opposite bank, German reinforcements heading for Augustów. The regiment engaged the enemy near the villages of Chodorki and Kurianki.[74] The Russians came under fierce enemy gunfire from across the river and shot back, protecting the crossing. The shelling continued for many hours, inflicting heavy casualties on both sides.

The battle continued throughout 1 October, with the Germans concentrating their forces in that area to break through. After hours of constant shelling, the enemy managed to cross the river in the dense fog and drenching rain. The Russians stood their ground. They needed to hold out and impede the enemy's progress until Russian troops could reach Suwałki.

Meanwhile, the regiment was outflanked and caught in the crossfire, forcing the men to pull back a few kilometres. They were exhausted after the two days of intermittent shelling, walking in the mud and being soaked by the rain without food or sleep. Staff Captain Avgustus returned with several men and reported that the 3rd Battalion, which held the extreme left flank, had been annihilated. But Colonel Izhitsky knew that his regiment could not fall back because they were nearly surrounded by the enemy. One more push and the circle would close. He arranged his men in orderly rows and led them towards the enemy. The sight of Russian soldiers marching out of the thickening fog in a downpour at twilight took the enemy aback. The Germans retreated, and, without a shot, the Russians occupied a neighbouring village and rested until dawn.

The next morning, on 2 October, they learnt that Avgustus was mistaken. His men had lied to him. They had fled from their unit while their comrades were holding out in the trenches until the end of the day. The 3rd Battalion had survived.

'It was a great joy for the regiment,' the colonel recounted. 'A few hours later, Staff Captain Avgustus atoned for his incorrect report with his death in a bayonet assault.'[75]

The enemy attacked at dawn, but the Russian regiment had no artillery support. They withdrew to a forest where the worn-out soldiers started roaming and staggering in a stupor. Then, the colonel received a message that Russian reinforcements were arriving soon. He realised that his regiment had to fend off the Germans for just another couple of hours. His men were heartened by the news, and the colonel led them in a bayonet counterattack. The bewildered enemy retired. The German assault was halted long enough for the Russian columns to reach the area.

'The small piece of land where these attacks took place was literally strewn with corpses of Russians and Germans,' remembered the colonel. One of those men was Yevgeny Avgustus.

During the four-day battle (30 September to 3 October) against an entire German division, two-thirds of the officers and nearly half of the lower ranks in the regiment were injured or killed or went missing in action.[76] They accomplished their mission and withstood the enemy attacks long enough for Russian troops to reach Suwałki. Their army drove the enemy out of the town, took the strategic initiative and crossed the border into East Prussia.

The end of an era

While Avgustus was fighting in Poland, and even after his death, readers of *Voyenny Sbornik*, a Russian military journal, received the issues containing the last instalments of his memoir of the Uriankhai crisis. Avgustus warned of an imminent clash between Russia and China over Mongolia and Manchuria. 'Sooner or later, the great fate will force us to accept the challenge of the gold-scaled dragon,' he warned. 'And by that time, we must be fully armed. We must work tirelessly to explore the borders, the operation routes and the possible sites of military operations, and prepare our lines of communication.'[77]

For many years after his return from South Africa, the imperial soldier longed for a war. With Kipling's fervour, he poeticised colonialism and the supposed inevitability of his country's southward expansion. Avgustus wanted to share in the glory of his empire, to help his country perform its 'historical mission' of continuous expansion. When the war came, it led to a great loss of territory, the collapse of the imperial system and the abolition of the monarchy. Three years after Avgustus's death, the Bolsheviks came to power in Russia, which would have been unacceptable to a staunch monarchist and nationalist like him. In the ensuing civil war perished the remnants of the ideology and the political system that he had supported.

Avgustus participated in two military conflicts: in South Africa in 1900 and in Poland (the Russian Empire) in 1914. Each time, he fought on the defensive. None of the invasions that he forecast took place in the 20th century. Still, his dream was achieved. A large territory, Tuva, became part of Russia thanks to his non-military contribution: research and exploration.

His best-known legacy, the memoir of the South African War, is now available to South African readers.

Notes

1   'Russian Boer officers', *Daily Mail*, 23 November 1899, p 4.
2   *Anglo-burskaya voyna 1899–1902 godov glazami rossiyskih poddannyh*. Vol 8, pp 16, 281; 'Otyezd v Transvaal', *Peterburgskaya Gazeta*, 1899, no 347, 19 December; 'Paris day by day', *The Daily Telegraph*, 9 November 1899, p 11.
3   *Anglo-burskaya voyna 1899–1902 godov glazami rossiyskih poddannyh*. Vol 6, pp 64–72, 80.
4   Davidson and Filatova, *The Russians and the Anglo-Boer War*, p 85; Voropaeva et al (comp and eds), *Anglo-burskaya voyna 1899–1902 gg.*, p 514.
5   Voropaeva et al (comp and eds), *Anglo-burskaya voyna 1899–1902 gg.*, p 514.
6   'Russian scouts', *The Morning Post*, 30 March 1900, p 5.
7   Izedinova, SV, *Neskolsko mesyatsev u burov: vospominaniya sestry miloserdiya*. Saint Petersburg: Tipografiya A S Souvorina, 1903, p 199.
8   Lecoy de la Marche, H-M-A, *Souvenirs de la guerre du Transvaal: journal d'un volontaire (mars-septembre 1900)*. Paris: A Colin, 1901, pp 25–26.
9   Gorelik, B, 'The role of Russian volunteers in the collapse of the international legion in the South African War', *Scientia Militaria: South African Journal of Military Studies*, 2021, vol 48, no 2, pp 34–36.
10 Davitt, M, *The Boer Fight for Freedom*. New York: Funk & Wagnalls, 1902, pp 334–335.
11 *Anglo-burskaya voyna 1899–1902 godov glazami rossiyskih poddannyh*. Vol 7, pp 382–383; Roubanov, V, *Ot Peterburga do Pretorii*. Saint Petersburg: Tipografiya zhurnala 'Stroitel', 1900, pp 40–41.
12 Pottinger, *The Foreign Volunteers*, p 280.
13 *Anglo-burskaya voyna 1899–1902 godov glazami rossiyskih poddannyh*. Vol 7, p 385.
14 Ibid, pp 385, 385–389.
15 Avgustus, Y, 'Briton or Boer. O polozhenii del v Yuzhnoy Afrike', *Varshavsky Dnevnik*, 1900, no 241, 3 (16) September.
16 Amery, LS and Williams, B (eds), *The Times History of the War in South Africa 1899–1902*, vol IV. London: Sampson Low, Marston and Co, Ltd, 1906, pp 24, 27; Pretorius, 'The Second Anglo-Boer War', p 115.
17 Avgustus, 'Briton or Boer'.

18 *Anglo-burskaya voyna 1899–1902 godov glazami rossiyskih poddannyh*. Vol 7, p 387; 'Hronika', *Varshavskiy Dnevnik*, 1900, no 200, 24 July; 'Obshtshestvo revniteley voyennykh znaniy', *Russkiy Invalid*, 1901, no 231, 24 October, p 3; Yanchevitsky, V, 'Polozheniye russkikh plennykh v Transvaale', *Novoye Vremya*, 1900, no 8826, 22 September.

19 Avgustus, 'V gostyakh u turok', p 634.

20 *Anglo-burskaya voyna 1899–1902 godov glazami rossiyskih poddannyh*. Vol 8, pp 306–310.

21 Ibid, pp 279–280, 284.

22 WK, 'Anglo-burskaya voina v Yuzhnoy Afrike. Vyp. II. Sost. A Vinogradsky', *Varshavsky Voyenny Zhurnal*, 1902, no 6, p 659.

23 Petukhov, 'Obraz Velikobritanii v rossiyskom obshestvennom mnenii', pp 87–90.

24 Avgustus, 'Briton or Boer'.

25 Avgustus, Y, 'Vospominaniya uchastnika anglo-burskoy voiny 1899–1902 gg.', *Varshavsky Voyenny Zhurnal*, 1901, no 1, p 58.

26 Avgustus, Y, *Vospominaniya uchastnika anglo-burskoy voiny 1899–1902 gg.* Warsaw: Tipografiya 'Bristol', 1902.

27 Gorelik, B, 'The Russian corps in the Anglo-Boer War: two months of misfortune', *Military History Journal*, 2020, vol 19, no 1, pp 10–17.

28 'Around the world', *The Navy and Army Illustrated*, 1901, vol XII, 27 April, p 127; *London Daily News*, 13 March 1901, p 5.

29 *Vestnik Obshtshestva revniteley voyennykh znaniy*, 1901, no 42, 15 October.

30 Avgustus Y, 'Iz vospominaniy russkogo volontyora v Transvaale', *Revelskiye Izvestiya*, 1902, no 120, 31 May, pp 1–2; no 121, 1 July, pp 1–2; no 125, 7 June, pp 1–2; no 126, 8 June, pp 1–2.

31 'Obshtshestvo revniteley voyennykh znaniy', p 3.

32 'Russian story of Boer War', *Aberdeen Press and Journal*, 2 July 1902, p 2.

33 Augustus, E, 'Sur la Tugela', *La Revue hebdomadaire*, 1901, vol IX, August, pp 235–258, 367–386, 530–551.

34 Porucznik Augustus, *Nad Tugelą: osobiste wspomnienia z wojny transwalskiej.* Warsaw: Drukiem Noskowskiego, 1902.

35 *Spisok izdaniy, vyshedshikh v Rossii v 1902 godu.* Saint Petersburg: Tipografiya Ministerstva vnutrennikh del, 1903, p 155.

36 Jēkabsons, 'Zabytiy latysh anglo-burskoy voiny', pp 104–105; Goppers, M; Goppers, K; Kažociņš, J et al (eds), *Ģenerālis Kārlis Goppers: 140 viņa laikabiedru stāsti ap septiņiem ugunskuriem Grāmatizdevēja Miķeļa Goppera pēdējā sastādītā grāmata 21. gadsimta redakcijā ar pielikumiem.* Stokholma-Rīga: Zelta Ābele, 2022, p 233.

37 Izedinova, *Neskolsko mesyatsev u burov.*

38 Gorelik, 'The role of Russian volunteers', pp 31–32.

39 Sergeyev, YY, *Bolshaya igra, 1856–1907: mify i realii rossiysko-britanskikh otnosheniy v Tsentralnoy i Vostochnoy Azii.* Moscow: KMK, 2012, pp 200–201.

40 Petukhov, 'Obraz Velikobritanii v rossiyskom obshestvennom mnenii', pp 78, 80.

41 Kuropatkin, AN, *Dnevnik generala AN Kuropatkina.* Moscow: Gosudarstvennaya publichnaya istoricheskaya biblioteka Rossii, 2010, p 80.

42 Avgustus, Y, 'Vospominaniya uchastnika anglo-burskoy voyny 1899–1900 gg.', *Varshavsky Voyenny Zhurnal*, 1902, no 3, p 227.

43 *Anglo-burskaya voyna 1899–1902 godov glazami rossiyskih poddannyh*. Vol 8,

pp 279–280.

[44] Sergeyev, *Bolshaya igra, 1856–1907*, p 202.

[45] *Anglo-burskaya voyna 1899–1902 godov glazami rossiyskih poddannyh*. Vol 8, p 285.

[46] Avgustus, 'V gostyakh u turok', p 633.

[47] Ibid.

[48] Avgustus Y, 'Materialy k izucheniyu turetskoy armii', *Varshavsky Voyenny Zhurnal*, 1902, no 3, p 330.

[49] Avgustus, 'V gostyakh u turok', p 638.

[50] Dostoevsky, FM, *Dnevnik pisatelya*, in Dostoevsky, FM, *Polnoye sobraniye sochineniy v tridsati tomakh*, vol 25. Leningrad: Nauka, 1983, p 67.

[51] Ibid, p 65.

[52] Yemets, V A, 'Problema Chernomorskih prolivov vo vneshney politike Rossii v period pervoy mirovoy voyny', *Rossiya i Chernomorskiye prolivy (XVIII–XX stoletiya)*. Moscow: Mezhdunarodniye otnosheniya, 1999, pp 337, 350.

[53] Avgustus, Y, 'Zametki o turetskoy armii (Po lichnym nablyudeniyam)', *Varshavsky Voyenny Zhurnal*, 1904, no 4, p 323.

[54] Avgustus, 'V gostyakh u turok', p 637.

[55] Ibid, pp 634–635.

[56] Baskhanov, MK, *Russkiye voyenniye vostokovedy do 1917 goda. Bibliograficheskiy slovar*. Moscow: Vostochnaya Literatura, 2005, p 8.

[57] Novikov, PA, 'Vostochno-Sibirskiye voinskiye soyedineniya v voinakh 1-y chetverti XX veka', PhD thesis, Institut mongolovedeniya, buddologii i tibetologii Sibirskogo otdeleniya RAN, Irkutsk, 2009, p 113.

[58] Avgustus, Y, 'S razvedchikami 30-go polka по Uryankhaiskomu krayu i Mongolii. (Dnevnik nachalnika komandy razvedchikov 30-go Sib. strelk. polka)', *Voyenny Sbornik*, 1914, no 1, p 152.

[59] Samdan, AA, 'The Russo-Tuvan conflict of 1908', *Bulletin of the KIH of the RAS*, 2017, vol 31, no 3, pp 31, 34.

[60] Kuzmin, YV, '"Uryankhaiskiy vopros" i russko-mongolo-kitaiskiye otnosheniya v rossiyskoy istoriografii i obshchestvennoy mysli Rossii na rubezhe vekov', *Rossiya i Mongoliya v nachale XX veka: diplomatiya, ekonomika, nauka*, vol 3, part 1. Irkutsk and Ulan-Bator: BGUEP, 2014, p 234; Samdan, 'The Russo-Tuvan conflict of 1908', p 32.

[61] Avgustus, 'S razvedchikami 30-go polka по Uryankhaiskomu krayu …', no 1, p 151.

[62] Ibid, p 153.

[63] Popov, V, *Vtoroye puteshestviye v Mongoliyu. 1910 g*, part III. Irkutsk: Shtab Irkutskogo voyennogo okruga, 1910, pp 18–19.

[64] Ibid, p 19.

[65] Avgustus, Y, 'Korrespondentsiya "Razvedchika"', *Razvedchik*, 1910, no 1020, 18 May, pp 302–303; Kuzmin, '"Uryankhaiskiy vopros" i russko-mongolo-kitaiskiye otnosheniya', p 235.

[66] Popov, *Vtoroye puteshestviye v Mongoliyu. 1910 g*, p 72.

[67] Ibid, pp 25, 52.

[68] Datsyshen, VG, *Sayanskiy rubezh. Yuzhnaya chast Priyeniseyskogo kraya i russko-tuvinskiye otnosheniya v 1616–1911 gg*. Moscow: Direct-Media, 2014, pp 187–188.

[69] Vasilenko, VA, 'Problema Uriankhaiskogo kraya v politike Rossii, Kitaya,

Mongolii (vtoraya polovina XIX v.–1914 g.)', PhD thesis, Irkutsky gosu-darstvenny pedagogichesky universitet, Irkutsk, 2006, pp 164–165.

[70] Kuzmin, '"Uryankhaiskiy vopros" i russko-mongolo-kitaiskiye otnosheniya', p 244.

[71] Suryayev, VN, '"Nelyogkoye sluzhebnoye dvizheniye armeyskogo ofitserst-va": chinoproizvodstvo i prokhozhdeniye sluzhby ofitserami russkoy armii nakanune Pervoy mirovoy voyny', *Voyenno-istorichesky Zhurnal*, 2014, no 9, pp 50–56.

[72] *Anglo-burskaya voyna 1899–1902 godov glazami rossiyskih poddannyh.* Vol 8, pp 306–310.

[73] Avgustus, 'Korrespondentsiya "Razvedchika"', p 184.

[74] Novikov, 'Vostochno-Sibirskiye voinskiye soyedineniya', p 181.

[75] An excerpt from the combat diary of the 30th Siberian Rifle Regiment, 4 September to 1 November 1914. Russian State Archives of Military History (RGVIA), f 3364, op 1, d 8, unnumbered pages.

[76] Kodinets, A, 'Slavnyi podvig 30-go Sibirskogo strelkovogo polka', *Voyenny Sbornik*, 1916, no 3, p 86; Novikov, 'Vostochno-Sibirskiye voinskiye soyedi-neniya', p 181.

[77] Avgustus, 'S razvedchikami 30-go polka пo Uryankhaiskomu krayu', no 9, pp 164–165.

[78] Ivan Gringof, a Saratov civil engineer of Lithuanian extraction.

Acknowledgements

I am grateful to:

Gennady Shubin (1966–2016), Institute for African Studies, Russian Academy of Sciences. He published Yevgeny Avgustus's memoir in its entirety for the first time, in a 13-volume collection of documents on Russian responses to the South African War, which he compiled and edited with his colleagues.

Annie Olivier, Jonathan Ball Publishers, for persuading her bosses that Yevgeny Avgustus's memoir deserves a wide readership and for her dedication to this project over three years.

Lucas Venter, for an English translation of the memoir that does justice to the original.

Alfred LeMaitre, the editor, for his incisive comments and attention to detail.

Fransjohan Pretorius, for the Foreword, as well as for pointing out errors in my manuscript and helping me to correct them.

Vladimir Shubin and Vasily Sidorov, Institute for African Studies, Russian Academy of Sciences, for their constructive criticism.

Ēriks Jēkabsons, University of Latvia, and Andrey Marmyshev, TASS, for sharing their unpublished material on Yevgeny Avgustus's life and career beyond the South African War.

Susanne Blendulf, Marjorie Dean and the South African Military History Society, for introducing the Avgustus memoir to South African readers in 2016 and for their support.

Doron Locketz of Bookdealers, Johannesburg, for convincing me that Avgustus's memoir should be brought out by a major South African publisher.

Boris Gorelik
Moscow
19 January 2022

Works by Yevgeny Avgustus
reproduced in this edition

The list comprises the texts that were used, partly or in full, in the reconstruction of the war memoir:

1   Avgustus, Y, 'Pisma s dorogi (ot nashego korrespondenta)', *Varshavsky Dnevnik*, 1899, no 333, 7 (19) December; no 334, 8 (20) December; no 337, 11 (23) December; no 340, 15 (27) December; 1900, no 32, 2 (14) February.
2   Avgustus, Y, 'Na puti v Transvaal', *Novoye Vremya*. 1900, no 8566, 2 (14) January; no 8582, 19 (31) January; no 8603, 8 (20) February; no 8605, 10 (22) February; no 8606, 11 (23) February; no 8624, 1 (14) March.
3   Avgustus, Y, 'Pisma russkogo volontyora', *Novoye Vremya*, 1900, no 8625, 2 (15) March.
4   Avgustus, Y, 'Vospominaniya uchastnika anglo-burskoy voyny 1899–1900 gg.', *Varshavsky Voyenny Zhurnal*, 1900, no 11 and 12; 1901, no 1, 3, 7, 9; 1902, no 1, 3, 6.
5   Avgustus, Y, *Vospominaniya uchastnika anglo-burskoy voyny 1899–1900 gg.* Warsaw: Tipografiya 'Bristol', 1902.
6   Avgustus, Y, 'Iz vospominaniy volontyora v Transvaale (ocherki i eskizy), *Revelskiye Izvesiya*, 1902, no 125, 7 June.

Bibliography

Allen, V. *Kruger's Pretoria: Buildings and Personalities of the City in the Nineteenth Century*. Pretoria: Protea Book House, 2007.

Amery, LS and Williams, B (eds). *The Times History of the War in South Africa 1899–1902*, vol IV. London: Sampson Low, Marston and Co, Ltd, 1906.

Anglo-burskaya voyna 1899–1902 godov glazami rossiyskih poddannyh. V 13 tomah. Moscow: Izdatel IB Belyi, 2012.

Atherley-Jones, LA. *Commerce in War*. New York: Appleton, 1907.

Augustus, E. 'Sur la Tugela', *La Revue hebdomadaire*, 1901, vol IX, August, pp 235–258, 367–386, 530–551.

Avgustus, Y. 'Briton or Boer. O polozhenii del v Yuzhnoy Afrike', *Varshavsky Dnevnik*, 1900, no 241, 3 (16) September.

Avgustus, Y. 'Vospominaniya uchastnika anglo-burskoy voiny 1899–1902 gg.', *Varshavsky Voyenny Zhurnal*, 1901, no 1.

Avgustus Y. 'Iz vospominaniy russkogo volontyora v Transvaale', *Revelskiye Izvestiya*, 1902, no 120, 31 May, pp 1–2; no 121, 1 July, pp 1–2; no 125, 7 June, pp 1–2; no 126, 8 June, pp 1–2.

Avgustus Y. 'Materialy k izucheniyu turetskoy armii', *Varshavsky Voyenny Zhurnal*, 1902, no 3.

Avgustus, Y. 'Vospominaniya uchastnika anglo-burskoy voyny 1899–1900 gg.', *Varshavsky Voyenny Zhurnal*, 1902, no 3.

Avgustus, Y. *Vospominaniya uchastnika anglo-burskoy voiny 1899–1902 gg.* Warsaw: Tipografiya 'Bristol', 1902.

Avgustus, Y. 'V gostyakh u turok. Puteviye ocherki i vpechatleniya', *Varshavsky Voyenny Zhurnal*, 1903, no 7.

Avgustus, Y. 'Zametki o turetskoy armii (Po lichnym nablyudeniyam)', *Varshavsky Voyenny Zhurnal*, 1904, no 4.

Avgustus, Y. 'Korrespondentsiya "Razvedchika"', *Razvedchik*, 1910, no 1020, 18 May, pp 302–303.

Avgustus, Y. 'S razvedchikami 30-go polka пo Uryankhaiskomu krayu i Mongolii. (Dnevnik nachalnika komandy razvedchikov 30-go Sib. strelk. polka)', *Voyenny Sbornik*, 1914, no 1 and 9.

Avgustus, Y. *A Russian Fighting for the Boer Cause*. Translated and edited by B Gorelik. Johannesburg: South African Military History Society, 2016.

Baskhanov, MK. *Russkiye voyenniye vostokovedy do 1917 goda. Bibliograficheskiy slovar*. Moscow: Vo stochnaya Literatura, 2005.

Baskhanov, MK. 'U vorot angliyskogo moguschestva', in *A Y Snesarev v Turkestane, 1899–1904*. Saint Petersburg: Nestor-Istoriya, 2015.

Beckett, IFW. *The Victorians at War*. London: Hambledon and London, 2003.

Bender, S. *Der Burenkrieg und die deutschsprachige Presse: Wahrnehmung und Deutung zwischen Bureneuphorie und Anglophobie, 1899–1902*. Paderborn: Ferdinand Schöningh, 2009.

Cloete GP. *The Anglo-Boer War: A Chronology*. Pretoria: JP van der Walt, 2000.

Cuthbertson, G, Grundlingh, A and Suttie, M-L. 'Introduction', in Cuthbertson, G, Grundlingh, A and Suttie, M-L (eds), *Writing a Wider War: Rethinking Gender, Race, and Identity in the South African War, 1899–1902*. Athens: Ohio University Press, 2002.

Datsyshen, VG. *Sayanskiy rubezh. Yuzhnaya chast Priyeniseyskogo kraya i russko-tuvinskiye otnosheniya v 1616–1911 gg*. Moscow: Direct-Media, 2014.

Davidson, A and Filatova, I. *The Russians and the Anglo-Boer War, 1899–1902*. Cape Town: Human & Rousseau, 1998.

Davitt, M. *The Boer Fight for Freedom*. New York: Funk & Wagnalls, 1902.

De Jong, C. 'Reports of neutral military observers on the Anglo-Boer War 1899–1902', *Scientia Militaria: South African Journal of Military Studies*, 1976, vol 6, no 1.

De Jong, C and Foxcroft, E (eds). 'Reports of neutral military observers during the Anglo-Boer War (The reports of two Russian military attachés, 1899–1900)', *Scientia Militaria: South African Journal of Military Studies*, 1975, vol 5, no 3, pp 1–21, and no 4, pp 49–61.

De Souza, FLH. *A Question of Treason*. Durban: Kiaat Creations, 2004.

Dostoevsky, FM. *Dnevnik pisatelya*, in Dostoevsky, FM, *Polnoye sobraniye sochineniy v tridsati tomakh*, vol 25. Leningrad: Nauka, 1983.

[Ebergardt, AK]. 'The Russian Red Cross in the Anglo-Boer War, 1899–1902. Report by a Russian doctor translated by C Moody', *Historia*, 1977, no 2, pp 112–129.

Fisher, J. *Paul Kruger: His Life and Times*. London: Secker & Warburg, 1974.

Gerdzhikov, M. *Spomeni, dokumenti, materiali*. Sofia: Nauka i Izkustvo, 1984.

Gillings, K. *The Battle of the Thukela Heights: 12–28 February 1900*. Randburg: Ravan Press, 1999.

Gooch, J. *The Boer War: Direction, Experience, and Image*. London: Frank Cass, 2000.

Goppers, M; Goppers, K; Kažociņš, J; Jēkabsons, Ē; Goldšmits, J; Laimonis, O (eds). *Ģenerālis Kārlis Goppers: 140 viņa laikabiedru stāsti ap septiņiem ugunskuriem Grāmatizdevēja Miķeļa Goppera pēdējā sastādītā grāmata 21. gadsimta redakcijā ar pielikumiem*. Stokholma-Rīga: Zelta Ābele, 2022.

Gorelik, B (ed). *'An Entirely Different World': Russian Visitors to the Cape, 1797–1870*. Cape Town: Van Riebeeck Society, 2015.

Gorelik, B. 'The Russian corps in the Anglo-Boer War: Two months of misfortune', *Military History Journal*, 2020, vol 19, no 1, pp 10–17.

Gorelik, B. 'The role of Russian volunteers in the collapse of the international legion in the South African War', *Scientia Militaria: South African Journal of Military Studies*, 2021, vol 49, no 2, pp 29–41.

Hancock, WK and Van der Poel, J (eds). *Selections from the Smuts Papers*. Vol I. Cambridge: Cambridge University Press, 1966.

Henze, P. *The Horn of Africa: From War to Peace*. Basingstoke: Macmillan, 1991.

Hillegas, HC. *With the Boer Forces*. London: Methuen & Co, 1900.

Izedinova, SA. *A Few Months with the Boers: The War Reminiscences of a Russian Nursing Sister*. Translated and edited by HJ Moody. Johannesburg: Perskor Publications, 1977.

Izedinova, SV. *Neskolsko mesyatsev u burov: vospominaniya sestry miloserdiya*. Saint Petersburg: Tipografiya AS Souvorina, 1903.

Jēkabsons, Ē. 'Zabytiy latysh anglo-burskoy voiny', *Otkrytyi Gorod*, 2019, no 7/8.

Johnson, RW. 'Rogue's paradise', *London Review of Books*, 1998, vol 20, no 14.

Kandyba-Foxcroft, E. *Russia and the Anglo-Boer War 1899–1902*. Pretoria: CUM Books, 1981.

Katayev, VP. *Razbitaya zhizn, ili Volshebny rog Oberona*, Katayev, VP, *Sobraniye sochineniy*, vol 8. Moscow: Hudozhestvennaya literatura, 1985.

Kodinets, A. 'Slavnyi podvig 30-go Sibirskogo strelkovogo polka', *Voyenny Sbornik*, 1916, no 3, p 86.

Kuropatkin, AN, *Dnevnik generala A N Kuropatkina*. Moscow: Gosudarstvennaya publichnaya istoricheskaya biblioteka Rossii, 2010.

Kuzmin, YV. '"Uryankhaiskiy vopros" i russko-mongolo-kitaiskiye otnosheniya v rossiyskoy istoriografii i obshchestvennoy mysli Rossii na rubezhe vekov', *Rossiya i Mongoliya v nachale XX veka: diplomatiya, ekonomika, nauka*, vol 3, part 1. Irkutsk and Ulan Bator: BGUEP, 2014.

Lebedev, VL. '*V Indiyu': Voyenno-statistichesky i strategichesky ocherk. Proyekt budushchego pokhoda*. Saint Petersburg, 1898.

Lecoy de la Marche, H-M-A. *Souvenirs de la guerre du Transvaal: journal d'un volontaire (mars-septembre 1900)*. Paris: A Colin, 1901.

Longland's Pretoria Directory for 1899. Pretoria: The State Library, 1979.

Lowry, D. '"The play of forces world-wide in their scope and revolutionary in their operation [JA Hobson]": The South African War as an international event', *South African Historical Journal*, 1999, vol 41, no 1.

Lowry, D. '"The world's no bigger than a kraal": The South African War and international opinion in the first age of "globalization"', in Omissi, D and Thompson, AS (eds), *The Impact of the South African War*. Basingstoke: Palgrave, 2002.

Lugan, B. *Ces Français qui ont fait l'Afrique du Sud*. [Étrépilly]: Bartillat, 1996.

Macnab, R. *French Colonel: Villebois-Mareuil and the Boers 1899–1900*. Cape Town: Oxford University Press, 1975.

Maphalala, J. 'The African people and the Anglo-Boer War', in *A Century is a Short Time: New Perspectives on the Anglo-Boer War*. Clydesdale: Nexus, 2005.

Maria Z. 'How I was a volunteer in the Transvaal', *Hertzog-Annale van die Suid-Afrikaanse Akademie vir Wetenskap en Kuns*, 1964, vol 11, December, pp 112–122.

Marks, M. 'War and Union, 1899–1910', in Ross, R, Mager, AK and Nasson, B (eds), *The Cambridge History of South Africa*, vol 2. Cambridge: Cambridge University Press, 2011.

Mommsen, WJ. 'Introduction', in Wilson, K (ed), *The International Impact of the Boer War*. Abingdon: Routledge, 2014.

Nasson, B. 'The war one hundred years on', in Cuthbertson, G, Grundlingh, A and Suttie, M-L (eds), *Writing a Wider War: Rethinking Gender, Race, and Identity in the South African War, 1899–1902*. Athens: Ohio University Press, 2002.

Nasson, B. 'The war for South Africa', in Giliomee, H and Mbenga, B (eds), *New History of South Africa*. Cape Town: Tafelberg, 2007.

Novikov, PA. 'Vostochno-Sibirskiye voinskiye soyedineniya v voinakh 1-y chetverti XX veka'. PhD thesis, Institut mongolovedeniya, buddologii i tibetologii Sibirskogo otdeleniya RAN, Irkutsk, 2009.

Okorokov, AV. *Russkiye dobrovoltsy*. Moscow: Yauza, Exmo, 2007.

Omissi, D and Thompson, AS. 'Introduction: Investigating the impact of the war', in Omissi, D and Thompson, AS (eds), *The Impact of the South African War*. Basingstoke: Palgrave, 2002.

Pap, L. Magyarország és a második angol–búr háború. PhD thesis. University of Debrecen, 2015.

Peltekov, AG. *Revolyutsionni deytsi ot Makedoniya i Odrinsko*. Sofia: Orbel, 2014.

Petukhov, LA. 'Obraz Velikobritanii v rossiyskom obshestvennom mnenii v period anglo-burskoy voiny (1899–1902 gg.)', PhD thesis. State Academic University for the Humanities, Moscow, 2009.

Popov, V. *Vtoroye puteshestviye v Mongoliyu. 1910 g*, part III. Irkutsk: Shtab Irkutskogo voyennogo okruga, 1910.

Porter, A. 'The South African War and the historians', *African Affairs*, 2000, vol 99, no 397.

Porucznik Augustus. *Nad Tugelą: osobiste wspomnienia z wojny transwalskiej*. Warsaw: Drukiem Noskowskiego, 1902.

Pottinger, B. *The Foreign Volunteers: They Fought for the Boers (1899–1901)*. Johannesburg: Scripta Africana, 1986.

Preller, GS and Engelenburg, FV. *Onze krijgs-officieren: album van portretten met levens-schetsen der Transvaalse generaals en kommandanten*. Pretoria: 'Volksstem' Kantore, 1904.

Pretorius, F. 'The Second Anglo-Boer War: An overview', *Scientia Militaria: South African Journal of Military Studies*, 2000, vol 30, no 2.

Pretorius, F. *Historical Dictionary of the Anglo-Boer War*. Lanham: The Scarecrow Press, 2009.

Pretorius, F. 'Welcome but not that welcome: The relations between foreign volunteers and the Boers in the Anglo-Boer War of 1899–1902', in Krüger, CG and Levsen, S (eds), *War Volunteering in Modern Times*. London: Palgrave Macmillan, 2010.

Romeiko-Gurko, VI. 'England's war against the South African republics', *Scientia Militaria: South African Journal of Military Studies*, 1981, vol 11, no 4, pp 5–17, and 1982, vol 12, no 1, pp 44–57.

Romeiko-Gurko, VI. *Voyna Anglii s Yuzhno-Afrikanskimi respublikami 1899–1901 gg. Otchyot komandirovannogo po vysochaishemu poveleniyu k voyskam Yuzhno-Afrikanskhikh respublik Generalnogo Shtaba polkovnika Romeiko-Gurko.* Saint Petersburg: Voyenno-Uchetnyi Komitet Glavnogo Shtaba, 1901.

Roubanov, V. *Ot Peterburga do Pretorii.* Saint Petersburg: Tipografiya zhurnala 'Stroitel', 1900.

Saks, D. *Boerejode: Jews in the Boer Armed Forces, 1899–1902.* Johannesburg: Charlie Fine Printers, 2010.

Saks, D. 'Jewish Bittereinders of the Anglo-Boer War', *Jewish Affairs,* 2019, Rosh Hashanah.

Samdan, AA. 'The Russo-Tuvan conflict of 1908', *Bulletin of the KIH of the RAS,* 2017, vol 31, no 3.

Schmidl, EA. 'Österreicher im Burenkrieg, 1899–1902'. PhD thesis, Universität Wien, 1980.

Sergeyev, YY. *Bolshaya igra, 1856–1907: mify i realii rossiysko-britanskikh otnosheniy v Tsentralnoy i Vostochnoy Azii.* Moscow: KMK, 2012.

Shubin, GV. *Rossiyskie dobrovoltsy v anglo-burskoy voyne (1899–1902) (po materialam Rossiyskogo gosudarstvennogo voenno-istoricheskogo arkhiva).* Moscow: Institut Afriki RAN, 2000.

Spisok izdaniy, vyshedshikh v Rossii v 1902 godu. Saint Petersburg: Tipografiya Ministerstva vnutrennikh del, 1903.

Spring, D. 'Russian foreign policy and the Boer War', in Wilson, K (ed), *The International Impact of the Boer War.* Abingdon: Routledge, 2014.

Story, D. *The Campaign with Kuropatkin.* London: T Werner Laurie, 1904.

Subjects of European nations (other than British subjects) who have taken full burgher rights under the Transvaal Government since the commencement of war: arranged under their different nationalities. Pretoria, 1900.

Suryayev, VN. '"Nelyogkoye sluzhebnoye dvizheniye armeyskogo ofitserstva": chinoproizvodstvo i prokhozhdeniye sluzhby ofitserami russkoy armii nakanune Pervoy mirovoy voyny', *Voyenno-istorichesky Zhurnal,* 2014, no 9.

Tanev, S. *Otvoreni pisma. Spomeni i ispovedi na glavniya redactor na v.'Utro' pisani v Tsentralniya zatvor.* Sofia: Universitetsko Izdatelstvo 'Sv. Kliment Okhridski', 1994.

Theron, B. *Pretoria at War, 1899–1900.* Pretoria: Protea Book House, 2000.

Tolstoy, L. *Sobraniye sochineniy v 22 tomakh*. Vol 19. Moscow: Khudozhestvennaya literatura, 1984.

Ustryalov, NG, *Russkaya istoriya do 1855 goda, v dvuh chastyah*. Petrozavodsk: Folium, 1997.

Uys, IS. *South African Military Who's Who 1452–1992*. Germiston: Fortress, 1992.

Van Aardt, JMH. 'Die aandeel van die Krugersdorpse kommando aan die Tweede Vryheidsoorlog (1899–1902)'. MA thesis, Potchefstroomse Universiteit vir CHO, 1950.

Van der Waag, I. 'Re-fighting the 2nd Anglo-Boer War: Historians in the trenches', *Scientia Militaria: South African Journal of Military Studies*, 2000, vol 30, no 1.

Van Niekerk, M. 'Adolf Schiel en die Duitse Kommando. (M.A.-tesis – Universiteit van Pretoria)', *Archives Year Book for South African History*, vol II. Cape Town, 1951.

Vasilenko, VA. Problema Uriankhaiskogo kraya v politike Rossii, Kitaya, Mongolii (vtoraya polovina XIX v.–1914 g.). PhD thesis. Irkutsky gosudarstvenny pedagogichesky universitet, Irkutsk, 2006.

Voropaeva, NG, Vyatkina, PP and Shubin, GV (comp and eds). *Anglo-burskaya voyna 1899–1902 gg. Po arkhivnym materialam i vosponiminaniyam ochevidtsev*. Moscow: Vostochnaya Literatura, 2001.

Voyennaya entsiklopediya, vol 5. Saint Petersburg: Tovaritshestvo ID Sytina, 1912.

WK. 'Anglo-burskaya voina v Yuzhnoy Afrike. Vyp. II. Sost. A Vinogradsky', *Varshavsky Voyenny Zhurnal*, 1902, no 6.

Wilson, K (ed). *The International Impact of the Boer War*. Abingdon: Routledge, 2014.

Yanchevitsky, V, 'Polozheniye russkikh plennykh v Transvaale', *Novoye Vremya*, 1900, no 8826, 22 September.

Yemets, VA. 'Problema Chernomorskih prolivov vo vneshney politike Rossii v period pervoy mirovoy voyny', *Rossiya i Chernomorskiye prolivy (XVIII–XX stoletiya)*. Moscow: Mezhdunarodniye otnosheniya, 1999.

About the editor

Boris Gorelik is a Russian scholar who has studied the history of cross-cultural encounters and interactions between Russia and South Africa.

He is Senior Research Fellow of the Institute for African Studies, Russian Academy of Sciences. His books, published in Russia, South Africa and the United Kingdom, include *The Past and Current Russian Immigration to South Africa* (2007), *Incredible Tretchikoff* (2013) and *'An Entirely Different World': Russian Visitors to the Cape 1797–1870* (2015).

Gorelik was born in Yekaterinburg, Russia, but has lived in Moscow since the age of 18, except for several years in Johannesburg in the 2010s, when he contributed articles to *Rapport Weekliks*.

About the translator

Lucas Venter studied Russian at the University of the Witwatersrand in the late 1980s and produced the first South African translations of poems by Innokenty Annensky, Alexander Blok, Osip Mandelstam, Vladislav Khodasevich and Leonid Pasternak.

In 1990, he settled in Moscow, becoming the first South African to reside in the Soviet Union for non-political reasons. Venter worked as an announcer and translator at Radio Moscow World Service. During his sojourn in Russia, Venter taught Afrikaans at the Diplomatic Academy of the USSR Ministry of Foreign Affairs and at the Institute for Asian and African Studies, Moscow State University.

Since Venter's return to South Africa in 1995, he has pursued a career in information technology while continuing to be active in the field of translation. He is the country's only native speaker of English with a professional knowledge of the Russian language and a broad experience in the translation of Russian fiction and non-fiction.

Index

www.ingramcontent.com/pod-product-compliance
Lightning Source LLC
Chambersburg PA
CBHW070528090426
42735CB00013B/2902